ON TOP OF
THE WORLD

By the same author:

I MUST FLY

ON TOP OF THE WORLD

by

Sheila Scott

HODDER AND STOUGHTON
LONDON SYDNEY AUCKLAND TORONTO

We that acquaint ourselves with every zone,
And pass both tropics, and behold each pole,
When we come home are to ourselves unknown,
And unacquainted still with our own soul.

The Vanity of Learning, SIR JOHN DAVIES (1596).

The contents of this book were more concisely and
beautifully expressed by Sir John Davies four
centuries before I tried to write it. My self is still
unknown to me, but I have been acquainted
with many people throughout Planet Earth,
and perhaps beyond, who helped to make many
seemingly impossible things possible for me, and
it is to them, even though their names may not be
written in this book, that I owe much.

Sheila Scott
May, 1973.

CONTENTS

ILLUSTRATIONS

4

ILLUSTRATIONS

ACKNOWLEDGMENTS:

[1] Syndication International, *Daily Mirror*
[2] Frank Woods
[3] The Press Association
[4] Peter M. H. Lewis
[5] *Evening Standard*
[6] Harris Morgan
[7] Keystone Press
[8] Ken Giller
[9] NASA photograph
[10] *Daily Express*
[11] US Navy photograph
[12] Eric Weller
[13] *Grimsby Evening Telegraph*

MAPS AND DIAGRAMS

FOREWORD

by Dr Philip K. Chapman
former astronaut

THE story Sheila Scott tells in this book has a significance which goes well beyond the records she established in her flight over the North Pole and around the world. It shows that the era of personal adventure in small aircraft is not yet over and that major feats of exploration can still be accomplished by individuals, without large-scale organisational backing, if they are sufficiently determined. Sheila belongs in the company of Lindbergh and Earhart and Saint-Exupéry, and she demonstrates that it is still possible to find in flight the challenges and fulfilment which they found.

The experience of being truly alone with nature, of being where man has not been, has almost vanished from the surface of this planet, and it seems to me that this is one of the most fundamentally important of all the changes in the human condition which have taken place in our time. There are still mountains to be climbed in Antarctica, and a few peaks still virgin in Nepal and Tibet, but mostly the world has become homogenised and civilised. There are tourist ships to Antarctica now, and it cannot be long before the hotel chains start building there. The snows of Kilimanjaro can be seen on a fourteen-day inclusive tour, and far Samarkand is becoming indistinguishable from Los Angeles.

It may be that we can solve the material problems of living together on this little planet, if we are prepared to pay the price for recycling our wastes and to accept restriction of the right to have children. Perhaps we can see to it that all men are fed and clothed and housed, but, within terrestrial constraints, there is no escaping the imminent and widespread curtailment of some of the joys of life, the things which raise life above mere subsistence, if they are not in fact the very foundations of our humanity. In particular, our children and our children's children must live in a world in which, if we are careless, each tree will have its surrounding pile of beer-cans, or, if we are wise, there will be preserved segments of wilderness, no doubt carefully manicured and with police to control the traffic. This is a serious problem, for the urge to explore, to be a pioneer, to seek a new and untrammelled environment over the next hill, is not just a superficial whim of mankind, but a deep-seated instinctual drive, part of the genetic endowment which has brought us up from the apes. As Robert Ardrey wrote in *The Territorial Imperative*, "In countless species there is an innate compulsion to explore, lacking either the pressure of deprivation or the seeking of economic reward." There is no way that the evolutionary traits which make us men can rapidly be adapted to the exigencies of the environment we have created, and we allow the urge to explore to be frustrated only at our peril: the surrogate which has always been adopted, when exploration and expansion have been denied, is savage conflict with our fellows, and that is possible now only at the risk of extermination of life on earth.

In the long run, of course, the exploration of space will provide an unlimited outlet for this human instinct. It is not coincidence that the breakout into space occurred just as man spread into the last corners of the planet: Everest was climbed in 1953, and Sputnik I was launched in 1957. That the technology was available is a consequence of the fact that, in this century, the time constants of technological growth have been much shorter than the thirty-five-year doubling time of population; and popular support of the space programme has surely been at least partly an expression of the exploratory drive which is deep within each of us. The exploration and then the colonisation of new worlds in Space is inevitable, for the simple reason that there is nowhere else to go, but the experience of spaceflight must remain for decades to come the privilege of a restricted few, backed by major mobilisations of talent and resources. Until the costs of spaceflight come down dramatically, as they inevitably will, alternative outlets must be found for those who need and will seek the self-knowledge which comes from personal confrontation with the unknown.

To be alone, to place oneself deliberately in a situation where success and perhaps even survival depend on one's skill and understanding and ability to cope with the unexpected is for me, as I think it is for most pilots, the essential fascination of flying. There is a wild world available within a mile of home, but straight up. The country of the clouds is always changing, and hence perpetually unexplored.

When the weather is clear, the view from a few thousand feet up is unfailingly magnificent, and flying is a serene and relaxed experience. When there are clouds, they bring their own alien and beautiful topography: the scenery around towering cumulus is unmatched by any mountains. When the weather closes in, the challenge increases—an instrument approach with low ceilings, especially in a light aircraft, is an exercise in close co-ordination of hand and eye and brain such as rarely can be found elsewhere and which, when well done, is very satisfying.

It is true, of course, that flying for the love of it is fighting a losing battle against the needs of aviation as transportation. As in other fields, the pressure of the crowd increasingly circumscribes the freedom of the individual. The areas and range of altitudes in which it is permissible to fly without being under radar control are decreasing steadily, especially in the more developed countries. The costs are also increasing, as the list of mandatory equipment grows: radios, navigation systems, radar transponders, crash-locator beacons, collision-avoidance systems, new and expensive items being added every year. Unlike other fields, however (such as driving for pleasure, where speed limits and traffic lights and police are, at best, necessary evils), the controls and complications added to flying serve a genuinely useful purpose, as well as merely allowing more people to share the sky; the calm voice of the controller is very comforting when the situation is tense. In any case, in a time when life is becoming more and more safe and synthetic, a light aircraft provides the only means I know whereby a man may go out on a Sunday afternoon and be as independent and as much in control of his own fate as was any explorer of a hundred years ago.

For those for whom the challenges of the local flying area are insufficient there are still many places in the world where there are no airways and no air traffic controllers and very few navigation aids. In such areas, the airlines may still be shuttling their comfortable cocoons back and forth overhead, but the light aeroplane pilot is on his own, and each flight completed is a triumph, not only over machinery and weather and terrain, but over oneself. There are very few people who understand the lure of such adventures better than Sheila Scott, and none who have tackled them more successfully.

Sheila Scott is a truly remarkable woman, an inspiration to

all who know her. Her contributions to aviation and to the preservation of the individual human spirit of exploration and adventure are almost unparallelled in our time. If *Mythre* had not been inundated when tropical storm Agnes flooded the Piper plant in Pennsylvania this year, she would now (December 1972) be in Antarctica, preparing to fly over the South Pole. I expect to see her there next Christmas, for she has never been deterred by setbacks others might find overwhelming. If so, I hope she will visit the memorial to her namesake, Robert Falcon Scott, on Ross Island, in McMurdo Sound, for she will find inscribed there a line from Ulysses which describes her perfectly: '. . . strong in will/ To seek, to strive, to find and not to yield.'

Philip K. Chapman

PART I

"I said I would do it"

Early life and learning to fly; Sheila's first records including her first solo 'round the world flight' of 1966 and the transatlantic 'Top of the Tower Race' between London and New York, 1969.

OVERTURE

1556 zulu June 18th, 1971

"GAYTO, GAYTO, Do you receive NHK? This is NASA."
Lee Field of the Naval Air Test Centre feverishly twirls his dials,
blowing everyone else off the air. He has nine minutes to make
contact with a small civilian aircraft—to transmit the most important radio message of one woman pilot's life.

"Aircraft *Mythre*, do you read me? NASA is calling you."
Lee in the Navy Yard of Washington DC, turns on more power
—as much power as he dare lest he blast the entire station off
the air.

1602 zulu

"SHEILA, SHEILA, I am not receiving you. If you receive
me, please activate your mike. Once for 'yes'—three times for
'repeat message'. Please acknowledge. I have a message. You
are estimated three minutes from the Top of the World. Continue heading for twenty minutes before twenty degrees left."
Alaska, Hawaii, Australia, all the world answers Lee, except the
little light aircraft now far out of human voice range. The heat
from the ultra-powerful transmitter is unbearable to Lee. He
quickly opens the door to try and cool it down. 1603 zulu. Two
minutes left to patch in the call from Goddard Space Flight
Centre to the elusive GAYTO.

1605 zulu

"GAYTO, This is November Hotel Kilo—NASA calling
you." Lee tries once more before,
"Sheila, you are on Top of the World, hold that heading,"
from astronaut Phil Chapman.

"Goddard indicates you on top," says Chuck Cote, the
Project Manager.

"Congratulations, Mother Christmas," exults Technical
Manager, Len Roach.

"Is your air pollution sensor working?" worries CBS special project reporter, Dick Hoagland. But neither GAYTO, *Mythre*, Sheila nor Mother Christmas reply. Lee wipes his brow and tries playing through the wave bands. He tries to go the other way round the world via his radio waves. The transmitter is boiling with furious heat and outside, Washington is in the middle of a sweltering heat wave. Insistent operators in far-off lands beg for mercy. Their eardrums are being blown out by Lee's attempts to find the elusive GAYTO. Where is she?

*   *   *

Two and a half thousand miles of ice surround me. Wires festoon me like a Christmas tree: three sprout out of my middle; another from my left ear; four more from my arms and legs and yet another around my neck. The safety harness cuts my shoulders and thighs. My hands are stiff with cold and from gripping the bucking controls. Thirty diverse lights once took turns at sending their insistent warning messages but now I need them, they stubbornly refuse to blink at me—all except one— the amber one winks but will not stay on—telling me a tale of two wheels out of three hanging down. The broken handle beside me can do no more—it can neither raise them nor lower the third. Dozens of useless dials reflect my despairing eyes. The airspeed indicator tells me of the cocoons of ice hanging below me; the thick twanging white rope that was once a fine HF aerial wire catches an aimless static tune. Ugly sounds of thudding chunks of ice assail my ears, and an army of ice crystals skitter across my vision. The light is grey and ghastly— suffocating—it is too close. I am nowhere on earth. I cannot see the Universe. I am nowhere. My only visible friend, the astro compass, sits helplessly before me without sun or star to bring it to life.

The second-hand on a clock creeps slowly round its dial— relentlessly slowly—even appearing to stop—moving again but much slower than can be measured on earth. Up here a second is an aeon—two are eternity. There are no human voices here, yet I know instinctively I must continue for twenty minutes. Twenty minutes seem more than my lifetime. But I am utterly committed by my words of centuries before—utterly committed at this milli-second of time to a grey cobwebby world like a ghost. There is no past, nor no future now. I am in awe. I am afraid. Yet I still feel my heart beat. Will there be one more emotion—one last sense yet—as fleeting in our kind of time as an electron?

I can see nothing—I can feel nothing through my frozen limbs—I only know I must transmit my message.

1605 zulu on latitude ninety north, a milli-second ahead in time of latitude forty north.

The grey ghastly light imperceptibly becomes silver; the clawing cobwebs part; the army of crystals retreat and there is a sea of grinding colliding ice; a rainbow glancing from a tiny emerald lake. The second-hand quickens with delight. The time is now and I am glad as never before. This is my own little piece of the North Pole. As though to pinpoint it for me, the tumbling ice has built a hill like virgin-white snow.

"I am on Top of the World. GAYTO—ninety north!" No one replies, but I did not expect it. I am used to my quiet world and have made friends with the sounds of the elements. Here in my enclosed cabin movements outside it become sound and through the sight of what looks like a blanket of earthly silence I can hear the very rumbling and pounding of the ice.

The cruel icy slipstream rushes in and bites my cheeks as I open the storm window, but the sheer delight of the moment makes me uncaring. The British flag unfurls with NASA's 'Snoopy' and whip past the window as I let them go. The camera strap catches my frozen hand, but, it is too late for pictures, the deep thick cloud embraces me. All triumph flees as it becomes a fight for survival. Turn, oh turn out of it, my second self and every nerve in my body yell in panic, but I cannot. I must go on. I must go on for twenty minutes. I must make sure this is the Pole, and the only way lies through this bumping hell. I transmit but again there is no one to tell. I must continue. Why? My frightened self argues, over one of the loneliest spots on earth on this day, June 28th, 1971.

My other self, the stubborn self, replies, "I said I would do it, so now I must try harder to get through, and then I must try even harder than I think I can!"

"But why did you say you would do it?" asks the first self. Why did I? How did it begin?

1

THIRTY-FIVE years before I had felt just like today—just as awe-inspired—alone but not lonely—challenged yet inspired by things I did not yet understand. The hill of long ago was earthy, wooded; a grandstand seat to an unfolding magical scene of endless changing colours in the boundless sky. The sun slipped behind a horizon of glory; a pale moon kept tryst with the evening star, Venus, my birth planet, and the birds in the trees kept me company with one last song before they, too, fell asleep under the mantle of soft sweet-smelling night air.

"What do you think you are doing—running away like this, worrying everyone to death." An angry voice disturbed my beautiful dreams. I was cold and afraid of its irate tones.

"I just wanted to be in the wide open space." I had not run away, I was at the edge of discovery—a new world that I had not noticed before—of new dimensions in my tiny universe. I had become aware of colour, of silence and quiet that was not silent, of the music and the rhythm of the winds as they carried the clouds far out into space, and the caressing touch of breezes as they passed, bearing the smell of wild heather. That was all—but it was an important discovery for me and worth the scolding.

Memory is merciful and I do not remember the monumental row that must have broken out as I was hauled back to a screaming bus-load of impatient children. The hills were the Malvern Hills in Worcestershire, England, and the school bus from the Alice Ottley School For Girls.

My parents were divorced, and my loving grandparents and aunts struggled to rear the unruly child that I had become. Later there was to be a kindly stepmother, but meanwhile I still had my father to myself on our days out. Days of glorious fun at the zoo, the circus, thrilling dares to ride the roller coaster —to dive from the top board in the swimming pool. Most thrilling of all was his sixth birthday treat—a ride in an aeroplane! Sir Alan Cobham, the great flying hero, who had flown all over the world was bringing his air circus to town, and for days the air had been full of new sounds and sights. Graceful yellow biplanes turned cartwheels through the air like birds, strewing rainbows of coloured smoke behind them. We could hear the engines, the music, the commentator's voice from miles away.

Banners in the air and posters on the ground led us to the deafening sound of newly started aircraft engines and the lovely smell of burnt new oil and aircraft paint. A leather helmeted being with a huge moustache glared at me as I objected to the restraining lap harness. But neither the glare, nor the roar of the engine could blot out the music as we careened clumsily along the bumpy green field to leap graceful as a bird into my wide open space. Below me, the houses became dolls' houses and all the people toys, and I felt the wind blow away my breath as it sang through the rigging wires. We were gods! It was the most exciting thing I had ever done. Too soon the day was over, but it remained a special memory throughout my life. It never occurred to me that I could recapture those moments every day.

How I longed to be grown up and free! I was always in some sort of scrape, though I never quite knew how, and it seemed I was always being punished for the wrong things. I was thrown out of school on at least two occasions, but each time allowed back.

My stepmother supervised the final growing-up stage—bought my first long dress and real high-heeled shoes—all of two inches—for my first dance. Make-up was still strictly forbidden, and my girl friends and I secretly experimented with talcum powder and carmine water colour out of the art room. I got caught using my stepmother's curling irons and lied about it in fright, only to be shorn of my Greta Garbo locks as a punishment. I had found a secret beau, and it had become important how I looked. For months I felt scalped and not like other girls.

One shattering Sunday in September 1939, the careless days were suddenly over. We were at war with Germany. I had to become more serious and pass my final school exams. My school reports still read 'does not try hard enough'! They obviously had a profound effect on me for later in life I changed. I was still always in trouble, but for trying *too much*.

Straight out of school with a head full of Florence Nightingale notions, I went into nursing. I was abruptly supposed to be grown up, but it was not the free life I had imagined. The discipline of the naval hospital at Portsmouth coupled with the restrictions imposed on us by a wartime government were hardly complete freedom, but I was excited and proud of my smart uniform and the new busy life on the wards. Sirens wailed continually, followed by inevitable ominous thuds. There were weekly rehearsals for meeting the German invasion and gas attacks when they came, as well as our work in the wards of wounded brought straight off the warships in the harbour. The wounded either died very soon after arrival, or were moved further inland after we had patched them up, which probably led to us living for the day only, and packing as much gaiety into our very young lives as possible. We needed to blot out the things we were seeing to be able to face the next convoy of men—boys no older than ourselves. Every moment of free time was deliberately spent catching 'liberty boats' to light-hearted fun with the constant stream of midshipmen on shore leave. This had its effect, and for many years I was to live for the moment, sampling everything for myself, never looking back or truly far ahead. Everything had to be fabulous or else not done at all—even if it meant being broke for months on end.

By 1945 I was stationed in London, which was to become my home from then on. Both wars came to an end, but I still lived for today and fun. The father of one of my friends was Alexander Korda, the great film producer, and at first, I only knew him as a kindly, most amusing man who spoilt us young things terribly with lavish presents, and somehow miraculously used to inveigle Claridge's into producing our favourite dishes at the meals to which he invited us. At that time everything was still rationed and special dishes were a great treat.

I wanted to act—I had had enough of discipline, and nursing was not for me. It was Alex who gave me my first job. He knew my character well and advised me to learn more about how films were made before deciding to take up acting seriously, and arranged for me to be a 'stand-in' to Deborah Kerr. I remember the ghastly early mornings and half-asleep journeys on the first train to the film studios at Denham. A rush to 'Make-up' followed by hours of standing around drinking endless cups of coffee, waiting, hoping to be called, dreaming of the day when

I might become a star like Deborah. When the film came to an end, I was really certain that I was destined to become a big star, and was absolutely furious with a fortune-teller who told me I would never be a famous actress, but would become famous in another field later in life, although I would never make a great fortune. I would have none of this, and enrolled for drama lessons for the following year. But how right she was!

When I left drama school, I landed several 'bit parts' in films and early television plays, but it was necessary to join a repertory company to gain sufficient experience to be given even a chance to audition for a West End show. Repertory was hard work. We rehearsed all day for the following week's show, performed the current week's show in the evening and spent the night cutting up old clothes and sewing next week's costumes—all for the princely sum of eight pounds a week. We all swapped clothes with each other and somehow managed to appear fairly elegant. Quite the most spectacular dress I ever had, and one which caught the eye of every camera at a sparkling 'first night', had been made out of a pair of old red velvet curtains, draped on top of pink satin, with a matching pink rose atop.

There were times when I was 'at liberty' and dragging around to dozens of agents' offices with my actor friends until our feet hurt. We lived on potatoes spiced with Worcestershire sauce (it is surprising how good this can taste if you are really hungry). We were never really starving. There were parties to go to nearly every night and usually food to be found at them. I invested in a course of modelling and I was able to turn to this for a living when there were no parts to be had.

Life was always fun but I was aware of a growing loneliness. I felt that there should be something more to living. My life held no real challenge, no excitement, no sense of direction and sometimes I felt a deadly boredom with it all. Maybe it was because of this that I made a most unfortunate marriage. But it did not help. We had nothing to give each other. It was wrong from the very first, and six long years later, ended in divorce. Alone, independent again, I tried a little of everything. I tried to write, still occasionally acting, or modelling, and even tried my hand at designing clothes.

A mixture of friends, mostly artistic, surrounded me and night after night we talked the dawn in with our ideas on life. I had become interested in philosophy, perhaps as a result of my search for something that did not pall within a few weeks. I was particularly interested in Buddhism, but found its rules and ideals too hard for me. I had become far too undisciplined. My early upbringing had been strict compared to these days, and it had been followed by the restrictions of war and hospital life, against which I was still rebelling. I wanted to taste life to the fullest—no matter what. Relentlessly I determined to try everything myself. I had been sheltered all my life, and in spite of it, was totally insecure. I was sure that life must be more than just earning money to eat and sleep, an endless cycle of meaningless days and nights. There had to be more to existence, some greater reason we were here, and I was determined to find it in my own way of living.

Then for a while I was completely happy for I became involved with a wonderful man. The complications surrounding us became too much, but the man concerned was one of the kindest and wisest of men, at that time for me. He was a man with a background of enormous moral courage, and sincere beliefs which he lived. Though he spoiled me and never tried to lead me, unknowingly he led me to a deeper awareness that all was not simple, and had to be looked for and studied.

My old fascination for growing things returned. I loved to observe odd things under a microscope; to watch a simple plant and the philosophy of its growth from seed to flowering; to care for strange animals—ours were chameleons, lizards and rabbits. We led a bohemian life, but books and music, my old loves, filled my life again, and I found new concepts through them. There were many coincidences that I was sure did not happen by chance, but I was afraid to face up to what it meant lest others thought I had taken leave of my senses. I was living in two worlds as though in a mirror. I read and experimented and even studied with a guru. When this turned to sexual experience, I lost faith in him. I was still too much the novice mentally to appreciate that the philosophies I tried to study included knowledge of many kinds of experience. I turned to other things —all dreams of an aesthetic life shattered. I was much too solemn then. A puritanical streak made me believe that perfect ethics could only be found by abstaining from living life to the full. It was years before I understood that for me it had only been by *living* life—sampling all the vices and virtues and discarding some of both, that I learned to recognise magical glimpses of a buried awareness, the missing dimension in my life.

And so, in 1959, I was still not sure what I wanted to do with my life, until . . .

"I am going to learn to fly." Somehow I had said it, not meaning it for a moment.

"I'll bet you the price of a lesson you won't," baited my amused friends. That bantering challenge and shout of derisive laughter did it and became the beginning of a whole new life. It happened at a Sunday brunch. Everyone was sleeping off a late party pretending to watch television, and I just wanted to wake them up with a controversial remark. I was showing off, but I was furious with their teasing that I was incapable of learning to fly—although it was true, as they joked, that I had failed my driving test twice.

"Just you wait and see," I retorted.

And so as I recorded in *I Must Fly*, I quickly rescued the women's magazine from the waste basket to look up the article from which I had just got the idea. I ostentatiously sat at my desk and wrote to all the flying schools mentioned in the story, but began to feel the joke had gone far enough. I felt like a wallflower addressing letters to herself as I enclosed the stamped envelopes under the grinning eyes of my friends.

Several days later a pile of envelopes arrived, all self-addressed. I looked in bewilderment at the glossy brochures they contained and found that most of them offered so-called cut rates in return for huge sums in advance. I foolishly left them lying around for my friends to find, and after further derisive comments, stubbornly rang up Elstree airport, who had advertised trial lessons for one pound only. I could not lose much for that small sum, and felt sure my friends would forget the whole idea by the time the day of my appointment came. They did not forget, and the day came all too soon. I consoled myself with the thought that I need appear only once, and that even after one lesson I could say I had been learning to fly. I started for Elstree on the tube, but in my apprehension missed all the connections by taking a train going the wrong direction. I finally emerged from below ground to hail a taxi. This proved to be the most expensive part of the day, but the admiring glance I got from the taxi-man when I told him I was late for a flying lesson was worth it. I began to enjoy the idea.

I was left amidst a strange conglomeration of antique aeroplanes, vintage cars, campers festooned with TV aerials and a bright new red fire engine. I found my way into a large hangar which was full of buses. This could not be the place advertised in the glossy brochure.

I heard a voice talking about 'two and a half' and 'five hundred' at Liverpool, and wandered through a door, half expecting to find a secret betting shop. Instead, I found a young man dressed in a very new pale blue flying suit talking on the telephone, while he nonchalantly swung a pair of radio headphones from his hand. He sent me to 'sign out' in the book in the hangar. By now I had lost my nerve again, and only wanted to steal away from this crazy remote airfield and return to my nice safe apartment. I sat for an hour, trying to hide my trembling fingers while listening to hair-raising stories from a crowd of cadets. A slightly more mature character arrived in old, oily overalls and I assumed he was the engineer. He barked:

"Where's this damned guy Scott?" I stood up reluctantly as he glared at me. All students, even if they were women, must be ready on time, signed out, preflight checks done, engines started, or they would be charged for any wasted flying time. I snapped back that I had already signed myself over. I pointed out that as I could not even start a washing machine without instructions, I did not think I should care to start on aeroplanes.

I was sent to find 'Romeo Charley' and told not to forget the cushions. I looked everywhere, but could not find anyone resembling this name. My instructor appeared, snapping, "She's on the line, of course."

Greatly bewildered, I followed him, and then saw that 'Romeo Charley' stood for the registration letters 'R.C.' on the aeroplane. Feeling foolish, I eyed the aeroplane with despair. It looked so frail and tiny. The instructor inspected the engine, discoursing grandly about carburettors, magnetos and other such mysteries. I nodded my head in pretended understanding. We squatted down and looked underneath, where I banged my head and emerged looking like an oily mop.

After pointing out that there was a fire extinguisher in the vicinity, my tormentor told me to get aboard. I managed to make it by bending double, hitching my skirt up to my waist and ruining my best nylons. We made yet another inspection inside the plane. I wondered what could be wrong with this antiquated aeroplane, that it needed so much checking. Then there were more barked instructions and what seemed like very rude gestures to the man waiting patiently in front to swing our propeller, and that was the end of any further attempt at lady-like behaviour.

The engine started with a horrible clanking din. I realised that one had to lip-read to learn to fly. As we bumped our way over the grass field to the runway, the radio let out an awful squawk, but the ogre seemed to understand its language.

"Are you sitting comfortably?" he hollered, reminding me of the dentist. With a deafening roar we were at last racing along the runway. A cloud of birds rose up before us, but fortunately outflew us, and as we left the ground it seemed as if we were scraping the tops of the trees. I looked down and there was the reservoir with its water skiers and dinghies. Ahead and all around me was more sky than I had ever known existed. I realised that I was enjoying the pleasant floating feeling, until I felt a rough bump which made the engine surge. My foot went down on an imaginary brake. But these were rudders, not brakes, and the plane gave a sickening lurch.

"Relax and learn to move with the aeroplane as though you were part of it. Please don't clasp the stick as though it's your last possession," said the ogre beside me sarcastically, "try and hold it as you would your boyfriend on a Saturday night."

This only made me clutch harder, and the harder I tried to unclutch, the more drunken became the course of the aeroplane. Finally the ogre took pity on me and took over the controls. I breathed a sigh of relief, but he asked me if I would like a real thrill. I felt nothing could be worse than what I had been through and weakly nodded. Another roar from the engine, and the nose went down a little and stopped there. We were turning over, and I felt inside out as I watched the horizon turn a cartwheel. I closed my eyes tightly and swore I would never again take on a bet. Then everything began to feel more normal and I opened one eye to see that we were flying straight and level again. I had survived my first barrel roll.

"Now that wasn't a bad effort at all," grinned the ogre. "Run along and get the list of checks, which I expect you to know by the next lesson." I looked up at him and thought he must have lapsed into sarcasm again, but his blue eyes were twinkling, and he had a mischievous smile. I decided to return.

AFTER a few lessons, I found another airport where I could stay overnight each weekend. Thruxton, near Salisbury Plain in the Wiltshire countryside, was an ideal green field for beginners, but I was very shaken by my first sight of the aeroplane I was to fly—a modified Tiger Moth biplane, renamed the Thruxton Jackaroo. It had one enclosed cockpit instead of the traditional two place open ones, and four seats which made it look pregnant but far too frail to fly. The noise was terrific, and the whole aircraft shook. I had to wear an old-fashioned flying helmet to be able to talk on the intercom to my instructor sitting behind.

Eventually, weeks later, the great day came when my instructor, John Heaton, got out of the back of the aeroplane and said, "You're on your own, ma'am. Now don't forget your tail trimmer!"

He slammed the door, turned his back on me and walked away. I taxied down the runway quickly before he changed his mind, but did not dare to think in case I might change mine. I did my take-off checks with extra care and began to sing in a flat, nonchalant fashion in mock pretence of confidence.

I looked at the vast expanse of green field before me and prayed that I could keep the aircraft straight. My hands were shaking as I pushed the throttle too quickly fully forward. With a bump the Jackaroo careened along a fairly straight path and then suddenly we were smoothly airborne. The aeroplane seemed to lift herself off without my aid and I realised that she and I were alone in the sky. There was no time to dwell on this romantic thought. There were things to be done if I were to stay up there.

"Remember to climb to five hundred feet before turning— throttle back to climbing power—retrim—oops—we're doing fine." But on turning downwind, I knew I was kidding myself and my legs were shaking so much that they were moving the rudder bars. The aircraft was swaying about like a ballet dancer. I breathed deeply and momentarily lost sight of the airfield. Staring wildly into the distance, I discovered that it was just behind and below me. All thoughts of normal airfield procedure and rectangular pattern forgotten, I made a diving turn on to the final approach. Somehow the aeroplane followed an erratic course towards the field. The ground seemed to be coming up too fast and I was sure the field was not quite the same shape as it had been when my instructor was with me. It had grown smaller. I remembered my instructor's patient voice telling me to watch the size and shape of the field and then I realised—I was too high. I throttled back the engine and remembered to trim back the stabiliser. That felt better and somehow I got my sights lined up on the runway after only a slightly zigzag path. Three enormous bounces later we came to rest safely if not smoothly. I could feel my face almost cracking with a smile of relief—a few seconds later I danced and sang with sheer happiness and triumph. A much-relieved instructor walked towards me.

There was an aero-club party that night, and we had a terrific champagne celebration which lasted until daylight. I remember racing my instructor's new white car around the perimeter track with sheer exuberance as the sun rose on a heavenly dawn. I was now longing for the next lesson. When we returned to the clubhouse, the few of us remaining upright surveyed the chaos and decided we had better clean up the mess. I rushed across the room to get a broom and slipped on a potato chip. My instructor picked me up, shaking my arm at the same time and said:

"Oh, come on now—you're all right." It hurt quite a bit and I snapped back:

"Oh yes, I've only broken my arm." Many a word spoken in jest . . .

By morning, I was nearly crying with pain and still unable to lift my arm. I really *had* broken it and they took me to the hospital where the other arm was found to have a suspected fracture as well. I returned to the airport trussed up like a chicken and unable to do a thing for myself. My hair looked like that of a wild woman's, and I was in utter despair. Ten minutes' solo in the air, and now I was grounded for heaven knows how long.

I nagged and nagged at the hospital in London until they took the plaster off one arm and put the really broken one in a

27

new plaster cast which allowed me to use my fingers. Finally the doctor got fed up with my nagging and gave me a piece of paper saying I was fit enough to fly an aeroplane providing a second pilot came too. I returned to Thruxton and inveigled everyone who had a licence into flying with me. This went on for two months until my arm healed, but I was to regret my impatience. Although they did not touch the controls and I did all flying, I got too used to having another human being up in the air with me.

When the plaster came off, I was allowed to fly solo again. Now I really hated every minute in the air alone, would make any excuse not to go, and called my instructor a sadistic monster. But he made me take off solo again and again, until I had satisfied him with a good landing. After three days of this sort of hell, he wisely sent me up during the last hour of daylight. It was a glorious still evening and I could see for miles. I was so engrossed in the fascinating view topped by a magnificent sunset—long after it had escaped from the view of the mere groundlings below me—that I forgot to be frightened. I felt a goddess—able to extend my vision. For the first time I relaxed at the controls and to my instructor's astonishment even landed later than I legally should. Till then it had all been rather a lark plus feminine stubbornness to win a bet, mixed with a great deal of doubt as to whether I would ever really learn to fly.

Now I had had a taste of what flying could really be like, I had caught flying fever which has remained with me ever since. I made many mistakes and there was much necessary bullying from my instructor for months, but at last I became the proud possessor of a private pilot's licence. However, this was not enough for me. Flying had become all I could think about, and I now wanted to obtain a commercial pilot's licence, which would enable me to fly larger aircraft and carry fare-paying passengers.

I found too, that it would be cheaper to buy my own Jackaroo, rather than to go on renting one in order to build up the two hundred hours necessary for a commercial licence. I could buy it on the hire purchase system just like a car. Every weekend I watched the hangar boys rebuilding the old RAF Tiger Moth into a Jackaroo. I fought with everyone until I got my own way

A Midsummer Night's Dream at Windsor Repertory Theatre!

The original *Myth* at Thruxton Airfield, 1960

Myth Too and *Mythre* flying together

and had her painted blue with silver wings and equipped with white upholstery. The men roared with laughter as they said it would soon be covered with black oil and that it would look ridiculous on such an antiquated aeroplane. But I wanted a strictly feminine aircraft and named her *Myth*, which is Greek for a female moth. There were some very rude interpretations of my own special sign, which I had painted on, but the real one has remained my secret to this day, and now for luck it is inscribed on every aeroplane I race.

At last *Myth* was ready and to me she was the most beautiful aeroplane that ever existed. At first she had no radio, or any such goodies. Navigation lights, brakes and such refinements were slowly obtained instead of new dresses, and a simple radio set as a birthday present. I began to collect radio crystals as others collect phonograph records. I was intensely proud of my new possession and I flew to the exclusion of everything else. I was no longer bored. There was something new to do all the time. I explored and began to stretch my wings. One of my first flights was down to North Africa making a dozen landings on the way to replenish the biplane's fuel tanks every two hours.

The men who had rebuilt her found she was an exceptionally fast model, and insisted that she should enter the handicap national air races. I took them on, but I still had to learn to fly well first. Once more I had impulsively reacted, and now I had to keep my word. I spent hours sticking bits of plaster over protruding bits that might slow her down, and trying out new propellers to make her faster, while my instructor scared me into a frenzy, with low-level racing turns round the airport trees which we used as mock pylon markers. Then there were the national race rules to study—some obviously dating from 1903—for one read, "No aeroplane driver shall interfere with another aeroplane driver whilst on the course!"

There is a special air of excitement about race days, quite unlike any other form of flying. I checked *Myth* into the race field, feeling very much the novice, but the friendly atmosphere was like a garden party. The competitors drank cups of coffee on the lawn while arguing the merits of their gleaming planes. Not daring to utter a word in front of these illustrious men, I unnecessarily polished *Myth* yet again in an effort to get rid of the butterflies in my tummy. Anxiously we all watched the weather, changing our plans and policies a dozen times until at last it was time to taxi to the start. Wingtip men held back *Myth* as I throttled forward as much as I dared to get a fast take-off, my eyes anxiously on the starter's green flag. The flag sliced the air and *Myth* leapt forward as her wingtip men let her go, and roared with fury down the runway to the beginning of a whole new world.

Unbelievably *Myth* won her races that weekend—my first race meeting—and we returned triumphantly with the De Havilland Trophy. Already the sky had captivated me, but now the element of challenge crept in and that, coupled with so many new things to explore, made me determine to make flying my life. The summer sped by as I explored Europe more and more with *Myth*, chasing every rally and race I could enter and soon it was autumn and time to learn to fly at night. The old clubhouse seemed cosy and homely as we students waited eagerly for the last remnants of fiery sun to disappear and make way for the cool moonlight. We collected and carried in logs and pine cones during the day to build up a blazing fragrant fire to return to and roast chestnuts. The field was covered with mushrooms, which we added to our feasts of bacon and eggs after we landed.

We waited around after twilight, incongruously wearing dark glasses to accustom our eyes more quickly to the darkness when we took them off—one flash of bright light from a cigarette lighter would reduce our night vision considerably. The shadowy shapes of the aeroplanes could just be discerned in the gloom outside, and the noise of the lorry stopping at intervals on its way down the runway, while the crew lit the 'gooseneck' paraffin flares, mingled with the last calls of the nightingales.

Those of us being initiated were of different nationalities, and I was the only woman; but, on that first night-flying exercise, all of us were excited in our individual ways. This is the effect that night flying has on everyone—a totally different experience from piloting a small aircraft in daylight.

There were no radios aboard the training aircraft, and we had to learn to read our charts by comparing the towns and aligning the chart in the correct direction. We checked our dead-reckoning exercises by the size and positions of the clusters of town lights and noticed that lakes and rivers stood out and shone like silver. The aerodrome identification beacons, lighthouses and marine beacons each flashed their identities by coloured Morse code, and we learned to navigate by each local town's street lights and neon signs. The winding coast was the broken strands of a diamond necklace, and it was easy to recognise the Isle of Wight standing independently away from the mainland—her necklace of lights was unbroken. The outline of surf bubbling against the rocks framed the fairgrounds—their big wheels and switchbacks looking like giant cast-off toys.

The navigation lights of the giant Boeings and Comets shone above us, seeming to chase the stars, but down below them the bumbling bee-like training aircraft of Hamble Air Training School seemed to jostle rudely in the sky in their attempts to land. The great ships under the floodlights of Southampton Harbour were as toy boats in a bath, leaping flames from the oil refinery reflected in the water; purple smoke drifted up to meet the scattered clouds, already tinged with silver shafts of moonlight, making dark pools of shadow on the ground. I felt I only had to stretch up to reach the stars; the old biplane was graceful and alive. I was in love with the whole sky, and never wanted this glorious night to end.

As we pulled our aircraft into the hangar, the mood changed; no one dared to express aloud the sentimental things we had all been feeling. One's first 'night-flying solo' is one of the memorable moments of learning to fly. The soft cockpit lighting and the starry night sky outside combined to give a comforting, secure feeling of one's own little world looking out on to another bigger world of serene beauty—yet awe-inspiring in its very vastness. A world I wanted to see all at once, but just like the student pilot that I was, I could only get a mere glimpse of what I was to discover through the window of that cocoon—the cocoon that was this night's cockpit.

On the ground no matter how hard I tried to conquer it, I was full of alternating moods of utter despair, or feverish happiness, but I discovered it was impossible to remain miserable or bad tempered in the sky. There was too much to see, to do and to feel, to think about. I looked down and became aware that there are many things on earth and its surrounding atmosphere than I had ever been able to imagine before on the ground—yet it all seemed part of a recurring pattern. The sky constantly changed my view; the very feel of the aircraft was a new experience on every flight. For me it was the discovery of a new dimension both physically and in my way of thinking. I had rediscovered the wide open spaces and beauty that I had found on a hilltop many years before.

By the end of 1960, I had acquired about three hundred hours—more than enough to start training for commercial licences. No pilot can have obtained the necessary basic experience in a more idyllic way, for mine had been by flying the gentle biplane leisurely throughout Europe, down to the very edge of the Sahara. Now at Oxford's commercial pilots' training school I had to spend hours around the same countryside perfecting a more disciplined form of flying. Later in London at the aviation college I nightly staggered home befuddled as though drunk from problems way beyond me—few of which resembled flying.

Somehow I struggled through and actually passed the flying examinations—all except one—my commercial pilot's medical. It took weeks to get a medical examination appointment in those days and so I had left it till last. I had a private pilot's medical and it never occurred to anyone there could possibly be a problem. The eye doctor at the RAF's Central Medical Board thought otherwise and grounded me for short sight. It was quite ridiculous for I had flown all over Europe without sophisticated radio aids—entirely eyeballing my navigation. Nothing and no one could persuade the wretched doctor he was wrong. My instructors tested me in the air without my glasses in different lights—at night and by twilight—which is difficult to land by at the best of times and found if anything my landings were smoother. It seemed the end of the world to me, particularly after all the hard cramming, but led to a far more exciting and rewarding life than I could possibly have dreamed of.

First the local Cessna dealer took pity on me and used me as a demonstrator of his aircraft at every race and weekend rally that came up. I could still fly these with only a private pilot's licence. I was lucky that year and as a reward ended up in the United States to attend the Cessna Aircraft factory's Sales Week in Wichita, Kansas, followed by the Aircraft Owners and Pilots

Association's yearly convention of some five thousand pilots. On hearing my sad story, they insisted that I retake my medical in America and start fresh. The American doctors could find no reason why I should not become a professional pilot—my near-sightedness was not as bad as originally reported. I was determined to stay airborne somehow, so remained in America to get commercial licences that would at least enable me to ferry and deliver aircraft to Britain for payment.

I had met Lee and Bill Whitesell at the Convention and they invited me to be their house guest at the then fabulous Flying W Ranch airport in New Jersey, while I worked at American commercial and instrument ratings. It had everything to attract the whole family to the airport, just like a country club, with swimming pool, horseback riding, restaurant, hayrides and all facets of small town American life. It was a wonderful introduction to life in the United States, and I very nearly stayed permanently. America certainly became my second home from then on, and still is. However, I was still determined to rout the beastly eye doctor and so returned to England brandishing my new licences, now backed by not a few official bodies in the UK. I was not the only victim, some very experienced airline men had been grounded too, but still the doctor would neither give in nor retest me.

Each time I returned to the States, my friends encouraged me to get another rating until in the end I had a smattering know-ledge of all forms of flight—from helicopters to seaplanes—on my commercial licence. I was getting tired of non-stop studying and ended up by making a complete mockery of the whole thing by flying an American registered aircraft in instrument flying conditions into London Airport as a commercial pilot, and then turned around to fly out a British registered one in the same airspace—the only difference was I had become a mere private pilot within an instant and could not accept payment for the second flight! Friends at the Ministry got so fed up with my non-stop barrage they finally called me and said:

"Things are changing, and if you'll just pipe down and not get up to any more tricks, we might send you a surprise in the post." The surprise was a request to attend CME for another medical—for a British commercial pilot's medical. This time I won the bright yellow cover for my licence, but already I was on the way to another form of flying—a freer form but equally disciplined in its way. The little biplane that had shown me vistas of further horizons could take me no further, and a home had to be found for her. I was now flying more sophisticated aircraft in order to keep up with my competitors.

I sold *Myth* to a parachutist group, the British Skydivers. I had been a drop pilot for a short time, and although I refused to jump out of aircraft myself, I had learned what great people they were. Full of laughter and usually living rough on the field, they had a special kind of bond—a feeling of responsibility for each other as well as their equipment. *Myth* was in good hands.

WHILE in the States again, in 1964, I became interested in a Mustang and a flight to Australia. My American friends sent me an official list of records that the Mustang could break, and on casually turning the pages my attention was caught by a list of fifteen light aircraft records around Europe which had not been attempted for several years. Once again just turning the pages of a book set me on a new path.

I decided to try, but it could not be in the Mustang, it had to be a light aircraft—so I borrowed a single-engined Piper Comanche 400 (which we called *Myth Sunpip* after Piper and the *Sun* newspaper who helped me) and broke them all within thirty-six hours. It was surprising how much work had to be put in beforehand to make those tiny records possible, but I learned much from them. As a result my next record attempt was to fly round the world to break American Jerrie Mock's record, though even this was by chance. I had not really planned to do it, yet when visiting Champion Spark Plug Factory in Toledo I found myself saying I might try it.

Jerrie Mock was the first woman to circumnavigate the world solo, closely followed by another American, Joan Merriam Smith. Jerrie had taken a northern route and Joan the longer route through New Guinea as she was commemorating Amelia Earhart's flight. It was time for a European to follow in their footsteps. I decided to take an even longer route. I wanted to see as much of the world and its continents as possible. Mine became a monster flight of 32,000 miles, though strangely all that is required to qualify for Fédération Aéronautique Internationale round-the-world claims is 22,000 miles—the equivalent of the Tropic of Cancer—not necessarily crossing below the Equator.

One would think it would be easier now than in the days of the great pioneer flights. It has become far more complicated—even if more comfortable to fly the world because of our modern love of paper work in triplicate, with visas, permissions to be sought, and it took many months of work to organise it.

I had fallen in love with the same Piper Comanche 400 which had broken my first records in the previous year. Still without a sponsor, I put my first deposit down on it—the princely sum of £100 for what in Europe was an £18,000 aircraft. There was a mass of equipment to obtain and my glossy aircraft had to be pulled to pieces, seats and all superfluous bits to be removed to make room for enormous fuel tanks in the cabin with me. There were months of flight planning, and in the midst of it all a change of aircraft. Some authority decided that the higher horsepower model of the Comanche would eat too much fuel, and I would never make it across the Pacific, so poor *Myth Sunpip* had to be abandoned and the lower horsepowered Comanche 260 obtained. By now there had been many borrowed aircraft, each one temporarily called *Myth* with a consecutive number for luck, but this was only the second aircraft I had ever owned so it became *Myth Too*.

Then there were hilarious sessions with the Aero-Medical Research people who had not dealt with a woman pilot in recent times. Their first telephone conversation was distinctly pompous, but after discussing the most personal aspects of the pilot as well as her aircraft, the speaker responded by saying how much he looked forward to meeting me in person now he knew me so intimately. Once there, they taught me all manner of things, from what to wear and eat, to isometric exercises (a simple thing like cramp could cost you a record), how to survive both in the air on flight legs of up to nineteen hours at a time, as well as on the ground should I be unfortunate enough to force land. Most important, they warned me that I would swell after a few days of such flying and that I must buy outsize clothes.

On the day I took off from London Airport, my friends had taxied *Myth Too* to just below the statue of Alcock and Brown, the first men to fly the Atlantic. I looked up into their eyes, and touched the statue for luck. I wondered if they had felt as emptied of all they had learned as I did at that moment, just before take-off. I felt totally incapable and unprepared, but as my wheels left the concrete runway it was as though everyone in the sky knew exactly how I felt. London Air Traffic Control placed me on that first airway with almost loving care, and with every official signal tucked in a little personal message of their own, and soon every airliner in the sky joined in. It started with BOAC, then in came Pan Am closely followed by Air India, Alitalia, Qantas—all the countries I was to fly to, and so it continued the whole way round the world whenever I was in radio contact.

My 'solo flight' became a whole 'world team' both of people in the sky, and the ground—people of every country, colour, creed and political belief, some of whom to this day have never actually met me, but who by their support spotlit the amount of happiness, laughter and goodwill that can be promoted by a little aircraft—by any international sport or traveller in fact. I learned as never before how very different the earth could be if we too could slice through prejudice in normal life.

I flew through clear nights full of stars, and in thick turbulent clouds, over sunny lands or parched deserts, and green seas always towards the East. Often afraid, other times happy and contented, sometimes hurting from being caged in my seat, with not enough sleep; certainly I was learning to fly as no amount of training could have taught me. Always physically alone in the sky—my only companions the disembodied voices of the kindly controllers, and the airline crews—strangely I was never really lonely, even over deserts and oceans far out of the voices' range.

Again and again I did not have a clue how to cope with various problems, yet somehow something always led me to a safe landing. Bill Hewitt, the ex-BOAC navigator, who was my flight liaiser in England always seemed to know where I was even when no one else did, and always got the right Telex through to encourage me. Occasionally it was bullying and telling me to get a move on, other times cheering; one glorious one reached me in the Pacific reading: "Sheila love, you are still ahead. Do not dawdle. Not time reversable arrival Nandi. If worried talk to rabbit, it can't bite. You are doing well. You promoted captain with four gold rings. Bill."

The rabbit was 'Buck Tooth', a toy rabbit which Bill had pushed through the window just before I took off from London Airport, and which sat atop my cabin fuel tank grinning with its buck teeth, however bad the flight became. It was Buck Tooth I turned to both in triumph and in trouble and his smile never let me down. Now he is an important member of my team, and has been part of all my flights, surviving all our dramas.

One day over the Pacific Ocean a cabin fuel tank burst, making the aircraft a flying bomb. It was Buck Tooth who won the day. Everything was immersed in fuel—my fear was a great paralysing stab of pain—the fumes were suffocating me. The most bedraggled rabbit you ever saw was swimming in the fuel, but still it gave me its idiotic grin. Involuntarily I grinned back —that grin took over and somehow in seconds I had done all the constructive things that could be done. That day I became two of me—one a robot performing the necessary actions, the other me observing the actions. Any moment the aircraft could blow sky high but I had learned to make use of the adrenalin that fear produces. I realised too that I was afraid of being hurt, not of death itself. I was lucky that day, and we reached land safely many hours later.

On such a world flight so much happens in a short space of time, yet each place—each incident is indelibly remembered far better than if you had stayed there for weeks as a tourist. You see the whole again just as you see the mass of the far off galaxy, yet you are aware of the individual atoms and protons that go towards making it something visible to us.

Memories like Damascus, where the Syrians had heard I used cologne to refresh myself, they had filled the cockpit with sweet smelling jasmine—a special flower for Syrian women for it means 'I love you'. Memories of the Syrian desert whose dust storms confused me, where like Lindbergh I made friends with a little fly trapped in my cockpit, followed by the loss of my little fly friend when the immigration men debugged me and the aircraft at Karachi!

Karachi at midnight, and the scene under a night of stars of my first big welcome. The movie cameras had caught up and I was at first blinded by the arc lamps but became aware of a sea of sound of feminine voices. As my eyes cleared, I saw dozens of beautiful women dressed in beautiful Pakistani costumes of loose pants covered by glorious coloured silk tunics, each one holding garlands of flowers, or golden symbols to welcome me with.

In contrast, the moonlight in Calcutta emphasising the shocking scene of hundreds of living bodies each lying on a rug on the street—the rug their only possession. One bowl of rice was given to them a day. They were the refugees from the earlier Indo-Pakistan war.

My own forced landing in, at that time forbidden, Burma owing to an electrical failure in monsoon conditions—and the Buddha in Shwe Dagon, the largest pagoda in the world, obviously working overtime for me that day!

The luxury of being given dozens of orchids at Singapore—the snake charmer outside Raffles Hotel contrasting with the very English RAF resthouse at Changi. The RAF warning me to take a certain airway otherwise someone might take a pot shot at me though they were awfully bad shots!

Arriving at Bali, then still off the beaten track of the tourists, with grass huts, graceful women with bare bosoms carrying baskets of coconuts and bananas on their heads, idols and temples wherever I looked and a seven-course Balinese meal for about forty pence!

A sunny, golden morning over the Timor Sea made me forget its sharks. My first thrilling glimpse of the coast of Australia when I felt like all the pioneers before me—talking to the women of the outback over HF radio, looking down and seeing their homesteads hundreds of miles from anywhere but complete with small aircraft and landing strip for transport.

Lonely and afraid over the storm tossed Tasman Sea, and a woman's voice in my ear saying, "Look behind you, Sheila." A flock of light aircraft had crept up on me under secret radar surveillance to give me the full VIP lead in to New Zealand.

Never will I forget the coral reefs, sandy beaches of the South Pacific isles with flying fish, sleepy lagoons and music wherever I landed; the old Fijian chiefs who garlanded me with necklaces of shells to bring me happiness and could not understand what records meant, nor why I could not stay to dance and feast for days.

Canton isle, once a Space-tracking atoll, where the whole population came out to greet me—all fifty-one of them—and I found I was the only woman that night on a Pacific isle with fifty-one Super Men!

Beautiful Hawaii, the land where you cannot remember what you came to forget. Then on to mainland America, land of surprises, with golden keys to the cities, police escorts with sirens blaring on the ground, and strangest of all, being made an Admiral of Space—the only other one being Bob Hope!

Newfoundland and the Royal Canadian Air Force's youngest cadet with huge yellow umbrella in one hand and the Union Jack in the other, who when I laughed, said, "There you are— I knew she'd choose the flag." He had obviously thought up his own way of greeting me as had the four Zontian members who had driven no less than a thousand miles just to give me a birthday present.

The last leg home and a message from the Channel Isles to return to them for a wonderful free holiday after the flight, and the welcome home words of yet another airline captain as we touched down together on parallel runways at London Airport. I had completed the longest solo flight around the world.

A kaleidoscope of waiting friends, flowers, customs officers, cameras, mikes—look here—look there, being so tired—oh so tired, but unable to relax. Non-understanding and sudden hurt when my beloved *Myth Too* was taxied away to be loaded on a lorry to be hung up outside the mighty newspaper office in Fleet Street. Only later understanding how many people saw and loved her too, whose thoughts over the years made many impossible things become possible for us both. Receptions, parties, charity requests and three secretaries in my tiny apartment trying to cope with sacks of mail and non-stop telephones, while I tried to earn the costs of such a flight.

For me only the sky remained reality. Life on the ground would never be the same again. These memories are only a small fraction of what such flights mean in material terms. But if flying becomes a vehicle to enable one to seek more to life, then the inner rewards are great enough to make one unwilling to give them up after just a few steps towards the blue expanse disguising the vastness of the universe. I am compelled to return again and again, striving to get higher and stay longer—at least in mind—for though I feel dwarfed by it, I find a purity of thought not always possible to recapture on the ground. I become as one with my aircraft—I am *her*—her every movement is mine as I freely fly through skies of changing hues and weather and diverse lands below. Even storms have magnificence and grandeur that no one can visualise from the ground, the colours of the seas are more vivid than ever can be seen from ship or port. The sense of smell is more intense—of new charts, a single rose, the spilt fuel—all are smelt separately, esoterically.

Up there I never feel alone as sometimes in a crowd of people on the ground; solitary perhaps but not lonely, not even in the worst moments of fear. In the sky, fear must be accepted as something known—an ordinary thing to be used to advantage. Far more important are the moments of an almost complete fulfilment; beginnings of understanding on a greater scale and smaller visions of a world friendship without prejudice; fascinating views of people and new lands—a beauty that is beyond description.

4

Was it chance again, the following year 1967, that led me to meet Ken Wood of food-mixer machine fame—a pilot himself? During the inevitable aviation conversation he barked, "I'm opening a new factory in South Africa in eight weeks' time. You could break the London to Capetown record to promote it. How much would you need?" That was all the business talk we ever had. The flight was on! My first visit to South Africa was certainly one of the most exciting journeys of my life.

The Israeli–Arab six-day war broke out during my preparations for the flight. The permissions for my over-flights were still coming in so I carried on with my plans, in spite of doleful predictions from my friends that I would never get there in one piece. The shooting was supposedly over by then, but the dramatic stories continued that there were six Arabs sitting on the end of the runway at Benghazi ready to shoot any aircraft down, and if I landed, I should still be stuck for lack of fuel and so on. But Libya reconfirmed she would still permit my flight.

When I landed, Benghazi was still maintaining the blackout from its recent war, and I was immediately surrounded by hundreds of excited chattering Arabs. Apprehensively I wondered if my friends had been right when the crowd refused to allow me to get out of the aircraft, but it soon turned out to be merely protocol. A suitable dignitary had to greet me first, and present me with a special scroll offering me food, free lodging— anything I needed. Not only did they give me fuel, but a choice of brand!

My next stop was to be at an oasis out in the desert in Chad, where barrels of fuel had been deposited for me by camel. But I had not taken into account that a Friday was a Moslem Sabbath. Although there are no control towers in the desert, one still does have to file a flight plan somewhere when crossing international borders. A controller, many hundreds of miles away from my route, received my Telexed plan and automatically replied, "No aircraft whose destination is South Africa may overfly Chad." There was no higher authority on duty on the Moslem holiday to confirm my previously obtained permission, and nothing I could do. Telephones and all communications north to Europe were non-existent because of the war. Then all hell broke out. The refuelling man came running to me shouting:

"Everything's changed—you are in trouble—you must go immediately. Try to get back to Malta. They've sent for the police to arrest you. You've had the Star of David painted on the aircraft!" I had done no such thing and could not think how they could imagine I would carry such an inflammatory sign in that particular area. The only national sign I carried was my own country's flag stencilled on the aircraft tail.

A furious mob milled round the aircraft. The secret police were already there and accusingly pointed to a sign I had not even realised was there, among the previous world flight autographs of good wishes painted on the wings. The offending sign was a year old and part of a signature from the Portuguese Azores islands. In vain, I tried to explain I had not written it personally, nor did I know it was there, and pointed out the fading paint while producing my passport to show where I had been. Finally the wily fuel man produced a pot of paint and after we had made a public painting-out ceremony, I was allowed to get into my aircraft. I did not stop for any more explanations and headed back to Malta fast. I had been lucky that the sign had been spotted in Benghazi where the crowd was more civilised than in my oasis. There they would have cut my throat without any questions, for the wounded Arabs were still left there from last week's war.

There was nothing to do but return to London and restart the record attempt via the west coast of Africa down to Capetown. The Congo had joined the eruptions now, and shot anything in sight but I could 'dogleg' out to sea. This time I went via Tripoli, and on across the Sahara desert to Kano in Nigeria. The heat was unbelievable, and the turbulence threw me all over the sky as I looked down at jagged rocks almost symmetrically arranged and at other times mountains of sand rearing up into a rusty-coloured sky until I could not tell the difference between land and air. Eagles and vultures from way above dive-bombed me until I was dizzy. One got bigger as it approached. It was no feathered bird—this one was gleaming metal—a jet fighter even more lethal than an eagle. A few unpleasant moments followed while I anxiously looked down wondering if I would be forced down or blown down. My pursuer disappeared behind me and a few minutes later the radio crackled and a heavily accented voice enquired, "Is that Sheila in the Piper Comanche?" Thank heavens for the writing on the aircraft today!

At Kano, I knew I was in the very heart of Africa—by the pungent odour, the sounds of chirping insects, the waves of heat, the tension of the people. But today there was an added excitement—the army had moved in two hours before. The airport was completely barricaded. I was warned to dogleg more new zones of fighting. Africa was erupting everywhere like one of her volcanoes, and I headed over Lagos. There was no chance of landing there now, but neither was there a way through the local tiger thunder storms. I had to edge into the highly active zone of Biafra before I finally escaped out to sea towards the island of São Tomé en route for Luanda in Angola.

Meanwhile Prince William, Britain's attaché in Lagos, received a furious message about the wicked aircraft, registered GATOY, carrying armaments and parachutists. What was it up to? Prince William recognised my registration number and with huge delight tried to explain there was hardly room for a revolver let alone a parachutist in my tiny tanked up aircraft!

Further on some of my charts read 'unsurveyed and uncharted', but I had filed at 9,000 feet and no one had even queried this. The night was utterly black; for no apparent reason I was very uneasy. Something not myself forced me to climb up higher as fast as possible. Twenty-four hours later other pilots told me about the uncharted mountain five hundred feet higher than I was flying. This was not the first time that I had such uncanny premonitions though I had not always acted on them. They had started long before I learned to fly, and I possibly became aware of them at the time I first seriously tried to study philosophy.

Normal communications still had been impossible when I left London, and so it was with great surprise that I heard the radio crackle with messages of welcome, congratulations and invitations as I flew over the border of South Africa. As I still

The start of the first solo round the world flight, 1966

Take-off from London Airport

Piper Comanche 260

MUSIC BY
WORLD RECORD CLUB

MYTH

Pioneer pilot Sir Alan Cobham and Marshal of the Royal Air Force, Sir Dermot Boyle, greet Sheila at the British Aviators' Welcome Home party at the Royal Aero Club, London

Sir Peter Masefield, Chairman of the Royal Aero Club, with Mr Gaisbacher, President of the Fédération Aéronautique Internationale, presents Sheila with the Britannia Trophy, 1969

The Royal Marines send Sheila off on a record attempt with a new tune to honour the occasion. London Airport, 1969

Zulu rickshaw in Durban

Refuelling African-style at Kilifi, Kenya

British Ninety-Nines, women pilots' party, 1971

struggled against the headwinds to get to Capetown in time to break the record, aircraft came up to meet me, with doors removed to make room for photographers on ropes to lead me on towards the great Table Mountain. My excitement was unbearable! I was going to make it this time, even though I had chipped only four hours off the standing record.

As I wearily but joyfully touched down at DF Malan airfield, the controller said, "Nice flight—nice landing Sheila. Look at my control tower, half of Capetown has come to meet you." I could not believe my eyes. What event was happening here? Ten thousand people could not be here for *Myth* and me? I had not known it, but from the border my whole flight and every word I spoke was broadcast over the national radio network, and my progress reports broadcast every step of the way just as they had done for aviatrix pioneer Amy Johnson who had flown this route in a Percival Gull Six aircraft in 1936.

"Well done—welcome home, lass," roared the crowd as I almost fell out of *Myth Too* into dozens of welcoming arms. What a greeting in this modern age, from a country I had never visited before—the same heady stuff that had greeted the pioneers before me. Everywhere I went there were laughing, teasing and cheering crowds, flowers, banner headlines, parties and most fabulous of all Table Mountain spot-lit that night in *Myth*'s and my honour. Even a Boeing 707 was detailed to fly over the Mount Nelson hotel to salute us.

And so it went all through Africa. Sometimes the methods of welcome changed, but always everywhere from south to north I found this fabulous enthusiasm and capacity for enjoyment regardless of political boundaries.

Now the increasing wars and worsening weather had closed me in, and the British Foreign Office officials dolefully told me *Myth* was marooned and I would never get her safely home that year. But there were the national races at home and all sorts of things planned. Also I was determined to return and see East Africa, now that I had come this far. Sudan had thrown out the British, and no British registered aircraft was allowed to over-fly, but I had already learned that if you can cut through official pomposity, you are far more likely to find a way. This is one of the advantages of private flying. So without telling the British, I sent a telegram directly to the Prime Minister of Sudan enlisting his help through mutual friends. He replied, not only permitting me through on the grounds of goodwill and sporting attempt, but with his greetings and his own personal representatives to meet me at Khartoum to see me safely on my way without any fuss or paperwork straight through the forbidden zones. At least a spark of friendship had been ignited there instead of the prevailing bitterness.

On my return I had to deliver the 'goodwill letter' I had carried from the Mayor of Capetown to the Lord Mayor of London. During the conversation the Lord Mayor told me of a special British Week being held in Toronto, Canada, and suggested it would be a good idea to fly a record flight to publicise it. So before I had even left Mansion House, yet another new opportunity had come to me and so the chain went on.

Long-distance flying had become the elixir that made me feel alive—a mere molecule in the universe, but nevertheless part of it. I was always struggling and having to work at anything except flying between the attempts, to raise enough to pay for the previous flight—never enough for the future, yet managed somehow to accept any long-distance challenge that arose. The flying was the positive charge, and the ground the negative, yet together they produced the energy needed to get a balanced view of life.

The sky had become my real life. On the ground I did not know who or what I was—me, the person, became completely swamped and I felt caged, and a negative thing. Everyone wanted my hand to shake, or sign an autograph book, or to open some charity do, but few realised I was weaker as a human being than they themselves. I could not live up to the inflexible being I was expected to be. The result was I had thousands of acquaintances and few close friends.

Throughout this time there had been another man in my life, but there was little chance for a normal life and times alone. He saw me in all the worst moods, and although not understanding them, accepted them. He did not fly—though bravely stuck it out with me on local flights—and had the strain of watching me go off for weeks without word to some wild place. He even tried to learn to fly too. Each time I returned he accepted the boredom of sitting six places away from me while I spoke my nightly piece to whatever function we were attending, but there were no lingering good-night kisses for him. I'd have to say, "I'm sorry darling, I can't stay up—I have to get up early to catch the train."

The train was usually to the north of England to give a lunch-time lecture—my main source of income for the flights. We stuck it out for three years, but we could not live two such separate lives. We quite literally and affectionately became the 'just good friends' we had always pretended to be. The truth was, he, like me, was not strong enough in all directions. My closest friend was my aircraft *Myth Too*. Whatever else had to be given up, it must not be the aircraft and I often measured more feminine frivolous things against how much fuel and flying hours they would buy. The aircraft always won.

Now a long-lasting love affair with the Royal Navy started at Biggin Hill Air Fair where I was being entertained by the Royal Air Force. Mumbling naval obscenities and remarks about spending my time with 'blankety crabs', a naval gentleman rushed me out of the airforce mess into a naval wardroom—a tent. I found myself inveigled into a corner and donning a pair of Fleet Air Arm overalls while being drilled in correct naval procedure and salute. I was to be part of the naval fly past crew in front of Prince Philip. As we flew past him in the lovely old torpedo dropper biplane, the Swordfish, my irrepressible friends pulled off my naval ratings cap and long blonde hair streamed behind. The comments on this new style naval rating are probably not repeatable, but the incident led to many marvellous opportunities—including being allowed to break the sound barrier in a naval jet, the Hunter, and eventually the formal presentation of Fleet Air Arm's wings as the Navy's only female naval aviator—honorary style. Now, wherever I fly, I am almost sure to find the Navy there ready to help.

5

AND so my life went on, with the sky always the reason for everything I did. My pursuit of records led me to most parts of the world, and now the great long-distance air races of the past began to be revived. The race that was undoubtedly the greatest fun was the *Daily Mail*'s 1969 'Top of the Tower', a race between London's GPO Tower and New York's Empire State Building. It was open to all comers in every type of transport, regardless of whether the competitor flew himself. The only restriction being that all competitors must cross the actual Atlantic Ocean by air. Anything could be used to get from airport to the top of the towers. The race commemorated the fiftieth anniversary of the first men to fly the Atlantic, Captain John Alcock and Lieutenant Arthur Whitton Brown, in the historic Vickers Vimy. The Vimy had won the challenge prize of £10,000 put up by the *Daily Mail* (which has always encouraged aviators) for the first aircraft across the Atlantic in 1919.

The race was to be run over eight days, May 4th to 12th, with each competitor choosing his own starting time, and favoured form of transport, from either side of the Atlantic. Three hundred and sixty of us entered—a more variegated group would have been hard to find. The aircraft involved ranged from airliner to the Royal Navy Squadron 892's fabulous Phantoms, and the Royal Air Force's incredible Harrier jump jet; glossy executive jets to Tiger Moths and even Mira Slovak's *Fournier*—half glider, half aeroplane.

The competitors were a glorious selection of extroverts, ranging from my favourite rival Tina, the chimpanzee, to Edward Drewery's team of sixty British businessmen complete in bowler hats, pin-striped trousers, furled umbrellas and briefcases bulging with export offerings for the unsuspecting American public! In the States, Commander Bill Martin, furious that his own US Navy could not challenge the Britishers because of Vietnam policies, made a private entry—and was to compete in the race from start to finish under a strange black hood in a bid to prove his extra-sensory perceptions! One of the first to enter was American Paul Friedman, who took his racing so seriously he withheld permission for his daughter to marry until race week was over! There were also the famous—flying grandfather, Max Conrad; Prince Michael of Kent; Olympic runner, Mary Rand; racing driver, Stirling Moss, with army parachutists, housewives, would-be balloonists and all! Their ingenuity was unbelievable, one girl was actually wrapped in a plastic bag to be airfreighted, and the gallant crippled Captain Alan Clarke travelled the whole way in his bath chair. The modes of transport varied from a 1919 Jenny biplane; a rowing boat; a Roman chariot; husky dogs pulling a sled; mules and even a penny farthing bicycle! All could enter for the price of £10. Well, I had that and somehow I had to be in it.

It was obvious the race was going to be won on skilled organisation and split-timing by an ace team. Lana St George Jeffers, then my secretary, and I carefully studied the rules. Lana decided to rope in every boyfriend she had (this was the easiest part of the preparations, for she has only to blink her inches-long, Irish eyelashes and the whole world gets tied around her little finger!). We would rehearse them so well they would be as good as any military professional team.

Naturally, I would fly solo in the beloved *Myth Too*; but how to get from her to the two towers—the start and finish points of the race? We tried everything, including *almost* persuading Scotland Yard to give me a Flying Crime Squad car. Next a racing motorbike was produced but I refused that on the grounds that I would undoubtedly fall off long before I reached *Myth Too*. Then we hit on it, a Navy helicopter could winch me down on a rope, but I was not the only one with that idea, and when the officials got wind of that plan, they very promptly issued an edict of 'No rope ladders, winches, or parachutes in the vicinity of London except on the River Thames!'

I quickly called David Brown, the manufacturer-designer of the fabulous Aston Martin cars, with a "Please may I borrow your Jet Ranger helicopter and also what about one of your glorious Aston Martin cars to get me from the GPO Tower to the helicopter?" David growled something back at me about women drivers who could not pass their driving test, but we were on.

Subsidiary transport now settled, it was time to drill our team. We decided to run our rehearsals at the same time of day as the time I would be really taking off. This was to be Sunday, the opening day of the race, but unlike the other light aircraft, I preferred to take the Atlantic stretch during the night on the theory that, in the event of radio failure, there was a better chance of seeing landfall the other side and of still continuing the race. What we had forgotten to plan for was the Sunday sightseers, for the race start line was in the Public Viewing Enclosure on the thirty-fifth floor. Lana's army of young things were stationed at every turn, each with a stop watch to time me reproachfully, but it took thirty minutes to get to the top! The high gale raging that day had put one elevator out of action and the other to half speed.

At last we were ready to rehearse. Stop watches synchronised. "Ready, steady, GO!" the team yelled. Full tilt at the elevator, but the wretched thing slammed its doors in my face and promptly gave up altogether. Nothing for it but to take the steps. I spiralled madly down, the walls whizzing round me as though I were in a spin, but opposite rudder would not help me today. Stick forward all right. I emerged like a spinning top into the arms of team member Number Four.

"What kept you? You took six and a half minutes. That's not good enough!" Oh hell, I thought, we have trained these boys too well. Still grumbling and bullying, he dragged me down the steps like a broken rag doll. The two Aston Martins roared off (for now we had two, one as leader and reserve!) A racing driver drove each one, led by Roy Pumphrey, the Aston manager, but no sooner had we whooped with joy at finding no lurking London Bobbies, than we were forced to a screaming halt! Trafalgar Square had been taken over by a monster demonstration again. Deftly and quickly into reverse to find another diversion, only to find we were back where we started!

"Oh, these closed-circuit racers," we murmured from the back. At last we caught a glimpse of the Thames. The heliport was actually in sight. Many minutes later I simply had to say, "Don't you drivers have to pass a navigation test? You are going so darn fast you've missed the turning!" We were lost in a maze of Battersea streets, and all the time the great power station next to the heliport maddeningly teased and beckoned us on into cul-de-sacs, and one-way streets. Somehow we made it, only to find a furious second half of the team waiting by the helicopter which had stopped its blades in utter disgust. It had only taken us three times as long as normal!

The days that followed got more and more complicatedly hilarious, and my apartment was full of people (even someone's baby) all clamouring with new and better theories. Meanwhile I could not think how to make *Myth Too* go faster, for she was up against all comers—most of them very fast twin aircraft. Well, we certainly cannot win anything and we are in for the fun, I said for both of us, but we are not going to be last either! Even the London bookies started accepting lighthearted bets as the day of the race approached.

Then a flip of the mail box spilled an ominous message. It said it was a taping of a séance! Hesitantly I played it. The medium's voice warned Sheila that her engine was spluttering, phut, phut and stopped over the sea like Amy Johnson! Amy had lost her life in the Thames Estuary during a wartime flight. The tape had been sent by some very kindly well-meaning people. I was horrified, but I could not give up because of it. I have always felt very positively that once you have announced an intention you must try. How often have I said things on the spur of the moment and then had to go through with them! Fortunately they have usually been the right things, so something must be guarding my thoughts.

I knew the tape was negative thinking, but still I was afraid of it, and my eyes kept straying to the drawer that I had hidden it in. I called the airport, and my down-to-earth engineers told me to get on with my flight planning and not to listen to it. Nevertheless they would give the aircraft a much more extensive check than I had ordered which was what they had wanted to do all the time anyway, had I not complained about the cost. The strange thing was that we did find little things that could have led to a ditching! *Myth* had stood unused for too long in a hangar while I spent the winter trying to earn enough for her keep.

Lord Donegall, a friend, once conducted a great psychic investigation some years ago in his role of newspaper correspondent. Now he checked out the group for me and found they were very dedicated sincere people. He promptly removed the tape from me saying, "Stop the negative thinking, Sheila, this is but a warning to take care. It does not specify the race anyway!"

At this stage, the Navy had put their blessings on the flight, and the BBC television film crew also decided to follow us in the race. And so I and my unsponsored team found we had the most enthusiastic support we could ever have imagined for ourselves. The glorious naval Phantoms would undoubtedly be the fastest in the race, and my Comanche one of the slowest, so *Myth* became everyone's pet. The frigate HMS *Nubian* was mid-Atlantic to guide the Phantoms and now would keep a protective eye on me too! The BBC worked out camera stations all along the route, including a live radio tie-up in the air, so I was not going to be very lonely on this flight. What a lovely send-off for any small aircraft pilot!

May 4th dawned, and we listened eagerly to the radio's hilarious reports of how the other competitors, belting down the Post Office Tower, were faring. They were scattering to all parts of England and our American friends were tumbling out of their Empire State helter-skelter on their side of the ocean.

I stayed lazily in bed laughing at their reported antics instead of collecting sleep before my night flight. Then came a call from an indignant foreman at our temporary base, London Airport.

"Somebody smeared your aircraft with some nasty red sticky stuff," he complained. "Don't they ever wash it? I have done it for you now!"

"Oh no!" I shrieked. "That was my super de luxe de-icing fluid and I got it specially for the race all the way from America!" Thank heavens for the spare can, but poor Doug Bianchi, then *Myth*'s engineering boss, who was seeing us off had to spend the whole of his Sunday putting it back on!

To my joy, the news that the first naval Phantom was doing well and about to set a new world record came through. A good omen! Time for us to go and now it was up to *Myth* and me to do our best in the smallest class. *Myth* and I, too, were out to break our own records on the direct Atlantic crossing. As I left my apartment, Sandra Collins gave me a big hug and whispered the words, "Fly high and safe. You are returning a godmother!" What a marvellous way to send someone off on a long lonely flight. I was as thrilled as though it were my own child.

Time to check in! A kaleidoscope of trailing wires, milling people, zooming cameras, cardboard cups of coffee, abandoned luggage met my eyes and feet as I rushed into the Post Office Tower. Our split-second timed take-offs had to be declared in advance and my wonderful team had got it all timed to perfection. They were strung out along the entire route. Even their girlfriends were stationed outside the public telephones, ready to call and alert the next teammate the moment our cavalcade streamed by. The helicopter, in turn, would inform our progress to the teammates waiting beside *Myth Too* at London Airport. There, too, pilot John Mercer would start *Myth*'s engine and take down the flight clearance minutes before we landed alongside her, so that we could quickly change places and I could proceed into the air without any delay.

"GO, Sheila," they screamed again. Head full of excited impressions and trembling hand tightly holding my race card. The Omega time-machine clattered and punched my time, and I was running helter-skelter for my life into the elevator. Whoosh, it was at top speed today. My ears popped and protested! I almost shot out of the elevator like a champagne cork as the team hauled me through a huge goodwilled crowd, who yelled, "Beat them, Sheila, beat them all!" Tears of excitement came into my eyes as I tumbled into the sleek blue Aston Martin. Ahead of us, its sister smartly drew away from us, but today a gorgeous tubby figure sat beside the racing driver—a London cab driver. What better navigator could have volunteered? Great walls of sound screamed above the cheering crowds. I nervously looked back. We were surrounded by white-helmeted motor cyclists!

"Ouch, the Bobbies have got us already, Heavens we'll be disqualified," I horrifiedly exclaimed to Roy.

"I thought that would surprise you," laughed Roy. "The Marines have arrived!" Indeed they had, and bless their hearts had returned from seeing their own competitors off to escort us too. The girls patiently waiting by their phone booths could hardly miss us now, nor did the rest of London! Every time the lights flashed red, great battle cries of wrath came from my gallant knights on motor cycle mounts, and magically the lights changed to green.

I leap out of the car and scramble under the great whirling blades of the Jet Ranger. A Movietone camera man hauls me aboard as the batsman slams the door, and waves us away up over the glistening Thames. Within moments, we are talking to London Airport, and within minutes can see it. There is dear Myth Too, *shimmering in excitement too, as her propeller whirls and catches the arcs of sunlight. We had taken all of six minutes. Now just six seconds to get out of the helicopter and on to the bathroom scales! The scales are a most important part of our equipment. The timekeeper has to check my weight as well as* Myth Too's *for light aircraft records. Three more steps and as fast as John slams the door I am safely sitting inside* Myth. *Brakes off and microphone in hand.*

"Darn it! What is wrong." No reply from the control tower! Precious seconds galloping away. I furiously open the door, then remember John had used the headset and the switches are up instead of down. Slam the door again. Air traffic's voice soothingly woos me through the speaker, clearing me straight to Runway 23 Left for an immediate take-off. We skim over the black lines between the grey concrete blocks like children playing hop-scotch. All of London Airport is behind us, and even the VC10 on finals makes an extra graceful curving approach to give my wheels time to gain momentum to leap for joy into the air. We are away, just Myth Too, *me and the sky.*

I did not know that the great announcer Raymond Baxter was up there in air traffic control, broadcasting live television of *Myth Too's* every quiver, and mine too! Undoubtedly it was thanks to his magnificent but utterly undeserved tributes that half the women of England say that they lay awake willing us on that night! I believe it was their concerted thoughts added to those of my own team that sped us faster than we can fly so heavily laden with ice.

This evening, the sky is in a welcoming mood and encourages us with its heavenly panorama of late afternoon sunlight over the green rolling English countryside. Even the thunderstorms have gracefully moved to one side to let us through. Their broody outlines make a sombre backcloth against the brilliance of the silver lakes and lengthening purple shadows below.

"*It is like our life,*" *I murmur to* Myth Too. "*One moment full of doubt, unsure, dark and threatening, and yet as suddenly full of soft happiness like an iridescent cloud.*"

Can this be Ireland already? Ireland, land of the 'little people' and pixies? The 'little people' are with us tonight, for it seems my watch has magically moved a whole two hours in a mere few seconds. We are fifteen minutes ahead of schedule! There is but one aircraft in the sky. It is a VC10 landing before us. But even that is a help, as he shelters us from the eager interviewers until I have safely set up the next leg's checks. It is now that poor Myth Too *must make her herculean effort to carry her almost intolerable burden of fuel up over the Irish hillocks towards the open sea. Bert Goodchild is with us, tending* Myth *carefully as he always does, slowly filling her with the thin green liquid that is her life blood.*

"*What are you waiting for?*" *grumbles a thick Irish brogue. Cameras are whirring and microphones are crackling. I retort that the aircraft will be thirsty if she is to remain airborne for hours.*

One last wave and I am aboard securely in my little cabin, harness done up and door tightly shut. The familiar smells of gas wafting gently with the aroma of bananas, and I touch the velvety smooth control stick as I check the elevators. My cockpit lights are warm and golden. Outside the sky allows us only enough light to reflect the silver chromium puddles on the dark runway. Look, the runway has become edged with a line of amber jewels to lead us out. I give one more glance over to the staring faces, and my rotating beacon is casting long fingers of red, lighting one face in particular. He frowns. "Don't worry, Bert!" His face breaks into a friendly grin, as though he heard. Myth's *engine smoothly roars as I push the throttle gently forward to taxi out, as though from the wings of a stage to the runway, which is our prelude. Just like an actress, I take three huge gulps of steadying air before the first entrance. We almost lumber forward,* Myth *awkward at first, with her unaccustomed weight.*

Remember to keep the pressure forward on that throttle, Sheila, no easing back or you'll fall in on your tail. Slowly, oh so slowly, it's taking an eternity. We are free again from the bonds of the sticky tarmac. We are at the gateway to the New World again. No Pilgrim Father ever felt as gloriously free as us, even though we must climb to eight thousand feet as the air traffic controller has bidden us. I wonder if he is working all night, will he return to one of those lighted cottages below? He has a nice furry Irish voice, so I am sure he is handsome. Only fairy princes can be near us this magical night.

Suddenly I am momentarily afraid. The night has grown dark. There is no friendly cottage light ahead, only the icy black depths of the Atlantic. I cannot even see my friends, the stars. I am lonely. "Oh no you are not," purrs back my trusty Lycoming engine. Why do I always imagine it as a lovely tubby thing, a rounded comforting person like an old nanny? It is as though there are three of us, old nanny Engine, Myth Too *and me. "Soon the moon will be up to cheer us on our way," the engine sings. "There's HMS* Nubian *out there waiting for you, and a radio telephone call. Time to let that trail aerial out and stop day-dreaming."*

For days now I have had dozens of people around me egging me on and leading me like no flight before. Heady wine for a solo pilot who must learn to be reliant on her own decisions, I chide myself.

2200 hours and time to tune into the GPO's radio beam. An unhappy high-pitched squawk greets me instead of the lovely gurgly voice of Raymond from Broadcasting House. Perhaps it is too early. But my watch tells me it is now. "Whatever happens keep talking," they had said. I talk and talk. The stars have come out and I can see Venus, my birth planet, up there. I thank my team and say we are doing fine. We are ahead of time. I hope they are not too tight, and aren't they lucky now they have got rid of me. They can go to bed now. I am back to the stars again. Still no one answers me! Thirty minutes later a woman's voice tells me to do it all again, they may use it later!

Poor Raymond sat in front of live cameras simply begging *Myth Too* to answer him, but we had escaped the GPO's beam and were far ahead. The team did not go to bed after all, wondering which part of the ocean I might possibly be in!

The outside air temperature is minus twelve and I am freezing. The heater does not work! Icy sand particles seem to sting the windshield. I shine the torch along wings, grown strangely white, bare of their usual friendly autographed greetings. I call air traffic control. He answers me, but refuses my request for a lower level.

"Why not?" I query, "I am all iced up."

"Because you are one of the ones in contact," he cruelly replies. "To-night there are too many little aircraft coming the other way without reporting!" I remember it is true and below 5000 feet you can still fly the Atlantic without too much surveillance. I think of the brave Arthur Brown who crept out on to the wings of the Vimy to scrape the ice away. Well I am not about to emulate him but I know if we get much more ice,

we will tumble ungracefully out of the sky. I turn around and grab an old shawl, huddle into it like a little old lady. I pour myself a comforting mug of hot coffee and warm my fingers by its heat. I have lost normal communications now and am in my own little world. Is there an outside world, or am I the only one left?

There were great dramas going on in other parts of the lonely ocean, which I could not know about until later. An American aircraft was in serious trouble. Little single-engined Mooney, Fred Clauser of Pennsylvania—was beaten down to a very low level by the ice and completely lost track of where he was. Aircraft in radio contact all around him tried to help, including one-legged Korean veteran pilot, Bill Guinther, flying a Bonanza. I remembered Fred's remarks before the race: he had innocently said that it was only planning that would win, not dare-devilry, as all the chance had been taken out of light aircraft flying with our modern aids, and it was not like Lindbergh's day! Ironically, the man now desperately trying to help him, Bill Guinther, had also made the same comments. Obviously the Fates were offended by these remarks, and one man was to pay dearly for it, only scraping through with his life by minutes, through a forced landing in the sea just off the Faroe Islands—seven hundred miles off course. Thanks to Bill's reports, air sea rescue had alerted the fishing boats, so Fred hardly got his feet wet, though the poor Mooney got a very cold bath. Fred had the guts to continue the race by airline and still make the Tower in time to finish, which is the most important thing in air racing.

Then there was private pilot, Ben Garcia, an even bigger baboon than Tina herself, who behaved like a perfect little society lady in comparison. There were no high-minded causes for Ben: he was in the race for the sheer joy of personal gimmickry and made no secret of it. But, many an official did not enjoy the chaos he left in his wake, nor did the poor little Piper Cub he left upside down in a chicken coop! Nevertheless, he did get himself across by airline, and no doubt gave hundreds of people enjoyment from his crazy clownlike antics. As for Tina, the chimp, she was perfect. She checked herself in using a thumb print as a signature. Dressed in a gorgeous silver dress, she posed for the photographs, went on her way, and at the other end was having none of the hullabaloo until she had very seriously checked her card at the finish!

I fly on through a dark desolate night so miserable that even the moon had deserted it. The frost on my windows has made the cockpit seem very small, and huddled in my shawl, I feel even more like a witch peering nearsightedly through the melted streaks. I have another cup of coffee and find a tube of sticky sweet condensed milk.

What's that I hear? Bang-snap-crash. Another thud! . . . It's the ice flying off the propeller. The engine is making a funny noise! My anxious eyes note the drop in manifold pressure. I give it some more power to warm it up and cautiously exercise the propeller. "Most of this is imagination," I chide myself. "It's the towering alps you fear, not the sea. Soon you can go lower. It may have to be fifty feet, but we've done it before." I tune in the Naval frequency. It's much too early, but incredibly I hear voices.

"HMS Nubian, do you read Golf Alpha Tango Oscar Yankee?"

"TOY, I read you loud and clear. Your position is one hundred miles east of the ship. Steer 268 and you should see our lights shortly."

We chat away about things great and small; and as if to join the party, the moon abruptly pushes the clouds aside, playing hide and seek with the waves below. It lights the great silver cones of ice sticking out of Myth's wings where tip tanks should be! I ask Nubian to positively request a lower level. Success, and slowly I edge downwards. The emptying fuel tank twangs behind my head. I jump in apprehension at its sudden noise, then laugh to be caught by its well-known pranks.

The stars seem to dip into the very water. I see a finger of light pointing up into the sky. It's Nubian's search lights! I can see the fluorescent spray around her bows. I sing with joy. She gives me her position, and tells me she is south of Ocean Weather Ship Juliet. *I need not dead reckon now. I can work out my position. We are still ahead of time! Why head for Ocean Weather Ship* Charley? *We do not need its beacon. We'll head straight for Wesleyville.*

"You are flying out of our range now, TOY. Captain has a message for you!" Another voice says, "Captain speaking. Ship's orders are the party is when we return to shore base. Every man aboard is awake and watching your progress on the screen. We have the loudspeakers on throughout the ship and we are all listening!" The Captain's voice is that of a man used to taking command, but a very human one!

I grow so dependent on sound and colour in my world. Now it is quiet again and it is hours since anyone talked to me. I talk to Myth. *She does not answer me, so I talk to Buck Tooth, the rabbit, who answers me with his usual toothy grin. He is adorned to suit the occasion in a bright red, white and blue ribbon to match my patriotic flying suit. I am glad the Naval men on* Nubian *could not see me now swathed in my shawl—I look more like Queen Victoria than Britannia.*

There are no communications now. My aerials must be piled up with ice. I must go even lower to watch for the coastline below the cloud. The sky is lighter. The sun must have risen above the horizon, but where are we? Slowly, foot by foot, lest the altimeter has changed as much as I fear, down we go to take a look. Myth *noses through the swirling mist until I see a solid patch of cloud twenty feet below us. Cloud be damned! It's pack ice, solid and jagged! Well, at least I know what my altitude really is, but I hope this mist does not get any lower. Dreamily I see a great white galleon skimming towards me, and as though in slow motion, we leisurely swing out of its path. My startled eyes look up as we pass alongside the jagged peaks of a magnificent giant iceberg. Now* Myth *races across the snowy sea at subsonic speed it seems. The very closeness of the jumbled sea cakes heightens every sense of thrill, but I am well aware of the icy joyless arms that await if I lift my eyes even for a second. A faint sound of Morse comes out of the speaker—Wesleyville, Newfoundland. Nearly there, I sing with joy. I climb a little, and confirm it on the radio compass. A spotted net curtain of snow shields Gander from my sight, but we are over the coastline now. We have made landfall! It's only eleven hours and we're four hours ahead. Four hours faster than our own previous record.*

Gander coldly welcomes us with an extra flurry of snow, but the bright BP truck lumbers up with fuel. I stagger inside the reception area and a dishevelled sleepy face greets me. It's Jack James, the kindly manager of the airport, who has looked after us so many times before. "You are four hours early," he greets me accusingly!

On, on, towards the Gulf of St Lawrence, over Nova Scotia. The Canadian controllers at Monkton must know how tired I am, for now they know I am solo they flirt away the time. I irritably notice they seem to be giving me an awful lot of extra jobs to sort out and request numerous answers, and then I realise, they are keeping me awake! They have obviously sent word down the line, for their American colleagues soon join in too, and almost before I know it, I am flying over Boston. Mad hatter's tea party and all, my irresponsible brain thinks.

La Guardia field in sight. Myth *rocks in the air currents from the hot concrete buildings of the great city of New York. Towering close to the*

Chrysler Building's spiky tower and the square outline of the Pan Am Building is the Empire State and the finish line. I can almost touch it, but I have far to go on the ground before I can actually punch the finish clock.

We slide to a halt quickly turning the switches off. I am so hunched up and have gripped the controls so tight I cannot move. A small ring of people stand round the aircraft in excitement but not one comes forward. The customs man has the right of way, but he doesn't waste a second and cheerily wishes me luck. I try to scramble out but my usual problem happens. Those wretched tank restraining wires have got the seat of my pants in a vice-like grip! The Fleet Air Arm in the crowd jump up and down in impatience yelling:

"Show a leg, Sheila, get on with it, girl. Get a move on!" It was more than my leg that was going to show! Somehow, waiting woman pilot Dee Mosteller hauls me to the helicopter, and I tumble in head first among a tangled mess of arms and legs belonging to more photographers. We leave the ground so fast the door flies open, and whoosh, we have to land again!

Out, double quick march! Into another Aston Martin, full pelt to the Empire State. Out of the car, sliding across the slippery floor into the elevator. It stops at the eightieth floor. Sixty-two seconds gone. I skid out again, prodded now on all sides by the excited BBC camera team, and run slam into a blank wall. Ouch, wrong way. Do a one eighty! Lost five seconds. Back into another elevator. Eight more seconds. Fall up the dais. One more second. Dee guides my hand to the clock. Gobble, snap. We are here. We've done it. Twenty-six hours, fifty-four minutes and twenty seconds, tower to tower. Champagne? Yes please, but I am drunk already! I am happy, happy, happy!

Back at my beloved Plaza Hotel. A tap at the door, a single romantic red rose atop a magnum of champagne from the Plaza itself. A great bouquet of red roses from the Royal Aero Club, which has been traditional whenever I break a record. A lovely fragrant basket of delicious bath treats from Elizabeth Arden herself. I was a woman again. Telegrams and telephone calls galore. A very special signal from the Admiral, and yet another from the frigate, HMS Nubian, signed with love from 290 sailors! Telephone again. It's Bob Webb, the flight planner.

"What did you do with those two minutes?" he growls.

"The hell with you," is my retort. "You know perfectly well you flight-planned us much faster than we can fly. We are not one of your monster VC10s."

"Well, I'm going to get some sleep," he grumbles on. *"I've been up all night too. Air Traffic Control rang me all night, every two hours to tell me where you were, and then what with those sailor boys!"*

"You were better off than me then. At least you knew where I was!" I sign off at last.

Excitement was too great and still I could not go to bed. Life was glorious and there was fun to be found in New York before setting off on some return records. We had won our section prize, and the second bit of sponsorship of my career was about to start from Whitbreads, the brewers, enabling me to just fly and fly that year.

So there followed another glorious year of flying; from close to the Arctic Circle down to the tip of South Africa again, entering races and sometimes chasing an elusive record. It was one of the busiest flying years of my career, and it seemed I was flying through an everlasting summer sky and it would go on forever. Perhaps there was not enough time to think straight on the ground, for without warning my life turned yet again, even before the year 1969 was out. I became involved in yet another international long-distance race and record attempt, a very different one that was to change me forever, and never again would I trust anyone lightly. It was a failure in a way, but not because of losing. After it, perhaps I would never fly again without a nagging fear of man-made problems, but also glimpsing miracles that truly happen. The ground caught up with my beloved sky and I was to become aware of two very positive but opposing forces, good and evil, as separate yet as attracting as the two magnetic poles. Forces, just like the earth's poles, very bewildering when one got too close to either. Nevertheless the sky and the aircraft still won above all other things, and I could not give them up.

PART II

"Memorable Christmas"

Sheila's story of the England to Australia Air Race, and on round the world again. 1969–1970.

"WHAT was your most memorable Christmas Day?" asked the woman journalist.

"The next one, as I shall be flying the England to Australia Air Race," I said, half in jest. It was December 1969, and competitors had come from all over the Western World in every kind of aircraft only to find England living up to her worst weather. Briefing day was held at the old wartime airfield at Biggin Hill on a turbulent Sunday. Rain streamed down on a bedraggled and miserable group of pilots; but the flying club tried to help us forget the weather by the warmth of their welcome. As I entered the crowded bar, I heard an official announcing through the megaphone that I was there: I assumed he was announcing the arrival of each race pilot. But that was not the case. He was making a fuss of me particularly—perhaps because of my sex—and it caused immediate antagonism from some men who had entered little international racing before. It was not a very happy beginning.

To make me even more uneasy my beret with its lucky naval rating's HMS *Nubian* cap ribbon had been swiped by the souvenir hunters. *Nubian* had adopted me after the 'Top of the Tower Race', and as there was no official naval entrant in this race, the Fleet Air Arm's 'honorary Naval aviator' was to be looked after by the Navy at the ground stops.

Take-off was four freezing days later, and by then snow and extremely bad weather had blanketed all of Europe. It would be tough flying the first leg until we reached the first compulsory refuelling stop, Athens. For some reason everything ran late for us and we were delayed by missing things, and I hurried along the taxiway only just in time to take off as the flag went down for my handicapped start. As I accelerated down Gatwick Airport's runway about to leave the ground, a knob fell off the instrument panel. It was obviously not my day!

Safely airborne, I discovered the missing knob was from the autopilot, leaving the bare metal spindle sticking out. Without it, this would be a very hard flight for me, a solo pilot; my competitors had co-pilots as well as autopilots. To do well, we all had to fly to Australia without time on the ground for rest which would take several days. Then I found that the magsyn compass, the transponder (an aid in controlled airspace) and the fuel indicator were also broken; and several other things were not working efficiently. For instance there was no indication from my long-distance radio (HF) aerial that it was reeling out to its correct length. Yet everything had been perfect when we flight tested the aircraft after the checks.

Of course, minor things go wrong in an aircraft just as they do in a car or even a kitchen, but normally it is one thing only, at the most two, or possibly a full electrical failure. There had to be something extremely odd for so many things to be wrong in a perfect aircraft. There was no question of turning back now, for once an aircraft's start time was passed, its elapsed time for the first part of the race ticked away regardless of what was wrong, or what delayed it. Fortunately, all my short-distance radio aids were working perfectly, and so was the aircraft standby compass. It was quite feasible and legal to get to Adelaide, Australia —the final destination for the first part of the 12,000 mile race— on short-range aids and had been done many times before. These snags just made me more determined: if anything, the very challenge urged me on. I could not do well in the race, but I had not expected to as a solo pilot. But I was not to be put off quite so easily—I would get there.

Blue skies emerged over the English Channel, and while it was smooth and clear, I tested everything again. By now there was no doubt that my normal 126 turns of HF long-distance radio trailing aerial had mysteriously become only fifty turns— not enough to receive or transmit voice. The set itself was obviously working but could not function without enough aerial. How could an aerial lose half its length by accident without its metal weight becoming unattached too?

Then, incredibly, unpleasant remarks and innuendos started in the air. This was the first time I had ever heard it actually during a sporting event. There are always grumbles before and after, but not while the race is on. At first I put it down to a different use of English language, but there could be no mistake when I heard:

"This race seems to be run for Air Race Number 99," from another competitor after air traffic control had made some necessary and normal comment to me, Air Race Number 99. The competitor burbled some more and I asked him to repeat his message.

"Air Race 99, ignore," came the instruction to me from a furious but protecting controller. He set me an example for much of the flight and I did ignore many things, but perhaps too many things for too long.

We were all stacked up through the layers of air lanes throughout Europe, most of us flying the direct route over the turbulent, snowy French mountains, and out over the Mediterranean through the night to Athens. The weather was appalling, alternating snow and thunderstorms. After Greece the climate suddenly changed to great heat over the shimmering haze and undulating sand dunes of Saudi Arabia's desert. I stripped off my woollen long johns and sweaters and stowed them behind the seat.

As the long smouldering day came to a close, and the moon shimmered romantically over the Gulf of Oman, I reached Karachi, Pakistan. There, most unexpectedly, I found I was only the second aircraft to check in, and the first was a Norman Britten aircraft. It was slower than me. But I lost the gained time struggling with the vast crowds waiting to greet us. Here, too, engineers found my trail aerial had been cut, and the two short pieces soldered together. I flew on over India and the mighty Ganges River—buzzards diving down on me, yet always managing somehow to miss my propeller—on towards Calcutta, to refuel. Here I was led into the BOAC office to meet the press. A camp bed had been left in the office for me to rest on during refuelling, and my interview was given literally flat out.

The Bay of Bengal was as turbulent and hot as ever, but as I neared the Malaysian coastline, the sun calmly slid into an orange horizon. I could hear that the leaders of the race were bunching up, fighting for air space into Singapore. Here the Royal Navy had provided another ace ground team, and in typically gallant fashion, gave me a gorgeous bouquet of orchids, which made me feel a woman again as I stumbled out into the darkness. Anrite Aviation took over *Myth Too* for refuelling and made her feel feminine again too by cleaning off a few of her travel stains. A very smart WREN jumped aboard to clean out the trash, while a Naval Commander filed my flight plan. The team knew if they could turn me round fast enough, I could save two hours' delay in the take-off queue as the traffic was building up. Competitors were streaming in now. The waiting nurse gave me a vitamin B_{12} injection and a new supply of multivitamins. I talked to the press through mouthfuls of steak for I was impatient to be off.

I was soon away, with a request for the longest runway into the wind, as the aircraft was overweight with the fuel tanks in the cabin behind me—needed for the long stretch from Singapore to Darwin, Australia. My preflight checks were done so quickly that I did not register the warning signs that something could be seriously amiss, even though my radio switches were out of their usual position, the position in which I had left them only a few minutes before. The old-fashioned standby headset I rarely use on long-distance flying (because the tight earphones give one a headache) was unexpectedly out of its box and lying on top of my storage chest. I vaguely thought someone had been service testing some of my equipment.

Five minutes after take-off, an irate controller demanded why Air Race Number 99 no longer replied to his questions. I heard him perfectly, so quickly switched radios to report in again. It was no use, 'Transmit' had gone in both sets. Then there was complete silence: the worst had happened and even 'Receive' was out.

I was stuck with no communications in thick, turbulent cumulus clouds in extraordinarily busy air space, on an active airway with no safe way of getting back. My long-distance aids were still unrepaired as there had been no time to delay anywhere. This time I suspected a complete electrical failure— every pilot's nightmare in instrument conditions, as it causes a failure of some of the blind flying instruments as well as the automatic under-carriage, flaps and indicators. I transmitted blind on all my radios, in all configurations, in case anything was still working and someone might hear that I would still try for Darwin without aids. I should be able to find the Australian continent—it was big enough—and as it would be daylight by then, could map read my way into Darwin. I had sufficient fuel to spare if I were slightly off course, and the onward weather forecast was clear in Australia.

At a safe distance out of Singapore, I left Oscar Advisory Airway and 'dead reckoned' twenty miles south of it to get out of the way of other traffic that might be following me. It was also necessary to climb to a higher level to avoid the volcanoes on the Indonesian land masses ahead of me. I chose 9750 feet to avoid being on an exact level with others, in case they too were off the airway course. (Aircraft under air traffic control on an airway fly at round figure levels with a minimum of 500 feet between them to prevent collisions.)

The dawn sun burned and scattered the clouds, and I felt more confident as I flew in the clear between them. By now I had verified that it was only my aids that were out and not a complete electrical failure. One radio—the long-distance communications HF set—apparently still worked, although it was useless with its damaged aerial. Wire had been cut, leaving too short an aerial. I tried once more to make the autopilot work with the tiny metal shank that originally held its missing knob. My thumb and finger became raw and bleeding trying to move it. I finally moved the wretched thing, but the direction was completely erratic and I found myself in a diving spiral.

"Oh well, the pioneers did it before me," I said aloud to *Myth*, "and we'll just have to do without aids too." The only difference was that solo pilots did not usually take on such long legs consecutively without rest. Somehow the sunlight refreshed me with renewed determination still to beat the solo feminine record, which stood at five days twenty-one hours from London to Darwin, Australia. When I left Singapore the record had been almost in sight in less than three days and would have been the best record attempt *Myth* and I had ever made.

There was no question of a solo pilot winning the whole race —there were only three of us, and the other two were men— against sixty-eight crews. A solo pilot has to overcome the physical endurance factor as well as spending more time on chores, while with a crew one pilot can eat, drink and sleep a little while the other flies. The important thing was not the winning but being part of this great race, yet I began to feel that luck had deserted me entirely as I tiredly struggled blindly on.

The weather ahead seemed equally determined to make the

flight as tough as possible and built up into towering cumulus clouds developing into severe thunderstorms. I had caught a glimpse of Borneo's coastline earlier so knew I was on the right track: recognisable land helped me fix actual times to positions and so work out my ground speeds. Unbelievably, I was ahead of time in spite of my problems.

The lovely calm disappeared as I approached the land masses and I no longer felt too optimistic. Suppose I was not on track, I thought, as the wind increased. There was no magsyn compass working to double-check on. I had passed through the equator region, so my standby compass could well be out in the southern hemisphere. Already it was continually moving with the turbulence and my unserviceable direction indicator recessed every five minutes. I was weary with trying to align the two.

I hastily took a long gulp of strong, sweet coffee to-ease my aching throat before the weather got too violent, but the coffee shot up into my face—brown sticky rivulets streamed out of my hair and down my cheeks. There were sandwiches, cold sausages and bananas in my insulated picnic bag, but my throat was too dry to eat. I took the special energy-making glucose tablets but the sickly powdery taste was horrible at this late breakfast time.

The sky had taken on an awe-inspiring mood, like a cathedral of towering arches—of silver-edged cloud frills backed by dark, sullen patches of torrential rain mist. I flew in and out of the lighter patches, wheeling and turning to avoid the worst solid black walls. A smoother piece of air would make me breathe a sigh of relaxing relief, but always a giant devil suddenly wrenched the controls and my temporary reprieve, leaving me gasping—hanging on tightly—seat belt and shoulder harness cutting into my shoulders and thighs. Again and again I had to turn out of the cruel grey charcoal solid mass looming before me, for it was like bouncing off a brick wall. Higher it was solid unflyable violent cloud. I feared what might be in them, and remembered such a storm only a few weeks before in Africa, when hail the size of golf balls had destroyed two light aircraft. Such conditions are quite different with radio aids, for at least then a pilot knows where the higher land masses are and can choose the best valleys to get through. The pressure needed to set the altimeter changes considerably going through fronts and so do the winds, and the radio provides the necessary information. Without radio it can only be a guess. This all conspired to bewilder me a little more after being twisted and turned in every direction.

This is damn silly, I thought. Here I was, a mere five or six hours away from Darwin, Australia, and the record. *There must be a way.* I would try to get out to sea around the north-east of Timor Island. I had been advised before the flight that it might be easier here if thunderstorms had built up over Timor Island, but it seemed to be blacker—the very eye of the storm. I was no longer sure of anything—not even if this *was* south-east of Timor. I could have slipped through somewhere south of Sumba Island, but it was impossible to tell without visibility or aids, or even a free hand to work anything out on paper. It all had to be done in my head.

All my training had always taught me when in trouble to climb, always to gain height, but the clouds were building higher and higher, black and unfriendly. I might well infringe an active airway, too, if I climbed higher. The evil glints of black mountain I had seen earlier were covered by vicious cloud. Indeed, it was time to get down and to do it without hitting anything.

I chose a lighter, straggly, kinder-looking cloud and slowly spiralled down looking in all directions for the jagged peaks it might be hiding. At one hundred feet I emerged from cloud totally disorientated into a torrent of beating rain.

All my charts were spread out but they are the size of a tablecloth and with one hand I desperately fought to refold them in the correct places. I tried to plot positions against the scanty times I had noted in my log. The large-scale map was long since missing—probably behind the tanks now—so I was left with only a small scale plotter. Surely I had to be south of Flores, of Sumba Islands.

I tried to avoid the heaviest rain and darkest patches of sea, but already the cloud was forcing me down to about thirty feet above the sea with no forward visibility making it impossible to concentrate on the office work in three feet of cabin space, and at the same time keep a look-out for anything that might be sticking up along our path.

71

Hopelessly, I switched everything on. Oddly, now one radio compass gave station identification Morse signals, loud and clear. Its needle turned drearily around and around, obviously affected by whatever was wrong electrically in the panel. Even the identification Morse signals were comforting. At least it was some contact with the ground, though heaven knows where those ground stations were—the identification letters made no sense with my radio charts. But who knows, I might fly within range of one of them, and it could be an airfield. I kept tuning Djakarta, Bali, Surabaja, Sumbawa, as I felt sure these were nearest to me but they did not respond.

The movement of the cloud had told me of the increased strength of the wind, which could have blown me miles off course. The HF long-distance radio with its too short aerial strangely came to life with static noise, though still no voices. I pressed my 'mike' button and that made a noise, so at least the set was really working both ways. It simply did not have enough aerial for range.

The weather was even worse, normal at midday. Suddenly the wandering radio compass needle hitched on to something strongly and definitely. There must be a beacon working nearby —maybe on an airfield. I turned to follow its direction. I was already down to less than thirty feet when the mist dipped down to the sea. I was too low to risk this direction lest it hid land with high ground, though the very fact that the mist was at ground level made me sure that land was there, and with it perhaps an elusive landing place. Four times I steadily followed the needle's direction, squeezed down by the cloud almost into the sea itself. The radio compass needle was so insistent that I talked to *Myth*, saying we must have the courage to go through it, but the mist was like a warning ghostly spectre. My wing tip almost touched the reaching, grasping fingers of the wave crests as I gently turned away, afraid to turn too tightly lest indeed the sea might capture and engulf us.

In the opposite direction, the cloud lifted a little and occasionally I saw brief patches of golden sun cloud through the dark, dark shadows. Up above there must be glorious visibility —but how high above was it, and how would I get down again? The bright patches were not big enough to be safe corridors.

This time I had pushed too far, and unless I found land with just a little cloud base left high enough to creep under, *Myth* and I must ditch or take the risk of hitting a volcano. I had enough fuel, if I conserved it, to take me on for an hour after darkness. We had flown through the night and almost all the day. I would do my best to hang on—no ditching yet—although my arms were aching with exhaustion and my legs full of cramp. I had been flying for two and a half days straight with only two hours of 'feet up' on a stretcher bed somewhere way back.

I was terribly hot, but I had to wear my lifejacket ready for the inevitable. I could smell its rubber as it stuck to my neck in the heat. My miraculous little Sarbi beacon felt heavy and became another weary-making thing; yet if I were floating in the sea it could bleep for two days without my doing anything; alternatively I could transmit to a nearby ship or aircraft). Either way it could save my life if I made an error of judgment and hit the sea too soon, so the added discomfort must be borne.

It was sometimes necessary to squeeze between steel grey sea and charcoal cloud in the mere height of a room. It is impossible to judge one's height exactly above the sea and without a pressure setting the altimeter is a very rough guide. I started one more search for visible land, first flying a square pattern, then triangular ones, but only endless surging, angry seas met my strained eyes.

I knew the possibility of death was now very near, at the most a few hours away, at worst minutes. I consciously faced up to this and felt, as always before, that whatever happened to me and *Myth* together was the right thing. Separately it would not have been right. There was nothing to regret and it was perhaps preordained. We, *Myth Too* and I, had tried and failed, but at least we had tried, which I felt most important in earthly life. To have been negative was a far worse sin than failure. I felt *Myth Too* would not let me down, but that it was I who had let her down. It would be all or nothing with *Myth*, and if it had to be, I felt she would let me die easily, quickly. I was afraid only of not having enough courage when the time ran out, and of crying.

I faced many things honestly and wondered whether I would have changed my life had I known this would happen. I remembered the good times, the incredible and beautiful times in the air, and I knew I had experienced more than most. I also remembered the unhappiness of recent days and the loneliness sometimes of my life on the ground—how few people knew me or even allowed me to be a human being. To thousands now I was a sort of name without being a flesh and blood thing—never me, the woman who could be hurt or elated, perhaps more than most; who could love a man; know moments of painful shyness, and gaucherie too; and who had many more self-doubts than they themselves.

And then I remembered the spontaneous gestures from strangers in the street, who simply called me Sheila and their thoughtful letters and good luck presents; my very close friends, Kay MacLean and the woman airline pilot, Elizabeth Overbury, whose support had often helped more than they knew; the engineers at Oxford who had looked at *Myth* and said she was too shabby to go to Australia like that, and so painted her in their own spare time; in fact all my long-suffering but expert team. In front of me was the card signed by all of the engineers at BUA, the airline that handles my flight watch. I thought of Geoffrey Edwards who, at the last moment, and without any questions had helped with some of the extra financing needed to make the flight, and I worried that he would think I had let him down. Because of his wonderful gesture alone, I could not give up—yet there was no apparent way to win through.

I peered out blindly, crouched over the stick, looking at endless ugly undulating waves. I forced myself to relax my tight grip, to sit up straight and to relax. My body was stiff. All seats except mine had been removed to make room for the giant extra fuel tanks there in the cabin with me, leaving no room to stretch an aching leg. All I could do, apart from isometric exercises, to relieve the pressures, was to vary my height an inch or two by sitting on a small cushion, and then removing it an hour later.

I stretched one hand into the black storage chest beside me to find the Thermos of ready-made coffee for stimulation, but there was none left, and I had to hold the controls so tightly that I could not spare the other hand to make some from a Thermos of hot water. I really did not need it: in such a situation, one's brain becomes unnaturally crystal clear and reacts at an amazing speed. I could smell the leather of my seat mingling with fast deteriorating fruit. *Myth*'s white wings scrawled with my coloured autograph pens, and her golden cowling now looked too frivolous and gay against the unrelenting sea that seemed to be waiting for the mistake that would send us plunging down into its depths.

I returned to my memories of all the sky had taught me and the experiences I had found there. The elements, far stronger than any human force and unbeatable at times, can change quite suddenly and, harnessed, become a help. It is in the sky that I find myself and know who I really am. In the sky I learn how much more the human mind is capable of, and not to ignore those depths and perceptions.

Now it had become stiflingly hot, and I was so low I could taste the salty dampness of the sea. Suddenly I shivered in spite of the humid heat with a foreboding feeling of evil around me. I was flying through an area of strange tribal religions and inexplicable happenings. Wartime pilots had often told me of their fears here and admit it was not just the knowledge of the enemy fighters lying in wait for them sheltered from sight by the eerie mountains, but that there is a distinct feeling of something bad here in the sinister night air.

Suddenly, a clear voice from the aircraft speaker interrupted these thoughts. It gave very clear instructions to an aircraft en route to Darwin. The short aerial must have picked up something at last, which indicated that I must be very near Darwin. But strange things can happen with long-distance radio, making it 'skip distance' near the end and beginning of the day. I transmitted my call sign and asked if anyone read me. Complete silence—only static air replied now.

I tested the mike button by its click and the HF radio test needle moved a little, indicating 'transmit' worked. If only I could make someone hear it! I tried reeling in and out my pathetic aerial, but the test needle always indicated too small a bounce. More indistinct aircraft instructions came through the speaker, until someone enquired about the Scott aircraft! "Heck, I am right here," I thought. "This is ridiculous." In vain I tried to tell them so but no one heard.

More crackling noises came through the speaker and the air seemed electrically alive. If they could not hear my voice perhaps they could hear the noises of my transmission. Why not try slow Morse on the button? Still very low over eternal, swelling waves, I tried to retain height with one hand while I laboriously pressed the button—long short, dash dot—giving my call sign, air race number and a Mayday that I was lost. I repeated it again and again to uncaring silence.

Then, minutes later, unbelievably, back came a Morse message. I heard it distinctly and struggled to write it down in dashes and dots with one hand still holding the wheel.

"What mat?" it said, but at first that did not make sense. Why did it not make sense? It could easily mean "What is the matter?" Old style radio messages were Morsed out in this shortened language.

Who could it be? A ham radio fan, or what? Surely not air traffic control—they all spoke English. The important thing was that there was somebody there. I started transmitting madly in my slow Morse and incredibly replies came back—much too fast for me to make sense out of them. Voices and snatches of conversation, including some bearings, interrupted the stream of Morse. Whatever I was receiving was too intermittent for me to work out where it came from, though Surabaja was certainly mentioned.

I signalled to my Morse friend, asking if he knew where I was and for advice, whether to try to get above cloud or to stay low. But now all I got was noise. I tried again for contact, in vain, but found the noise came immediately after I transmitted my poor Morse. I signalled in Morse again, "I can hear you occasionally, please repeat messages frequently, make two noises for yes, and one for no." I again asked should I stay low and received two noises. I repeated it and the same happened. I stayed low. Contact somewhere, somehow was established.

The sensation of some electrical energy in the aircraft increased and so did the high-pitched noise with an occasional metallic sound. My very fingertips felt alive with intense energy and my brain was full of sound. Now the main radio compass, whose needle had been stuck, was being affected and swinging cleanly, clearly and finally clinging to a definite bearing. My trembling fingers turned its audio switch up. The very loud Morse identification signal made no sense with any place I could trace on the charts. I turned the aircraft to follow the

Sheila receives the OBE in the New Year's Honours List, 1968

With the Hon. Edward Heath, on the day he renamed Ashford Airport, and (*on the left*) Gillian Cazalet, woman aircraft pilot

'Run for It'—from *Myth Too* to waiting helicopter to reach the Empire State
Building, New York
The *Daily Mail* 'Top of the Tower' Transatlantic Air Race, 1969

Sheila is somewhere in the middle of the scramble!

Prize-winners of the Transatlantic Air Race

Celebrating *Myth Too*'s victory after the 'Top of the Tower' Race at Oxford Airport

The great woman record-breaker of the Thirties, Jean Batten, with General Dick
Asjes of Belgium and Sheila at the England to Australia Air Race reception, 1969

Sydney, Australia, at last: England to Australia Air Race, 1970

direction the needle was pointing: there was nowhere else to go, so I might as well follow it.

The voices came back, but they were confused. They could not all be from air traffic control. What was I picking up? A ship, national radio, telephone, what? Could it be imagination? I tried to tell myself it was, but quite definitely the sound was coming out of the speaker, and when I put the headphones on, it was even louder. The unreal atmosphere intensified and I had a very definite feeling of being led. Most fantastic of all, I heard a woman's voice praying, and I thought she said, "Sheila, you must pray with me before you die."

"But I am still alive. I can stay airborne for a couple of hours yet. I am not dying." I thought, "This is not right. This is not what flying taught me. I must remain alert and fight to stay here." Then it seemed she said, "Oh, do be careful, Sheila. Keep still," and at that moment I *was* circling. I had climbed above a low cloud only to find I was enclosed by a circle of higher cloud which could be hiding volcanic masses. I descended again into silence. The voice did not return. I knew this voice could have been hallucination caused by my own thoughts fighting with early childhood teachings together with my definite feeling of being led, or maybe it truly was a mystical experience.

The babble of voices was decidedly real now, but masculine and arguing about two missing aircraft and a wrong heading. A very firm voice with an attractive burr, spoke in good English, though again not with a completely British accent; and with a second person was certainly searching for something or someone.

Was it an airborne pilot talking to an air traffic controller? Who was he looking for? Was it me? Then, amazingly I heard, "You don't think you are going to see her get out of that." More fantastic was the answer, "I don't care, I still want to find her." A heading of 150 degrees and 330 degrees was discussed and also an escape heading of two hundred and something degrees. I clicked Morse frantically on the button but received no reply, although I heard someone say they could not understand all the messages. Then I heard conversation, which sounded crazy to me.

"She seems to be in a coma," said one voice.

"That's the way I want her, nice and easy, relaxed," came the reply.

Then later, "It's a great situation. There's a huge Cu Nim sitting at the side of her." I had been flying low and straight on a steady course of 140 degrees straight under a thunderstorm, still following the mysterious signal on the radio compass. This was too much of a coincidence. The wings shivered but I held the heading firm. It was better than circling nowhere. So I crept on through the storm under lowering cloud. A long, low shape seemed to appear on the horizon far ahead, but it did not look like an island. I signalled once again in my slow Morse, "Ship or island ahead." Fantastically, again a Morse signal came back answering "Ship." Could it be? Was it an aircraft carrier? If it was, how could it help me with my crippled aids? There was no hook on my aircraft tail to attempt a deck landing. In moments a host of memories came back, and feverish new ideas mingled with them in my mind. The immediate thought of ditching beside a ship, if it was one, was quickly discarded. This was shark-infested sea.

I looked and looked. There was no ship, but there was an island, and beyond it many more—mere tiny beaches, perhaps fifty yards long, with coconut trees growing all over them. All of them too small to be of help. One even had a hut, and a strange little boat which had two huge bending leaves as sails. As I watched, it moved away with a man aboard. I followed and circled it again and again, but it led to nowhere but more ugly dark mist dipping to the sea.

I circled each island separately, desperately hoping for a beach long enough to land on. There were so many tiny dots of land, but none long or flat enough to get down without crashing back into the sea. There had to be a way of getting on to one of them while I had fuel and daylight and enough clear visibility. Perhaps I should ditch *Myth* close to one of them hoping that our momentum would carry us up to the beach. I flew backwards and forwards, wondering how to judge it—trying to find a patch of shallow sea into wind that could land me near a beach before all daylight disappeared. I had to risk it. I had nothing to lose for I was only alive on borrowed time already.

I took long, low runs over the waves which partly hid the dark shapes in the water. Submerged rocks? No, sharks! Oh my

God, the sharks were even close to land. Gone were any hopes of a safe ditching. Certainly I had one little packet of shark repellent attached to my life belt, but how long would this packet last? If one little scratch shed blood as a result of a rough landing, every shark for miles around would be on the scene even in shallow water. I would never make the shore in one piece, and at the thought of the sheer horror of being eaten alive, I lost all courage. There would be no voluntary ditching by me now.

A confused conversation broke out. "Can you save her?" "We don't know yet!"

Then I heard it, yet another voice giving a report, or was it a telephone conversation of the news of my death? I could not take it all in but I found myself protesting, "I am not dead yet. There are two hours to go. I am alive and I can hear you. This cannot be death if I can hear you." I talked to myself and *Myth*, for nobody on earth could hear me.

The voice said something about being "dedicated to flying and now she has given her life for it", and finished by saying, "This was the last photograph taken of her with her secretary in London at the race take-off." It *was* me they were talking about. Lana, my secretary, had been one of the last to talk to me through my storm window just before I started the engine and I remembered they had been taking pictures. Then another story telling about how I was fighting for my life. It must have been a newspaper man sending home two stories to suit the occasion.

During a lull in these conversations I decided to send one last message to my Morse friend, trying to explain what had happened. It seemed certain I would disappear eventually for no amount of determination could manufacture more fuel. There were people who would be concerned about what really happened to me and my aircraft. I signed off with my love.

Five minutes later my message was *read* vocally, even my love, and so was the fuel time remaining which I had attempted to indicate earlier! There was certainly a second male voice replying to it. It seemed to be the same reassuring voice with a burr in it and surely it was airborne. At some stage I had asked by Morse if it was the Navy and a voice said, "Let her think it is." There really was someone who cared, whether he was trying to find me, or just to give me confidence. Indeed he gave me needed strength.

"We could save her," I heard these words, but knew in my heart I could not be saved. I was afraid, desperately afraid, of what the last moments would be. Would it be a ghastly, grinding, noisy crash of only moments, or would we slowly sink to the ocean bed? It is said that drowning is a pleasant sensation, but what about the long minutes while the aeroplane slowly filled with water? Or would I be hurt and floating in the dinghy? Would I have the dignity not to scream, and remember the wonderful moments *Myth* had given me, the real friends she had found for me, or would the evil fish get me first? I was afraid I, too, would become an animal in terror and pain.

A gleam of light flashed somewhere, but where? Sun beaming on the water? No, there it was again right at the corner of my vision. I turned to look. It must be a mirage. The cloud had lifted a little and showed the base of a volcanic-looking, sheer mountain. Land yes—but solid and vertical. It was no mirage.

It might conceivably be someone signalling so, still rather hopelessly, I turned towards the land mass. Surely, that was not flat land I saw in front of the mountain? It was. Closer, I found it was watery, flooded land—rice paddy fields!

"*Myth*, we may get a bit hurt but we won't drown and we won't be eaten by sharks. Tomorrow someone will find us. There must be people if there are rice fields," I shouted aloud. My eyes strayed on a little further, and saw there, too, an aeroplane. It was low, but climbing. If it were real, it must have come from somewhere. It was real and it had, for straight ahead was a stretch of concrete, the most comforting, beautiful, long piece of ordinary concrete—a runway?

The speaker was crackling with my wonderful burry man's voice again. I spoke and Morsed again in my excitement.

"Sheila, air race number 99 okay, runway in sight." All formalities were forgotten, and the last airborne message I heard him reporting, "I received a message from her, but it does not make sense."

With only a quick circuit I went straight for that deserted and dirty, but wonderful runway. *Myth*'s wheels kissed it as we rolled the length of it—my legs were no longer strong enough to stand on the toe brakes. I thought an aircraft was behind me and had come from this airfield, so I swung off into the long grass as I could not see a taxi track. I switched off the engine so as not to damage the propeller in the long grass. There was complete silence all round me. No noise, no voices and no following aircraft. Where on earth was I? I could not see a moving thing. I was alone on an abandoned airfield, but where and in what country?

As I struggled out of my lifebelt I found I could hardly move. I lost all sense of time for a little, only to become aware later that I was no longer alone. Many sunburnt people moved through the tall grass towards me. A small truck bearing uniformed gentlemen came hurtling down the runway. Strange people pressed close to the aircraft, staring and gesticulating with excited high-pitched voices.

The aircraft door was roughly opened, and a gruff voice said in broken English, "Get out—come with me immediately." I tried and tried, but now my legs would not even lift up over the tin storage chest beside me, to scramble out of the door. Somehow I hauled my legs up manually with my arms and laid them like paralysed things on the chest, but it was no good. More unceremonious orders, but I could not move. Hands pulled and tugged me out to set me on my feet. Realising I was probably under arrest, I tried to explain my presence in a straightforward way.

"What country am I in?" I asked, but they did not reply, nor would my legs hold me upright and down I went, but still talking.

They hauled me up once again and I tried to explain that I would find the ship's papers. More and more people crowded around shouting and jumping; the children clapped and grinned. The grim officials eventually demanded that I leave everything here—I could hardly do otherwise—and dragged me with my useless limbs into the truck—with me chattering all the while—still trying to understand where I was.

Next I found myself in a basic airport briefing room, where someone had given me a drink. I began to feel more real, but I also realised, sadly, my rescuer had not come from here. These strange dark people did not seem to realise what I was doing in this part of the world.

I showed them the air race legal papers. I told them about the aircraft problems and circling the islands, but they only seemed worried that I had circled the town. I had not even seen a house, only waves for hours!

It turned out that an aircraft had been waiting for the usual afternoon bad weather to lift and as the cloud cleared, the pilot did his preflight checks, including switching his rotating beacon on for a few short moments. This is what I had seen and had I been facing the other way I would have missed it and still have been heading into nothing. So even my very heading had been a miracle—or was it guidance?

As the questions and explanations went on, the feeling came back into my stiffened body and made itself known by the very hurt of it. My hair hung lankly from the sweat streaming down, and my clothes stuck to me in a wet crumpled mess. My broken nails were jagged, with livid fingertips and thumb swollen and sore from trying to turn knobless spindles. I was too tired even to care that many were staring at me—a poor white thing who contrasted pitifully with the good looking, suntanned people around me. I was finally allowed to know that this was a military airfield near Makassar, principal town of the Celébes Islands.

I began to recover a little. They insisted that my aircraft must be brought up to the apron for surveillance. They pushed and hauled *Myth* out of the muddy, long grass back on to the runway, but the village people crowded on the runway too. Some had even produced bicycles. They jumped and cheered and clapped and some called 'Sheila Myth' in a strange Indonesian accent—the words they had seen painted on the aircraft. Vainly I warned them about my propeller before I started up, but they did not understand and only yelled all the more 'Sheila' and 'Scott'. I yanked the propeller and mimed 'Buzz buzz, chop chop' and this enchanted them even more as though I were a clown. Indeed I was.

Thereupon the strangest procession took place the whole length of the runway. The van led the way immediately in front of me, obviously afraid I might try to get away, though where to, or with what strength or fuel, I do not know. The people danced around as though it were a fiesta and the bicycles raced on ahead. They shouted and sang, but I was afraid my whirling prop blades would catch one of them.

No one was really quite decided what to do with me, and whether I should be locked up. It was a male lockup! I had begged them earlier to send a message out to the race organisers that I had landed safely here. I found that had been done, but that any other form of communication was impossible and could only be made from the town, an hour's drive away, yet they would not let me go there. I suggested a telegram. They said that it would take two weeks. They finally decided to take me to the Commandant's house to tell him my story and talk to his wife.

The Commandant questioned me very closely and insisted that I show on the chart again and again exactly what course I had been flying, but what was the use? All I had seen for hours were waves, and sharks, a coconut tree and isolated glimpses of sheer mountain. His attractive wife unexpectedly spoke fluent English and begged him to let me rest. The fever I had caught plus no sleep for nearly three days combined to give me a feeling of almost being drugged.

She led me to an empty bedroom. Torn brown paper covered the glassless windows. She left a candle beside me both for light and to discourage the flies swarming in. The darkened room swung around me as I lay down gratefully, the fantasia of the last three sleepless days dancing in my mind. With less than three days since I left London, I could still break the solo record as it stood at five and a half days. If I could sleep a little and find fuel for the aircraft, surely I could get off at dawn without aids. Now at least I knew where I was; and Darwin was only eight short flying hours away.

I awoke bewilderedly to the sun streaming through the cracks in the paper-covered windows. The nightmares were true and it had all happened, but I was still alive. I was vaguely aware that conversations had gone on through the night. I must have been only semi-conscious until now, and my planned early start was spoiled. Still fully clothed, I had slept through it.

My limbs would hardly move as I crept out of bed. The Commandant had long since gone to his office, and his friendly wife to a meeting in the town. Her sister, who spoke no English, showed her sympathy by producing more powdery chocolate drink. Another military man arrived indicating that I was to go with him, giving me no time to refresh my fevered face. My handbag mirror reflected a puffy insect-bitten face and wild hair, but I was more anxious to get on with the race than to clean up.

We bumped along the mud roads to the airport, where I found many of last night's faces. But I had been too bewildered and could not remember which face belonged to which official. I tried to explain that I had to go on and that I could make it without aids to Darwin now that I knew where I was. If I left immediately, I could still make the Australian coastline in daylight for it was becoming summer there. But it was no use. They would not allow it.

There was still no way of communicating with the outside world except through the airport Telex, which only gives aircraft movements and sometimes weather, and which they did not wish me to use. Eventually I persuaded them to send a message out that I would try visually but the clouds building up to the south-east over the Gunung Lompobaton mountain were already indicating the daily late morning storms. Now today I knew this mountain was nine and a half thousand feet high. It was the mountain towards which, the previous day, I had unknowingly headed towards four times! It had been hidden by the cloud which I had tried to make myself risk going through, and each time an unknown force had made me turn back.

For a while, it almost seemed that I was getting full cooperation. Refuellers filled my tanks, and even accepted my credit card. But there was still my passport to rescue from another part of the field and other delaying processes. Soon all hope of reaching Darwin had gone—that day anyway, and dispiritedly, I knew I would not be allowed to go. Communication from the field was hopeless. They maintained that the telephone only went to the local houses.

The military pilot Isnain, of the Aztec, arrived with a message from a Mr Anderson—a missionary pilot with a Cherokee—saying he had been unable to continue with his flight that day owing to the fearful weather just ahead, but he hoped to see me before he left.

The pilot, seeing my distress, warned me that I should only fly with repaired aids and in early morning at this season. He offered to take me with him into the nearest town to see what we could organise. The military jeep was crowded with joking military men but I could not understand the cracks. We drove through milling streets of open markets, bicycle rickshaws and grazing water buffalo to the town post office. There he thought I might be able to telephone the British Embassy in Djakarta (which is on another Indonesian Island, hundreds of miles away).

At the post office, Isnain must have had influence, because after some argument and delay he had got me through to the British Air Attaché in Djakarta, who greeted me by saying, "I'm glad you are here." I did not quite know how to take that, but at least he promised to let my team at home know where I was before we were abruptly cut off.

Isnain then took me to his house to meet his wife, Prijah, and two children. The family did not speak English, but we managed with gestures as she illustrated the way they lived with the aid of old photographs. Coffee, made of a half-filled cup of ground coffee, topped up with boiling water, was produced with Indonesian-style banana fritters. This was merely the appetiser, preceding an Indonesian dish of fish, eggs and rice. The flies are so thick here that even the fruit juice glasses have to have covers. I noticed they lit candles in daylight when we ate, and at first thought it was a Hindu religious rite, but it was just to keep the flies away.

The children and their friends came back with me to the airfield to see my aircraft. They did speak a little English—parrot fashion—gleaned from the European pop songs they listened to on the radio! They chanted, "I love you, do not forget us." Later this was taken up by all the children I met there and must have been their standard English greeting. What could be more charming?

Rain came down in torrents again and I watched in horror as the water streamed literally through *Myth Too*'s fuselage and the roots of the wings. Stray dogs nibbled at her tyres, and I was terrified that their teeth would go right through. There were no spares here. One moment her paint was literally baking off the aircraft from the enormous heat, and the next she looked like an amphibian swimming in floods of water. Somehow I had to move on, for there was no shelter for the aircraft here.

Sadly, I returned to the Commandant's home for another night. Everyone had now become extremely kind to me here, but I was most concerned about *Myth Too* standing out in the vicious weather, and I knew that as each day went by, she would deteriorate a little more. I was also frantic to get back into the race as, although there was little hope of a prize, at least there were several more days in which I could qualify for the final, and could even still break the women's record.

Late that night a Mr Anderson, American owner of a missionary aircraft *en route* to Manila, visited me. With him was colleague Morris Bliss, resident missionary, and his Indonesian assistant. They talked for many hours, lecturing me severely that I had been saved by a miracle the day before, and would be deliberately throwing my life away on a suicide attempt if I did not get things mended before I left. But how could I get things fixed, I argued? There was no way of getting any spare parts. They promised that next day they personally would escort me to the PT Nickel Company, a mining concern, equipped both with private HF radio, and a helicopter. The helicopter was up in the bush but they might have spares and an engineer here.

The missionaries again questioned me closely about the events of the flight, and argued that all of the things that occurred had probably been my tired brain rebelling and telling me it was overstretched. I did not believe the answer was quite as simple as that. Finally they prayed, in a very natural conversational way, asking that I feel better, that I should find my spares and make Australia safely and happily, and in time to qualify for the race. I was greatly touched. The prayers fitted with my own positive thought beliefs, even though I did not believe their earlier explanations.

I tossed and turned, sleepless, wondering through most of another night about the inexplicable things that had happened. I must have finally fallen deeply asleep because next I awoke with a terrible headache to the sound of an American voice. I rushed out, too late, to find he had gone. Now my thoughts and feelings had changed and again I was deeply depressed—even today I still could have just broken the record. I should have taken a risk and tried somehow to escape without my passport. I burst into tears. It seemed now I was making all the wrong decisions.

But soon Morris Bliss returned to drive to PT Nickel's office.

There, Bob Hamilton, the courteous Managing Director, offered every available facility from financial help to communications. First we tried their private HF radio set but that too had broken. Next we tried normal telephoning to Australia, England, Singapore, Calcutta, Karachi, right back along the route I had flown, and finally in desperation, to America for them to get a message back to England! Everywhere, anywhere, to try and organise a message home or to Singapore for spares, but every time the answer came back that the lines were closed.

Morris took me home where his wife was decorating a huge Christmas tree. Outside Chinese firecrackers reminded me that it was the day before Christmas Eve. In the brilliant sun and steamy heat, I had quite forgotten. At the airport the Bristow helicopter arrived to load up with turkeys and Christmas supplies for the mining men up country but still no engineer. One might arrive from Djakarta tomorrow or in a week's time! I waited all night but no telephone calls came through. Meanwhile Bob Hamilton had managed to communicate a long message to Djakarta requesting the British Ambassador to relay it on.

Much later a reply communication via the aeronautical Telex system arrived, requesting that I send full detailed messages instead of the abbreviated arrival messages usually allowed and that each message be repeated to Darwin, Singapore, London and Adelaide networks. Although I did not know it then, this repetition went on for several days. My private messages to my personal team and engineers found their way to an organiser of the race, which accounted for the surprising answer that they could not help as it would be unfair to other competitors!

I was alone in the briefing room when a telephone rang, so I answered it. Imagine my surprise when a voice said, "Sheila Scott? It's the *Daily Mail* here." How had they managed to get through? A roving reporter had reached Djakarta in search of me but could not get across to this remote island. Someone came into the room but I had already made contact with the outside world, and hung on to the phone.

Arthur Brittenden, the editor, had heard the confusing news that I had reached Darwin as flight planned but had not broken a record. He guessed something must be very wrong and checked, only to find I was, in fact, missing and had not arrived at all. He set one of his women reporters to work together with British United Airways. It had taken three days to communicate directly to me.

But after this call, days of messages and Telexes were given to me and things really started to happen fast. Now the Indonesian Air Force provided radio engineers. At first, it was difficult with the language problem, and some of my equipment was very different from theirs, but the radio officer was as determined as I was. He refused to give up, in spite of the Christmas leave and eventually sorted out the working of the VHF set. He found some broken fuses. I was back in business, with one short-range radio working—in a distorted fashion. It was better than nothing. I could take off the next day—Christmas Day—for Australia at last.

In the middle of all this, a Telex arrived reading, "Can route Surabaja, Makassar to escort Air Race 99 to Darwin request immediate answer or Air Race 34 will divert Den Pasar, Kupang, Darwin." It was highly probable that my radio would quit again. We still had not found the basic reason for the failures, and as the other aircraft was obviously out of the race prize money, we Telexed back that the very kind offer was appreciated. To my delight, on checking the race runner list we found Air Race 34 was the unofficial Red Arrow team with television film man, Arthur Gibson, flying the Italian Marchetti. The pilots must be Terry Kingsley and Peter Evans.

The afternoon weather presented its worst self but later a speck appeared from the west, circumventing the thunderstorms. I raced and splashed through the puddles, laughing and shouting for joy at seeing them, not meaning to be ungrateful to my Indonesian friends.

"Come let's see how good an actress you are—mock that scene up again, in case I didn't get it," greeted Arthur Gibson from behind his camera. And we did, for the drama was played out as far as we were concerned. More telephone calls now poured in on previously unusable telephones from the British press representatives wanting the story of our race epics—but our race was not yet finished. We could still get to Adelaide for the start of the short speed race on January 2nd.

7

It was Christmas morning but Morris and the Commandant and his wife, with several of our newly found friends, had risen at five o'clock to wave us off. Terry filed our flight plans for Kupang on Timor Island halfway to Australia for the Marchetti had only a short range owing to its passengers. Planning to land with them, I only put in my usual amount of fuel, although it was still far more range than they had. Just before I started the engine, Morris tapped on the storm window, and said another of his little prayers for my safe journey and future happiness.

That morning the sun was hard and bright. My eyes were soon watering, as I tried to formate on the other aircraft. Almost leisurely we flew over Maumere airfield on Flores Island, the terrain wide open and clear below us—on towards Timor Island. But in no time, the clear skies became thick, wet murk again, and we were forced to descend rapidly over the churning sea, still approaching Kupang on the next island. We almost kissed the waves at a mere thirty feet. The low rain clouds reduced all forward visibility. Spray leapt to meet us, and ragged patches of mist dipped down into the sea. I hung on at top speed to the tail of the Marchetti, trying to keep up with it, as it was ten knots faster than my normal speed.

Now we were concentrating too hard for talk on the radio. In any case, my speaker was so distorted again I could hardly hear a thing. The storm water was still caught in the inner shell of my aircraft, and I could see it seeping through my light covers. Uncomfortably I felt the cold drops dripping on my face and soaking my shirt. Again and again, we tried to get into Kupang from all angles but it was hopeless. Kupang was covered by unrelenting fog cloaking sinuous coastal mountains.

There was no time to waste. The Marchetti could barely have enough fuel to return to Flores Island and Maumere airfield. We turned around smartly and headed back towards Flores. I could stretch mine with economy speeds, but now I was gobbling it up to keep my speed up to that of the Marchetti. I tried to tune various beacons while still keeping my eyes on the leader aircraft, but nothing responded. As the follow aircraft, I did not have a clue by then exactly where we were. You cannot formate solo and make a note of times and tracks under such circumstances. I could only guess where we might be. Forward visibility was fifty feet at the most, and after what seemed hours later, a coastline of undulating beach covered with coconut trees appeared to shoot under us.

"Turn left, head 270, Sheila. On to 270, Sheila," crackled the radio, and, as I did, a coconut tree on a hummock scraped so uncomfortably close, I doubted there were any coconuts left.

As I turned a headland loomed above and ahead of me, disappearing into cloud. To hell with flying on a heading of 270, I thought, I will climb high on instruments back over the sea. I was skirting too low over the edge of ragged beach and trees. The Marchetti flying close beside me looked like a tiny blue jet as angry foam of gun-metal sea flashed beneath her. Her navigation lights comfortingly gleamed at me. But trying to look both at her and the bits of land under me was vertigo-making; and far better for us to separate. In formation, the follow aircraft must not take eyes off the leader but we were too low for me, a non-trained formation pilot, to keep this up. I had experience of close air-to-air filming, but never tight formation at low level with nil forward visibility. It could have been fun if the weather had not been so rotten.

I radioed that I would fend for myself at a higher level as I climbed up and out to turn on to 180 degrees, hoping that the coast did not curve round to meet me head on. My last glimpse of my pals was of them heading directly towards more barbaric coastline. They appeared to say on the distorted radio, "Head west, Sheila, it's better."

The severe turbulent cloud indicated only too obviously the vicinity of embedded thunderstorms, as I fought to control *Myth Too*, at one time quite out of control. An ugly silence followed on the radio, and there was no reply to my calls. The worst must have happened. Where was the other plane? Had it crashed, or made a beach? I descended full of misgiving back over the furious sea—hoping it was sea and not mountain—but at twenty feet I saw the angry swell below me and turned back to the island to look, but there was no sign of anyone or anything except the jagged coastline. Visibility was worse than ever and I could not remain so low without hitting the trees. There was no way out, and nothing I could do but to turn south again and climb back up over the sea. Down draughts hurled me down then straight up again—at one time quite out of control—until I somehow managed to remain high enough to avoid the volcanoes. I decided to head back over Flores Island to attempt to try and find more skilled help from somewhere for my missing friends.

I crept through unbelievable turbulence to the northern side of Flores, to let down again over the sea. Here the cloud base was higher. My distorted radio, now tuned to the emergency frequency, picked up nothing. Maumere must be miles behind me in the thunderstorms. I continued on around the island until I met a solid wall of swirling violence and clouds. There had been no sign of anything or anyone, neither was there any place to land. I had to turn back yet again. My chart indicated that there were two small airfields on the next island to the West. I must make for one of these and, if they were still in existence, ask for help. Volcano tops crowned with bubbling cloud reared above me to port. I hoped to find a certain creek leading to a little airfield, but it was hopeless. Fog reached down to the ground inland.

Suddenly ahead, hints of sunlight peeped through the cloud and I picked up the headland—just where it should be according to the chart. The little town of Sumbawa must be somewhere ahead.

A house appeared, tucked under the storm. I circled round and eventually saw animals grazing on a long grass field—it was a runway, otherwise utterly deserted. Not a car or anything seemed to move near the small control tower as I circled. Nothing apart from the animals running from the aircraft noise, yet before I had finished taxiing up to the deserted control hut, dozens of people had emerged from nowhere like ants out of an ant hill. I almost fell out of the aircraft in my haste to explain the emergency. Fortunately some of the airport people spoke pidgin English, and I asked to signal Maumere immediately to find out whether the Marchetti had landed safely there. But in Sumbawa, there truly are *no* external telephones or Telex system—only telegrams which could take up to two weeks. Outside communication is by Morse when the weather is suitable—rather like bush telegraphy.

Today, a holiday, no one was working, he explained and frustratingly went to argue with me that the other aircraft must be all right if I myself had managed to find Sumbawa. Again and again, I tried to get it across to him that the second aircraft was certainly in trouble as it was out of fuel. Once again I showed him the chart and the impossible coastline where I had last seen it. Outside now the heavens had opened up like a giant waterfall. My throat was aching with thirst but I was frantic with worry, for it was hours since I last saw the missing crew. There was no fuel here to even refuel so there was no hope of finding better communications.

Somehow I persuaded them at least to try to find the communications man. But the storm interfered with radio reception to the receiving station at Bali Island, Java. Hours later we received the grim reply that nothing had landed at Maumere, I requested the Air Search and Rescue Services, they could be lying hurt on some deserted coastline, or floating in a dinghy in shark-infested waters. Worse all three could be dead.

I had already signalled the latitude and longitude of where I estimated I had last seen them. There had been no way of telling exactly where we crossed the coastline; all I knew was that I had last seen them heading two-six-zero and their last readable message to me had been—"Head west for the weather is better there."

Signalling by Morse takes long enough, apart from the language barrier, with its misunderstood words and numerals. The delays made me realise how much we, in more sophisticated countries, take such services as telephone, voice radio and Telex for granted. I was impatient with anxiety while Sumbawa argued that there was nothing else to be done and wanted to close up for the day. Help tonight could possibly still save lives.

At last more replies clattered in—the Morse too rapid for me to follow. No sooner was one message written out when in came another, now with urgent requests from Darwin and Singapore too for further details of exact positions, until finally a message from Singapore said "Message understood!", but that was all. I still did not know if anyone was actually doing anything constructive.

Many faces pressed against the windows of the office, all staring, chattering and laughing as they watched and commented on every move I made. I was aghast at my inability to do anything towards finding the Marchetti. Oh, for some fuel. Tears in my eyes, I turned away so that the watchers should not see how shocked I was. But the tears were seen and the atmosphere became almost threatening as the crowd became cross. It was some time before instinct told me that this was because they thought I did not like *them*. I learned then, as never before, that the hardest thing is to smile and act a pantomime of explanation, when in reality your head is full of fear and your eyes of tears.

I was at my wits' end to know how to keep this station open. The maintenance man grumbled in Indonesian that the generator was too hot and would break down. I thought it was an excuse and grumbled back that as long as we could help any rescue operations it must stay open. I needed the reassurance that rescue had really started, before all communications became impossible again. Affirmation came through from Bali—just in time—before the generator gave its final groaning objection and stopped for ever. Crowds still milled around outside, only kept out of the office by the manager flicking a giant feather duster thing, accompanied by shooshing shouts of fury.

I paddled barefoot through the torrent over the flooded field to get my few possessions and to settle poor *Myth Too* as best I could. We squeezed into a very ancient jeep; the people pressed closer and children held on to the sides of the truck completely unaware of any danger. We lurched off through muddy, deeply pot-holed roads, lined by austere bungalows, nestling against old-time homes on stilts sheltered by coconut matting.

My friends talked of how angry the village priest would be that they had worked on such a day. I replied that I was sure he would forgive them, as it was perhaps to save some peoples' lives, and asked to be taken to him. Unfortunately, the priest spoke no English and so my hopes of help there were quickly dashed. They then suggested visiting the seventy-year-old German doctor—the only European in the area. After hearing my sorry plight, he suggested that I return that evening to his house for food and to listen to the household radio news, broadcast from Australia. There might be some news of the missing plane.

I could stay at the local resthouse—which was hardly a tourist spot. Life is fairly primitive here compared to Europe and America. My dark hot room had one glassless window which could only be veiled from prying eyes by shutters, leaving one in stifling blackness. A wooden bed with kitchen table, one broken chair and fly-brown mirror over a wash basin with no water completed the room. I tried to turn on a light switch as I stumbled in the darkened room, but that too was only for show. I was streaming with sweat and fever again. Opening the shutters was the only way of getting air into the room, but it also attracted strange flies and inches-long bugs as well as the entire flock of village children shouting and mocking as children will. There was absolutely no privacy. Everything I did was closely observed. I coughed and coughed, and even my coughs were imitated. It sounded like a tuberculosis ward. I opened the aircraft first-aid pack to find anti-insect cream and somehow publicly cleaned up with dry tissues.

Back at the old German doctor's house, the smiling Indonesian wife welcomed me and led me to a bowl of warm water, soap and a towel, and even wooden clogs to wear. It was the first warm water and soap I had had to wash in for a week.

Christmas dinner consisted of rice, shredded dried deer meat, buffalo mince, tomatoes and tea. I tried to eat to be polite to my kind hosts, but could only swallow the tea gratefully. I was still too ill and worried to eat.

The old doctor talked of the people who had visited there— all of twenty-six in a whole year, mostly archaeologists or geologists. He talked much of a visitor, Emil Zatopek, the great runner, but my mind was straying to the missing aircraft. At nine we were able to tune into Darwin on the household's radio set, but all I could hear from the distorted reception was long descriptions of how the rest of the world had celebrated Christmas Day and that the Pope had given away dozens of toys to children. No word of the air race or my friends filtered through.

Studying the doctor's local survey charts did not help as he showed me the only beach on the south coast of Flores where an aircraft might land safely. Everywhere else was so rugged and tightly layered with trees they could never have got down safely. I got increasingly distressed, sure that we had not been as far east as the safe beach he pointed to.

On my return to my shuttered room, the doctor had sprayed my room with his special strong insect spray—so strong that the room had to be left unoccupied for half an hour. I sat, lonely and afraid of the fate of my friends, outside on the communal balcony, but this was obviously the local signal that I wished to be picked up. The local men kept gesturing for a light until I realised the same cigarette had been lit many times. The buzzing and chirping of night insects mingled with the drums of the village revellers. Another time I might have enjoyed the romantic adventure of it all, but now I had too many dramas of my own to appreciate it.

I tried to think of homely things, remembering that it was Christmas Day, and that once again, a miracle had happened—I had got down safely. Was it because of Morris prayers or positive thoughts, or why was it? Before, I had not been able to help the troubles I had got into, for most of them were due to outside physical destruction of certain aids. But today, I could perhaps have prevented further mistakes if I had not allowed myself to be led. Why then should I be saved, and perhaps the others not? Was it even being saved—to be the one left with the intolerable burden of not knowing what had happened.

I finally went to bed, wedging the doors and shutters closed, otherwise anyone from the street could walk straight in during the night—there were no locks—but it was stifling without ventilation. In desperation I pinned my dirty shirt over the holes in the mosquito net to ward off giant-sized bugs.

The day after Christmas started at 6.30 a.m. when a rousing bang at the door wakened me. The doctor had heard on the radio that a search party was being organised for the boys, and that Darwin knew I was here on Sumbawa. So they had not reached Maumere airfield. Depressed and utterly miserable I struggled to get dressed quickly. My cold and dysentery were worse, and now there was not even a tissue left from the aircraft's emergency supply. I was bitten all over and barely human. Tea was provided that morning, and as it must have been made with boiling water, I risked cleaning my teeth with it! Even the soles of my shoes were peeling off and my clothes were steaming. I would have to get some wooden clogs, though I had very little Indonesian currency—only traveller's cheques which no one understood as money. Fortunately the room cost only thirty-five pence a night.

At the airport, I found a message from an Air Vice-Marshal Iskander, of the Indonesian Air Force, that he would arrange enough fuel to be sent in a drum by the DC3 air transport in the next day or so, to enable me to fly to the customs field at Bali.

Someone came rushing in with excited gestures. The ordinary radio had broadcast the news that the boys were safe in Australia. I felt light-headed—and drunk with relief sat down. But all around me remained ruffled and angry, obviously blaming me for insisting on a search when the other aircraft had been perfectly all right. In fact the men did have to force land—on the only bit of beach I had seen on the doctor's chart, and would have still been there, had it not been for a friendly isolated village. It was a while before I realised that if fuel did not come for forty-eight hours, I was absolutely out of the race. Now the worry of my companions was solved, I must try and get myself there. Having gone through all this it would be too frustrating to let down my own team at home by not even qualifying as a finisher.

The supplies in the aircraft were finished—except for two unexpected packs of cigarettes and an old piece of muslin which I ripped up for a towel and hankies. It was like finding nuggets of gold. Two eggs and some sour bread were today's food ration —but the eggs were pickled probably five years old.

That night I spread my charts all over the balcony as the moonlight was brighter there, to plot new courses to Bali and Australia, as the village drums competed with the howling dogs. The insects crawled all over my charts and flies bumped into me, but now they were old friends! I still felt extremely ill physically, but comforted myself with the thought that if I could just make Adelaide in time, there would be four days to recover in, before the fast segment of the race began to Sydney.

By early dawn, I was impatiently waiting for the jeep. Three hours later it arrived, with its usual impossible load and we trundled off to the airport to wait for the old DC3 supply aircraft now signalled to arrive today. But first we had to clear the runway of wild buffalo with the jeep.

The old DC3 aircraft flying over the field was one of the most comforting sights I have ever seen and seemed like the most modern of transport after the last few days. The crew dragged out a drum of fuel. They had thought of everything—even an umbrella to keep water out of the fuel in case of rain. "Miss Scott, I presume!" said an attractive young man who had somehow talked himself aboard with the supplies. "The British Embassy said you were a heavy smoker, and the first thing you would ask for would be these." He pulled out dozens of packets of cigarettes. This was Hugh Lunn of Reuters. It was like a gay fiesta as we filled the tanks, but the DC3 was in a rush to beat the midday storms, and so was I.

Large raindrops were already falling heralding the thunderstorms grumbling over the far volcano, as I quickly climbed aboard. I felt a glorious sense of freedom as I headed slightly out to sea where the sunlight still danced on the waves, accentuated by the black cage of clouds and emotions I was leaving behind. Today there was much activity on the VHF radio, and several enquiries where I was. I heard three other race aircraft also going into Bali, so unbelievably, even though a week later than I had planned, I was not the only competitor yet to qualify.

Bali had become so modern I hardly recognised it, but I was reassured to find many old friends from my 1966 World Flight still there. The customs man who welcomed me showed me his signature still in my passport. Even the same airport manager was there—now a very important man with his big new shiny airport.

The line boy cheerily filled my fuel tanks, I told him to fill them to overflowing, as they often look full when they are not. He cracked back that he was BP and not 'Brand X', and therefore would look after me well. It was in good humour, and yet someone must have been half listening and, as so often in this race, jumped to the wrong conclusion. Later, I was to discover, someone had duly reported that I said I was given bad fuel from Bali. What utter nonsense! It is now a very civilised glossy field, and I was exceedingly grateful for the good service they had given me.

A Norman Britten aircraft being ferried to Port Moresby by Keith Sissons arrived. He had been about to load his aircraft up with spares and fuel to come down to Sumbawa to rescue me.

I had never met him before, but he had heard of my plight and had the imagination to know I was stuck, and to do something positive about it. This spotlit the bond that there is among genuine pilots who really love long-distance flying, and helped me to forget the mental bruises I had received from others who were certainly not in the race for love of anything.

It was now late afternoon and I had only one short-range radio set partly working. I was instructed to leave early next morning, when, at least, I would remain legal (and there could be no criticism) as I could visually map-read the coastline of Australia if necessary. The Qantas manager took us to the new Hotel Continental that had risen since I was last here. On the way, I looked for the Bali I had known with its beautiful, bare-bosomed women in the gaily coloured, flowing skirts. Now they wore mini skirts and blouses. The hibiscus and palm trees were still there, but the grass huts had become concrete boxes and the uninhibited village drums had become pop music from transistor radios.

The Bali Continental Hotel can never have opened its door to a stranger female sight than me as I entered the foyer with Keith and Hugh. Glamorous women draped over the sofas looked very startled when they saw my insect-bitten image with its wire-wool hair walk in. The manager was magnificent and greeted me as though I were swathed in mink from head to foot. With both arms outstretched, he welcomed me through the parade of beautiful people, and said the hotel was mine to command! What would I like most? "Bacon and eggs?" I asked wistfully. He immediately led me to the restaurant, and a huge plate soon was put before me. They knew I had missed Christmas, could not find any Christmas pudding, so they found a dessert with raisins and currants in it and stuck a candle on it for celebration. I drank gallons of coffee and recklessly smoked innumerable cigarettes, an absolute joy now I knew I no longer had to ration anything. In my room, I luxuriated in a bath of sweet-smelling bath oil from the drug store, washed my clothes and draped myself in fragrant towels, and turned all the switches and buttons on and off again like a child. I savoured every single thing, in a way no guest could possibly have done before, or since.

At last I arrived at Darwin, Australia, unsuspecting and

happy, to be met by old friends in the Aero Club, headed by Peter Denholm, the chairman. Even the customs men filled in the forms for me and made me feel welcome. Qantas had laid on food supplies for all the competing aircraft (with real Christmas pudding at last!). Among friends, I was lulled into a secure feeling of happiness and relief, and quite unprepared for the shocks that were still to come.

The press had gathered, most of them warm and friendly except for one very large gentleman who attacked me verbally in a way I had never before heard in my entire career. He accused me of deserting the other aircraft—hardly desertion when I had gone back into what were impossible conditions to find them. He went on to say that *Myth Too* was not fit for the race, and neither was I and so on. The fact was that *Myth Too* was a well-proven aircraft that had done far more in its short lifetime than any other aircraft in the race. A few minutes later, I heard the radio announcing that I had arrived after a bad time, but no word of my message of thanks to the Indonesian people, who would be listening for news. What was going on?

What a joy to be able to telephone England, to tell them I was here, but all was not right there, either. Lana, my secretary, had been worried first by reports that I was dead: then, when I was found to be alive, warned by an official in England that I had tried to obtain ten thousand dollars *in cash* from the Singapore Royal Aero Club. She did not believe it for such a demand could only mean I was up to something bad. Who could have planted such a story?

Now I, too, really did panic. I had no need for such a horrific sum of money, even if I could have raised it. Luckily I had never been alone for a single second in Singapore. The British Navy had been with me all the time. Only my aircraft had been left alone and that with what undoubtedly should have been fatal results for me.

This latest fantastic story, and the fact that an official who knew me well should believe such nonsense, was grim. I told her to contact the Royal Aero Club immediately, and to tell them I knew nothing whatsoever about it, to investigate the report and, if necessary, put it into police hands. I did not care for the implications. This was too serious an accusation and too large a sum of money to ignore any more.

Early in the morning I found kindly Peter Denholm, Chairman of the Aero Club, had been up half the night to change my oil and plugs himself. This was Australia as I remembered it, welcoming, sporting and helpful. Air Race competitors were still arriving and taking off, as I took off for Alice Springs—the last compulsory stop before Adelaide.

As the heat built up, the turbulence grew greater, and grappling with the controls, I throttled back, only to find the dial was not registering any manifold pressure. What else could go wrong? Now it was to be the engine. At Alice Springs we found a clean cut in the manifold pressure pipe—fortunately only the one leading to the dial.

During refuelling, I was still being showered with food and enjoying the good things of Australia, when a mysterious message arrived for me from Adelaide. It read, "Police in attendance—do not fear for your life. We will be there to meet you. Glad you are here!"

There was something very wrong. I could no longer console myself that I may have been oversensitive, or imagining anything. Inexplicable incidents and remarks had now been occurring since the first briefing day. In previous flights I had always found enormous kindness and friendliness from all people as a whole, no matter what their political belief, colour, creed or personal ambitions. I could not imagine who could be going to such lengths or why, but whatever the reasons, I was not prepared to give in to them and had to see it through even if it did kill me.

I flew on over the great mass of red desert, occasionally hearing Air Race Five, John Wynn and co-pilot, Keith Buttrey, in the Victa Airtourer, the smallest aircraft in the race. They were a great-hearted couple, and were two of the best sports in the race.

As I flew over the dried up salt taking in the cool of the evening, towards Adelaide, air traffic control picked me up on radar and led me to Parafield, Adelaide's airfield. I joyously thought the most frustrating flight of my life was over. But there was much more to come. I was ordered to remain in the middle of the runway and not to leave it until the DCA cars reached me. This was a very odd arrival instruction and again, I wondered why. Peter Lloyd, and Beverley Snook, both officials of the race committee, descended round the aircraft with a flock of cars, and after climbing on my wing to greet me, directed me to follow their cars, but not before a heavy built gentleman had wedged himself in the door of my aircraft, and stayed there while I taxied the aircraft off the runway.

Thousands of people waited, but *Myth Too* and I were diverted away from them into a huge empty hangar, and the door slammed behind us. There *Myth Too* was to be kept under guard, but even stranger was the police guard on me too, as well as the 'plain clothes' escort. Not that I could complain, for they had certainly chosen a handsome Aussie.

As I got out of the car some people said, "Congratulations, well done!" I nearly cried then, and clung to a friend's hand, half sobbing. "It almost was," I said, recalling how, when trouble hit, I was only four hours from Darwin and from halving the record. He put his arm around me, and told me to keep smiling. I think perhaps this was the worst moment—to be congratulated when I knew we should, and could, have done so much better.

They took me, still closely guarded, to the Club House to the crowd's fury. Hundreds of shouting people pressed close while Bev literally dragged me through the mêlée. This was no choice of mine, for if the people had been sweet enough to come and see me, then I wanted to meet them too. Fortunately one of the club officials realised this, and found a table for me to stand on so at least I could say hello to them. Australia had done much for me during my first round-the-world flight three years before and I was truly happy to be back. I did not yet know the extent of the misquotes which had been magnified by days of gossip without my being there to try and straighten it out. Nor did I know hundreds of people had waited for me at Parafield, but had been hustled away by non-thinking officials, and gone away angry and disappointed, believing I had refused to talk to them.

Many press and cameras again, mostly sympathetic. One question was thrown at me: "Is it true that you believe your aircraft was sabotaged?" What could I answer? This was serious, and not good publicity for the race, or anybody. On the other hand, I could not let down my loyal engineers who had sent me off in a perfect aeroplane. I tried to explain that I personally had not used the word 'sabotage' originally, but that

I had a very good and very well-equipped aircraft, which had flown all over the world many times, and which had been a hundred per cent perfect on flight test.

I was accused of asking for police protection. It was conclusively confirmed that I did not. But who did and why? Was it to keep the race in the headlines? It also came out that remarks had been made that I had deliberately given up the race four hours out of Darwin, because I could not win it and could cash in on the publicity by coming in at the last moment. In fact I was doing well in the race at that time. It was unbelievable that while I was going through the biggest headache of my career, the record snatched from my grasp, people could think up such a story!

There were public remarks that I should not enter the race if I did not expect adventure, and that I had no right in it in a badly equipped aeroplane. Okay, I wearily thought, sneer at me. I was too sick to care much about myself, but when they attacked an aircraft as great as my Piper Comanche, it was going too far. This well-equipped aircraft had flown the deserts and oceans of the world many times and never let me down. But this was to be the way it was for several days. There would always be one unpleasant person to a hundred other warm-hearted people. The more professional pilots tried to smooth things and told me the truth of how some were using me as an excuse to promote their own protest to get extra points in the race.

I tried to help the situation by replying personally to every telephone call or argument that came up as calmly as I could, and by appearing at every official function. I was almost delirious with fever. The telephone never stopped even for a minute during the day, and during the night it rang at least once an hour from Europe. I had to answer these calls myself, as I could no longer risk misquotes. Once I woke up to answer the telephone and found myself talking live on British television. My brain was so exhausted that I did not even recognise the names of some of the friends they mentioned. On the other hand whenever the hotel staff of the South Australian Hotel saw what looked like an attack from a critic, they gave me a great bear hug saying, "Don't listen to them, they are jealous. We love you." Looking back, it may have been a nightmare, but I did also find many people who became friends and who loyally stood by me.

On January 1st, New Year's Day, 1970, everyone was feeling a little jaded after the New Year Ball held in the Aero Club hangar. We listened to the briefing for the next day's race, not feeling very pleased with the weather man who gave us a miserable forecast. Take-off for Griffith and Sydney the next morning was delayed and delayed to allow the weather to improve before we were flagged away with a handicap start. There were six Comanches taking off together—me last (because I was solo, and therefore considered lighter, in spite of the load of steel tanks that I carry instead of passengers). *Myth Too* was performing beautifully as though to emphatically refute the things said about her, and immediately overtook a Comanche in front of us, and the next as well.

After that I did not see anyone until Griffith, where too many of us emerged and converged from every direction at the same time and altitude. Storm clouds had driven us down to between fifty and three hundred feet and it was sheer luck none of us collided. The controller coped nobly until for a time the weather was so low the airfield had to be closed. Those of us left in the air circled and circled and somehow avoided each other. Plaintive pleas about not enough fuel came from some of those who had now been caught out. He directed those of us with enough fuel to go to Narrandera, thirty miles south, which we did. It was reported that Sheila Scott force landed at Narrandera. It was now becoming a joke.

There was no question of the race going on to Sydney for the finish that day now, and somehow Griffith's Aero Club managed to cope magnificently with the unexpected housing of two hundred extra people—no easy job in a small town. They drove backwards and forwards ferrying us non-stop into the little town. The reservations were set up by telephone using the surnames only of the competitors, and somehow I had been booked into a room for four with three men I had never even met. I do not think they would have appreciated me as a bed fellow as I hacked and coughed my way through the night.

The BP representative, Antony Howard, gave me his room in the one modern Irrigana Motel by doubling up with someone else. The kindly local chemist reopened his shop to get me cough mixture and medicines, refusing to take any payment. I certainly needed this night's respite. Next day fortunately the weather was still too bad to continue the race and so I had time to recover.

Two days later, just as we were about to take off a very furious gentleman, the Chairman of the Aero Club, loomed before me almost about to hit me, saying how dare I say such things about Griffith town. I had been in bed most of the time, and had done nothing but praise the magnificent job they had done, but this time the papers said "Sheila Scott says Griffith is a bum town!" This reverberated around the world on radio and TV. Although I am quite capable of using the good old English language, this was not one of my words. I had heard a young, unthinking man use these words in the car, but both Arthur Wignell and I had answered him back and reminded him of the spontaneous hospitality Griffith had laid on for us. It was all so untrue and petty that I should have been able to laugh at it, but I was beyond laughing any more. It was ludicrous, but the pettiness was whizzing around the world and hurting others. I was as near to suicide as anyone could be. How can one live knowing innocent people are being hurt, and some reputations being destroyed, just because one exists?

A jinx was on me even though obviously a 'man-made' one. Tears rolled down as I left the runway because there was no way of convincing this friendly little town that I, at any rate, had been happy there. But there was a race to finish. This was what I had struggled on to do, what I had said I would do even if, as it turned out, ignominiously. The elements were gentle today, and the clean sky gave me back a little happiness for an hour or two. We do not yet understand all that that great wide expanse holds, but at least one knows there is tough honesty even in the roughest levels of the sky.

My competitive spirit asserted itself as I saw the aircraft ahead of us, and gradually *Myth* overtook some of them. The exhilaration of the race had caught up with me and I felt stronger in mind at least. At last, after the most misunderstood three weeks of my life, Bankstown Airport, Sydney, lay in sight, and all the race seemed to be streaming over the white finishing line at the same time. *Myth* and I were fourth in our class in this race which was not so bad for such a battle-weary pair.

Crowds of well-wishers mingled with the yellow and green mini-skirted BP girls to greet us all. Old friend Ken Holt of Ansett General Aviation who had done so much on our first visit here was there to hand *Myth Too* over to his engineers to cosset. More cameras and microphones zoomed up at me, but this time I was not going to be bullied, and determined to get my word in first. I promptly told everyone of them about the Griffith episode, so perhaps the people there did eventually get the true message. Only one interviewer tried to draw me to retort angrily, by saying, "Sydney thinks of you as a Prima Donna, what do you think about that?" That was the last of the bullying. Some of the same press told me personally that they knew the true story—one being that large sums of money bets had been the reason for the sabotage. Some people had gone too far. It was more like murder than betting!

The scars of that race are still with me and always will be. Much of the strange experience over the Indonesian seas can be explained simply. For example, HF radio often behaves in unpredictable fashion owing to skip distances and sky waves, and the actual HF set was not damaged—merely its aerial cut and shortened so that under normal conditions it could not work— but obviously the conditions were not normal that day, and by freak I had received *some* transmissions. A newspaper man later confirmed that reports of my death, and a further one that I was still fighting for it, were indeed filed and transmitted, but by the time the papers went to press, at least my whereabouts had been ascertained. Furthermore, my aircraft equipment was proved to have been damaged in a way in which no self-respecting engineer would leave it. So had certain misleading reports been sent to strategic places quite unknown to me, or my team long before I reached Australia. There were large bets made on the race, and undeservedly I was among the favourites to win. I can only draw my own conclusions.

But there are stranger things than human physical behaviour. Undoubtedly we all have an inner knowledge—which if we could only develop it is powerful enough to link all mankind. Whether this power—extra-sensory perception—will be retained for good only in the future, or used just like other more physical discoveries as a weapon, which could finally destroy us, is far from sure, and may well be why many are reluctant to recognise it. Undoubtedly some kind of perception entered into my story for me to have survived those weeks.

Over the Bandu Sea I had been more aware than ever before of two poles of opposing forces—to the point of actually believing I heard the two forces arguing. Oddly I was near the Equator when all this was happening—midway between the magnetic Poles—maybe midway between mental concepts. Some would prefer to believe this part of my story to have been hallucination—but even if it were I have never since been without fear of the evil part of it—even to the point of dreading sometimes to recognise either force lest I get taken in by the false one. Some of the influence I felt could well have been extra-sensory perception as a result of the positive thoughts of my worried team.

I myself remain entirely unconvinced that more than a fraction of my experiences were hallucination—if any at all.

Great strides have been made in a relatively short time in Outer Space—yet we are only just beginning to understand the fantastic capabilities of man's mental perception—a perception that is not reliant on visual proof. Scientists, psychologists and theologians are beginning to work together already, and realise they are complementary to each other in new ideas and future discoveries. These new scientist psychologists have long had to extend their philosophies beyond that which can be observed visually, or proven in any laboratory; just as the modern theosophists have to admit that most of their teaching has been lost in the maze of parables, according to individual men's stories over the ages, coupled with dogma.

Some old philosophies state one must become almost neuter within oneself to observe impartially what goes on both around one and in oneself before one finds any spiritual guidance. If that is so, then the voices which said, "She's in a coma"—"that's the way I want her, nice and easy, relaxed," would make mystical sense, along with the praying women's voice which also implored me to keep still. On that day I was very near to death, perhaps as near as I could be without physical injury, or disease: however calm one might become in such inescapable circumstances, a certain amount of emotion must be present in one's thoughts—and certainly was in mine, and many consider it to be all imagination and extreme fatigue.

Indeed I had been awake for three days, but I do not believe this is the complete answer to all the things I heard alone over the sea.

How so much damage actually occurred to the aircraft, and exactly by whom, or why it went so far, is better not to know, but the incident was important to me for it was 'the vehicle' which enabled me personally to think far more consciously than I would have done had things always worked out easily. After extensive overhauls we believed that we had removed all the damage, but in fact there were to be two more serious incidents resulting from untraced faults. My story and life should have finished a few weeks later in the Pacific Ocean. The magnetic force set up by offset voltages inside two pieces of equipment pulled my aircraft compass off by many degrees. We did not trace this damage on our flight tests as it only occurred after being several hours airborne. There is no point in retelling these further epics, as I made it safely—though not through any technical skills of my own—I do not have any even now. Luck? No—it's happened too often to be luck!

I continued with my plans to fly on around the world again across the Pacific, the USA and the Atlantic, but this time I wanted to spend time exploring and photographing many of the Pacific Isles, particularly Fiji and the Gilberts.

I flew on eastwards from Brisbane, Australia, via the New Caledonian Islands to Fiji, for an unforgettable few weeks. During the time I spent here the Fijians, and indeed all the people who lived among these islands, became real friends, and their kind understanding, too, refreshed me and gave me back some of my confidence. I explored the villages in the hills, and sailed to the outer islands, and would willingly have settled there for life.

When it was time to leave, it was as though the Fijians knew how I felt, and they had planned one more surprise—this time for *Myth Too* and me together.

At dawn the sun had burst forth from the other side of the earth and watched from just above the horizon the time-honoured, hundreds-of-years-old ceremony that now took place on the charcoal tarmac of Nandi's sophisticated airport. The hard, ugly concrete was softened by the surrounding patchwork of green sugar-cane fields, and distant red hills. Shining, gleaming jets silently surveyed, as though their blasting noise had been suddenly cut off by the reverence of the scene, the little 'Te Wanikiba'—the flying canoe—which is what *Myth Too* had been affectionately called in Pacific parts. The woven ceremonial mats, on which I sat bare-footed and cross-legged, contrasted with the tiny modern white aircraft, and the daytime *sulus* of the Chiefs showed up the dull grey trousers of the watching Europeans.

I was leaving, perhaps for ever, these islands, where for far too short a time I had relaxed most and found great happiness from among a whole world of flights. Tears were in my eyes as the age-old island words were spoken—words I could not speak myself and yet there were no barriers between us—not even those of words. We were of different beliefs, different colours and born at opposite ends of the earth, but I inexplicably understood what they meant.

Gently, a genuine Tabua was placed in my hands, and with it, the positive thought and power of love and affection behind this historic gift. They gave it to me with the words, which in English would say, that they felt I belonged to Fiji, that it would guard *Myth* and me across the great Oceans, and would bring us safely back to Fiji. At that time there was no possibility of my returning to the Pacific, but the Tabua was to perform its magic.

This huge yellow tooth, with its necklace of woven grass, had played its part in life again and again over many years as the symbol of great ceremonial occasions. Nowadays, a genuine Tabua is used only to honour, or install a great Chief, and is rarely allowed to leave Fiji. Over the decades this one, like its fellows, had been used to secure the hand of a great lady, on other occasions as atonement for a crime, or even to secure the death of another man, or to assuage the temper of a person of rank as well as for great honour. Now it was to be used in much more homely fashion—to keep a lone woman pilot company, and to remind her of past happiness.

The sun was high in the sky as I flew out over emerald sea dancing over coral reefs, heading north for Tarawa atoll in the Gilbert and Ellice Isles. Somewhere across this track Amelia Earhart and her co-pilot, Lieutenant Commander Fred

Noonan, had fought for their lives against adverse weather and faulty radio during their last flight in July 1937. They had left Laos in New Guinea for Howland Island and only had the Pacific to cross before finishing their flight round the world. I was to be more fortunate than they, for I too lost once again my radio aids later *en route* to Hawaii and yet again to the American coastline, but I made it. Once in America *all* the faults were finally solved and *Myth Too* became her usual wonderful self, still to capture more records and lead me to new adventures and dreams.

PART III

"On Top of the World"

The story of the first light aircraft in the world flown solo over the True North Pole, Equator to Equator, and of NASA experiments via satellite during the same flight, 1971.

> Were I so tall to reach the pole
> Or grasp the ocean with my span,
> I must be measured by my soul:
> The mind's the measure of the man.
> *Horae Lyricae*,
> Isaac Watts, 1706.

8

"WHAT ever happened to your plans to fly over the North Pole next spring?"

"The Advertising company still has not made up its mind about sponsorship and so I'll have to call it off—maybe for ever this time. It's almost too late for this year, as the best time to go is April before the icing fog sets in up there," I sadly replied one snowy December day in 1970.

For many years I had longed to make this flight, and again and again various companies had indicated it was the flight they would be most interested in sponsoring and had led me on, but when it came to the final decision they had always backed down. It certainly was not the finance needed, which, although more than I could raise myself, was still far less than companies spent on promoting other ventures. I wondered if the reason could be my sex, for there are no sponsored female venturers, though many sponsored teams and individual men.

There is also the problem of personally convincing the would-be backer that what one is doing is worth while. As he becomes sympathetic towards what one is doing invariably the personal side comes in, as he does not want to feel responsible for any-thing bad that could happen. This time I had sadly almost given up for ever any hopes of flying the Arctic or Antarctic regions, but had felt complete disappointment in myself. Now incredibly and unexpectedly I was happy again as I heard the words, "Some of us have been giving some thought and dis-cussions to your attempt, and feel it would be a good thing for Britain. We have formed an 'Adventure Trust' and will sponsor you!"

I feverishly worked out whether I could still be ready in time. I knew there might never be another chance to do it, and all who had helped me prepare previous flights were unanimous in their offers of help and advice that I must do it. We were on, but barely three months were left for the preparations.

First of all a twin-engined aircraft had to be obtained to make the journey possible, for my little single-engined Piper Comanche *Myth Too* could not carry all the extra equipment needed to fly over the icy cold wastes of the Pole, nor was it possible to fit suitable de-icing equipment on her. She had broken ninety-four world class records for me, won races and flown me round the world twice. It was almost unthinkable to do anything without her—she had become the focal point of my life. But there was nothing for it but to obtain the Piper Aztec twin—a well-proven aircraft, still within the required weight-limit of light aircraft; yet a good work-horse which was large enough to carry the extra fuel, and capable of standing up to extreme conditions. In spite of doleful predictions that we could never modify one in time or ever get delivery in time, somehow I managed to inveigle the Piper factory in America to produce one within weeks instead of months and persuaded Oxford airport in Britain that they could modify it in time.

The Fédération Aviation Internationale, world governing body for the verification of aviation world records, confirmed the rules of a polar attempt and accepted my bid to make the attempt. Charles Blair, Pan Am airline captain and ex-fighter pilot, had made the first epic solo long-distance flight over the North Pole from Norway to Alaska in a P51 Mustang in 1951. However, no one had yet succeeded in flying a light aircraft Equator to Equator via a Pole according to rules of the FAI and certainly no woman had attempted the Arctic Ocean solo. The major differences between Charles Blair's fighter Mustang and a light aircraft are weight, cruise power and altitude. A light aircraft has to remain airborne many more hours for sufficient range, and is unable to climb high enough above the weather layer to avoid its severe icing.

The approved route flown from Equator to Equator via the True North Pole had not been successfully flown by a light aircraft before by anyone. There were also some other standing records I wanted to capture—with a little luck maybe I could gain my hundredth record since 1965—so I decided to continue on around the world to the west—which is virtually the wrong way round for aviators as it is against prevailing winds.

If successful it would be my third solo flight around the world; but, for me, gaining more air records had become the catalyst fusing the wider knowledge I was finding through the physical action of flying. Now actual record breaking is a public reason for making such flights, but although I still enjoy the challenge of long-distance flights, and undoubtedly at the beginning patriotic spirit entered into the ingredients of the adventures, this has become less as I find myself involved with people of all nationalities, colour and belief—involved in fact with planet earth. The basic reasons have become more intimate with personal compelling desires to explore further the deeper experiences that I pushed aside in my earlier life, which are now insistently making me very consciously aware of what flying and the sky can lead me to, both physically and metaphysically. This is not just beautiful thinking which we all day-dream in suitable surroundings. It is a more positive influence than that— an awareness of an energy, a vibration like a sound, or an actual force propelling me to look further. Others, I know, find it elsewhere—some on mountains or oceans—but for me it is most distinctive after the pure concentration that long-distance flights require, both in their preparation and doing. It is as though every molecule of my body must work to perfect a single thought—or action—almost as though every muscle and movement, emotion and sense must be exhausted, before one can get a glimpse through the barriers of thought.

Sometimes in the sky I am on the very edge of understanding, but by the time I have touched down on earth all my thoughts have elusively vanished again. Yet in spite of this, after every flight, no matter how short or long, my thoughts still seem to be airborne as though separate from the physical me. No matter how hard I try to concentrate on the people around me, my reactions and replies remain automatic and it takes time before I feel completely back on solid earth. I have not assimilated enough of this new (to me) learning and therefore cannot yet retain all that the philosophy of the sky can teach, but it has been enough to make me restless on the ground, and for me to grasp at any excuse for a new flight. No matter how lazy I have become, each time a challenging flight is presented I am filled with euphoric energy I did not know I had, and sleep and recreation become insignificant; material things and security become unessential except in making the flight possible. Then I am happy, even in discomfort, and yet when I am discouraged

I lose all energy and have to force myself almost physically out of a cabbage-like lethargy.

It is not that I wish to be alone for all my life, but simply that I have to spend some time conquering—using my emotions and senses to advantage without distraction. I enjoy to the full the team-life that must go with the preparations of a big flight for a little aircraft, but that is maybe heightened because we all have the same single-minded purpose. When I leave the team I know they are still there with me, even if in mind, and undoubtedly it is their collective thinking willing success that brings me home safely. Then, too, there is the entirely different, yet still emotional relationship between pilot and aircraft when the aircraft seems a living thing sensitive to one's reactions.

When this new flight to the Pole was first planned, I did not dream that more tangible experiments could also be attached to my flight. These too were to add greatly to my own personal interest in research, as well as giving a point to my flights that others are able to use constructively to advantage. Although my personal philosophy has nothing to do with some of the scientific people involved with me, I feel very deeply that scientific reasons are partly responsible for the creed I am trying to follow.

There have been many gallant attempts to cross the North Pole since Robert Peary's historical first crossing by dog-sled, but perhaps the most gruelling venture was that of tenacious Wally Herbert and his team who walked across, and the most significant the daring journey under the ice by the nuclear submarine *Nautilus*, captained by Commander William Anderson.

But there was still little first-hand advice about Polar aviation to be obtained in England. Robbie Robinson, Chief of BOAC's Navigation Department, and the Royal Geographical Society were pillars of strength, and as interested and encouraging as though it were their own attempt. They produced wondrous charts for me to peruse and dream over—nothing thrills me more than unrolling a new map to plot a new venture —the very smell of the paper is as good as Arpege scent.

Next there were weather analyses, charts and equipment brochures to be studied; dozens of check lists to sort out, and worst of all, thousands of letters to write. An avalanche of paperwork flowed into all rooms in my apartment, and the telephone once again never stopped ringing. Numerous permissions and visas for landings and over-flights, had to be obtained. It is no longer easy in this modern age to fly a direct course around the world. There are always new wars or political boundaries to circumvent, or else countries who will not allow over-flights but insist on landings (to collect the landing fee one suspects!). I had to consult aviation governing bodies and obtain help from the Foreign Office.

Most important of all, the Air Registration Board, which governs the safety of aircraft, and is responsible for issuing the Certificate of Airworthiness without which you cannot fly, had to be referred to many times. The Aztec's normal eleven-hundred-mile range fuel system had to be greatly modified with extra tanks installed to give it a range of three thousand miles. Again my past records helped here, and Paul Whicher, a chief there, eased my problems, though he sternly warned me that the overweight figures I was applying for, in order to carry sufficient fuel, would mean the aircraft's performance would be seven hundred feet below sea level if I lost an engine.

The speed of our preparations was not improved by our usual English malaise—strikes—and now the electricity men plunged us into darkness from time to time. It is necessary to use electricity even in daylight in my dark apartment, and many a laborious and quavering letter written by candlelight was sent out to lighter parts of earth from darkest England. Successive meetings took place at Oxford airport, about the lightest weight equipment to be installed aboard the aircraft, but in the end it came down to what could be obtained quickly, and what room there was for it. What began as an impressive list became very basic indeed, and I realised I would have to navigate by the sun alone for much of the way up north. Certainly I could not afford a sophisticated inertial platform as used by large aircraft for Polar flying. An astro sun compass, a watch and a simple direction indicator were eventually to be my only aids on the Polar journey. Greek navigator Pytheas, first known Arctic explorer of 310 BC, had used a form of sun compass to navigate and now it would be my only actual navigation aid—twenty-three centuries later. I could claim to be the first woman to navigate the same ocean by any form of transport if I made it.

There was much to learn for I had never used grid navigation or a sun compass before.

The worst part was trying to make actual space for the vast amounts of fuel I would need. Even with all the passenger seats of the aircraft removed, it was difficult to design tanks large enough which would still go through the aircraft door, and yet allow the plane to remain balanced correctly in order for it to fly!

The bosses at Oxford grumbled that the work simply could not be prepared in time. Would I please do the Polar flight *next* year? Their engineers, the men who would actually do the work on the aircraft, had different ideas, and supported me to the hilt. Like me, they were excited and knew I should make the attempt while I had the chance. Will I ever forget their words, so unusual in these modern days?

"Sheila, there are seven days and seven nights, and a week-end in every week. We'll be ready!" said the chief engineer, Les Baston.

The flight was certainly on now, for it had been declared officially, and in a few weeks I had mustered as much help as usually takes three months to arrange. Even the official authorities were enthusiastic and rounding up as much help as could be found at short notice. But in spite of the monstrous ground work, I think I had always known that this flight was being made too easy for me financially. My sponsors had re-thought their proposition, and decided they were scared of the Pole and thought they were underwriting my death! They would sponsor anything else whether flying or sailing but not the Pole. Not only had I now announced the flight formally, but had longed for the chance for six years. What I was trying to do was worth staking my life on—a decision which I had made years before anyway.

Many people had already donated their precious time and gone to great lengths to obtain help for me; others had already been engaged for jobs; a large financial consideration was already incurred towards the flight, and I knew I personally was already committed to the flight. There are very few rules in my restive life, except that once I have said that I will attempt something, I believe I must try to go through with it.

That night I talked with the engineers, who would be working on the new aircraft. Once again it was *Myth Too* and those who loved her that I trusted. It was Chief Engineer, Les, who again voiced it, and said, "Girl, you must do what you say you'll do. You always have. Somehow we'll all do it." Those words were the spur that made me absolutely determined to go on.

We wandered across to the hangar where *Myth Too* lived. Previously it had seemed *Myth Too* had not wanted to know about this new strange flight without her, and she had seemed self-contained. To me, she is almost a living personality—not a piece of machinery. We had shared a very strange and wonderful life full of extremes, sometimes of heartbreak which always ended safely, and at other times shared more happiness than most humans have ever known. Uncannily that night her door was open inviting me aboard. The engineers went away and left me, sitting in her, in the dark hangar full of shadowy shapes of wings and propellers of the flying chariots of other pilots' dreams and adventures.

My mind was blank—yet thousands of thoughts struggled to fill it and I did not know what decision to make. The very feel of the stick, the smell of the fuel and the sight of her familiar dials comforted me and reminded me of the dozens of disappointments and hurts we had taken together and how every time we had come through. I had always believed that everything that happened in *Myth* was right, whatever it entailed and that night it was as though she told me she was a part of the new flight.

The engineers drove me to the station as they were to do many times in their spare time to save money to help towards the flight, even down to buying me steaks to fatten me up! The journey home seemed like seconds as I debated and planned how to raise a large enough loan to make the flight. It was too late to get a commercial sponsor, for promoters need at least nine months to prepare their own promotions. What was there left to sell? I was already accepting almost any kind of paying proposition to pay for the extra secretaries and things needed to organise it, but I could not earn enough to buy the new aircraft as well. That was the only reason that I had not made this attempt years before when I first dreamt of it. Although I had no idea how I could possibly raise even the minimum amount needed for the aircraft, I continued planning during the next few days as though my backers were still there. If we had stopped work for even a day, the flight would have absolutely no hope of taking place, even with all the money in the world. I talked it out with someone very close to me. Twenty-four hours later her voice on the telephone quietly said, "You must keep your word. You cannot end your career with a broken word. I have sold some shares today, enough to start you off. You must raise the rest, as that's all I can do."

It was a most generous loan, and it was enough, with what I could raise myself, to start bargaining with the hire-purchase people. Meanwhile, I had talked to my understanding bank manager at Barclays Bank. They trusted me and would give me the overdraft when I needed it. How different from 1966 when they had refused to have anything to do with such nonsense as solo world flights. Now they were believers and firm allies.

Next I approached Lombank, the delayed payment bank, with whose help I had already bought two aircraft in my career. Surely this would stand me in good stead? But no, they wanted a guarantor. By now I was hypersensitive about any supposed guarantor. I had had too many entries but 'non-starters' in the past to even consider another. I argued stubbornly that I had fulfilled all the conditions without failing them in the past. Fantastically they gave in, but only if *Myth Too* stood in as my collateral. They explained she would be 'put in charge'! My overactive mind horrifically thought of *Myth Too* in prison and behind bars—neither of us could ever survive a cage! However, Victor Cannock, then a Lombank director, went on to explain that merely meant she could not be sold, that I could fly her or do what else I wanted with her. In my heart, I thought it was a fair deal that *Myth* and I should be solely responsible to pay for the flight, though it now meant that if I were unable to pay the hire purchase instalments Lombank could take both aircraft. The loss of capital would be nothing compared to the loss of *Myth Too*. She was the ultimate I personally could stake. In the whole of my life nothing was of greater value in terms of loyalty.

9

PHIL CHAPMAN, the astronaut, whose family I had previously visited, had invited me to Cape Kennedy at the beginning of February 1971 to watch the launching of Apollo 14. Fortunately I already had the ticket, so I decided to combine the opportunity with a business trip to arrange final aircraft details with the Piper Aircraft factory, and avionics equipment makers, and also to collect personally all the spare bits that could no longer be mailed in time because of a postal strike in England.

Watching a launch on television is exciting, but to be there during the last few days and actually to see the launch in the company of NASA's personnel must be one of the unforgettable times of a life. The immenseness of it is much greater than any television cameras can show, and the air is electric with hyper-excitement and high tension. The spectacle has now been described so often and by far more lucid writers than I—there is nothing I can add—except that it was probably the spectator experience in my lifetime that I shall remember best.

It was during a night excursion to the very base of the rocket with Dick Hoagland, at that time with CBS and the TV crew, that Phil started one of his 'way out' Space conversations, and we all joined in adding more and more delicious ideas. Many joking comparisons were made about my forthcoming flight, and Dick teased that I could never escape even in my little aircraft in this electronic age. We became serious and talked about how a small aircraft could be used for experiments, and my passage over the Arctic regions tracked, as proof that I actually flew over the North Pole. This was something that had been practically impossible for anyone in the past for there are no low-level radar stations or permanent landmarks up there in two and a half thousand miles of ice-topped sea and there is little a solo pilot can do to provide actual proof of an over-flight of the North Pole—a necessity to claim a first, or a world record anywhere. I was astounded a few days later in New York to discover that Dick had indeed taken our ideas and presented them seriously to various authorities in Washington. They were interested! My flight might possibly be used to some advantage in the biomedical and environmental fields as well as for a satellite tracking experiment.

The new aircraft had now arrived in England and much of it already had been stripped down into many different pieces all over the hangar floor ready for its conversion for cold weather and long-range flying. Just like my original *Myth Too*, I never saw it in pristine condition on arrival, nor could I fly my new acquisition yet. I looked at her with some doubt. Would she ever really fly? She looked like a plump white pouter pigeon without its feathers in comparison to my slim elegant Comanche. Les Baston was specially designing her new livery as a surprise for me. The paint was to be turquoise and gold in my favourite colours. In fact green is my lucky colour, but the engineers were adamant and refused to have a green aircraft in the hangar, so they compromised and allowed me to have turquoise on the understanding it was more blue than green. A deep turquoise table-napkin and the belt of one of my flying suits whizzed backwards and forwards for matching up with bits of every shade of paint until we were all satisfied that it was turquoise. They decided that *Myth*, the female moth, should be a kind of heraldic sign and for a while hundreds of moth and butterfly pictures festooned Les's office instead of spark plug advertisements and manufacturers' calendars. They painted the prettiest one they could find on the new aircraft's tail and above it the intertwined flags of Great Britain and America. Many weird and wonderful names were thought up for her and we finally settled on *Mythre* which could mean a multitude of things.

Myth Too's registration was GATOY so for years there had been many a jokester in the air quipping, "Gee—a toy!" By chance we obtained GAYTO, the same letters jumbled, for *Mythre*—obviously a lucky omen and 'Gay Take-off' we decided. There were hundreds of flight plans to be made up in triplicate and prepared before the flight. Friends were sandwiched between aircraft spare parts and textbooks in my tiny guest room while Fiona MacGinley, my secretary, had the nonstop shrilling telephone for company. I camped out on my bed, which became my office desk, surrounded by mountains of charts, brochures and endless cups of coffee, cigarettes and multivitamins. Edwin Franklyn, who normally trains football players, came every morning to massage my muscles back to fitness: there was no time for country walks and all the things that are supposed to make you physically perfect.

RAF Northolt's flight planning department, and Major Warren Bishop of the American Embassy, tracked unobtainable charts and chased impossible information about strange landing places. RAF Manby, the Air Force School of Air Warfare, took me on as a student for a concentrated Polar navigation study course. Once there, Wing Commander Freddie French and Flight Lieutenant Eric Stafford with others tried to instil in my by now somewhat fluffy brain the theory, methods and techniques of Polar navigation. They disapproved heartily of my almost non-existent aircraft aids, and said it could hardly be done but nevertheless set to in good military fashion to improvise.

As a fugitive from mathematics, I desperately tried to assimilate complicated algebraic figures and several months of study into two days, watched by movie cameras and the news interviews which had now begun, and constantly interrupted by non-stop telephone messages from home.

My RAF instructors found more and more problems. The astro compass cannot be used as easily in the high latitudes of north and south because there are more mathematical conversion sums to be made—easy on the ground but not in the air without a navigator or plotting table, with numerous other chores to do apart from the sheer physical and mental exhaustion of sitting, unable to move for up to nineteen hours at a time. There would be no room for reference books in the aircraft so they concocted instant ready-reference charts for me to use.

An almost insurmountable problem was keeping the basic instruments warm enough to perform should the aircraft's one and only heater fail. The loss of heat inside the aircraft could mean a snowstorm literally in the cabin within minutes, and windows layered in thick frost. Eventually the very controls of the aircraft would freeze up. Institute of Aviation Medicine at Farnborough set to work to solve my physical frostbite problems, while Robin Montgomerie-Charrington at Oxford scoured the world to find some catalytic standby miniature heaters (unspillable flameless portable heaters) which do not give out carbon monoxide fumes. All normal fresh air inlets in the aircraft would have to be sealed against the intense cold.

And so it went on until late one Friday evening, I was so utterly frustrated and exhausted by trying to mould everything together as well as forsaking all pride by begging and borrowing, that I just gave up and turned to Jackie Williams, who now donated all her spare time helping with the secretarial work too, and said, "It's no go Jackie, I can't go on. The odds are too great to surmount this year and yet I cannot afford to hang on to the new aircraft in pieces and unusable for another year. What's worse, for the first time in my flying career, I cannot see the picture in my mind of the aircraft flying or my goal. We have run out of time. I am not going to make it."

For the first time since I had known her, she replied, "No. I don't think you are this time, Sheila!"

I think at that stage we stopped work, and she probably made me my eternal cup of coffee. All I remember is the devastating misery of a complete failure before I had even had a go! At exactly midnight the telephone shrilled and as I glumly answered it, a voice said, "It's Go, Sheila—Go, Sheila!" It was Phil Chapman telephoning me from Houston, USA, with the unbelievable news that our proposed experiment had been approved. He went on to say the whole idea had been voted on one hour before (the same hour when I gave up in England four thousand miles away) and then reconsidered after certain arguments had been put forward, and that I would be getting further telephone calls that night. We did and stayed up throughout the night, all exhaustion forgotten. Jackie immediately opened a bottle of wine and we drank a toast to NASA for nothing on earth was going to make me give up now!

NASA's Goddard Space Flight Centre in Greenbelt, Maryland, was to try a small IRLS (Interrogation Recording and Location System) experiment on me during the flight. Goddard was built as the original Houston—training home of the astronauts, but politics moved them to Texas. Goddard homes the computers that assemble the multitude of data from a launch as well as operating the semi-permanent satellites.

A small electronic package (weighing only 10 lb) known as a

BIP (Balloon Interrogation Package) would be installed in my aircraft. This package, using its own batteries, could actually transmit to the polar orbiting space satellite, Nimbus! The satellite in turn would transmit the collected data to the computers in Goddard Space Centre and Fairbanks, Alaska, and they in turn could also give it new commands for further orbits. More scientific explanations of this system can be found in the appendix of this book. This particular system had never before been used on a mobile platform such as an aircraft. This one was to be called the Scott BIP system! It was to be a threefold experiment—location, environment and biomedicine. General Instrument Corporation of USA were providing the equipment and NASA electronics experts would supervise the installations. Oxford airport boggled, and I am sure did not believe me at first. The flight would have to be delayed to enable all this to take place, but I was certainly not going to pass up this chance. Though undoubtedly the toughest flight to take on with so little solid help behind me in my own country, it was going to be the most exciting flight that any light-aviation pilot, man or woman, could hope for.

The complications had been that the 'powers that be' in Washington had thought it was a great idea, and it was a woman involved (after all, we women were always getting at them for not allowing us into Space!). But I was British and America could not experiment on a British subject unless a government agency from her own country represented her. My American friends argued that I had American licences as well as British, and spent much time there too, so providing I found a suitable British agency it was agreed we could go.

The problem was to find a British government agency fast enough—one that could take an immediate decision without three months' red tape. I called a friend in the RAF, the sensible and non-pompous Chief of Air Staff, Sir John Grundy, for advice on whom to apply to without reams of time-wasting triplicate paperwork. To my surprise he replied that it would be of interest to the Royal Air Force and the Institute of Aviation Medicine at Farnborough would like the biomedical side. Various things started to straighten out.

To facilitate the various conversations that had now to take place between me and in the UK Goddard Space Centre in

USA I was introduced to the SCAMA (Station Conferencing and Monitoring Arrangement) line. I arrived at the General Post Office's Electra House, a Victorian-looking building on the Thames Embankment, and hesitantly asked for NASA, not believing this could be the place, nor what was happening to me! I was led to the innards of this building and there was a door with the NASA sign! I hardly believed I could still be in England. This small area held all manner of exciting computers and communications, and the walls were covered with the smiling faces of the astronauts.

Larry De Hays, American Manager of the station, greeted me, and asked, "Do you want a Conference to talk to Alaska, Goddard and Houston at the same time?"

How simple life could become as a result of the spin-offs of Space flight. He showed me the computer which in a few seconds could ask a question of Houston and answer while I watched. In the weeks that followed, and during the many SCAMA line meetings, this place was to become a sanctuary. It was the only place I could get immediate and straight answers to many problems.

That day I met Charles (Chuck) Cote, the USA Project Manager of the Scott IRLS experiment and Technical Manager Len Roach, on the SCAMA line. I could almost picture them by their voices, always calmly efficient but with overtones of sympathetic amusement, giving me an enormous team sense of security. It was as though I knew them well in person. The months of preparations became more and more delayed, and without this enormous mental backup I doubt that I could have continued alone with the 'battle for Scott to make her North Pole Flight'!

Things began to take shape but there were still a host of minor details to arrange such as unbreakable sun glasses that would shut out all the glaring sunlight and yet be light enough to wear twenty-four hours at a time. It is surprising how complicated the minor details can get, and yet one can surmount the larger issues quite smoothly. The £10 second-hand astro compass took months to find, and we scoured the world for the small catalytic heaters whose value was only £20. Both very necessary things for the £50,000 aircraft!

I spent a fantastic day at the Institute of Aviation Medicine where they tested my survival gear and Arctic clothing. Dressed in five layers of clothing topped by an insulated bright orange mountaineering suit, I sat in the pressure chambers while they 'deep froze' me down to minus twenty centigrade like a packet of garden peas! I felt rather like a giant fish in an aquarium as people squinted at me through the portholes of the chamber. To add insult to injury, they then turned on freezing wind to simulate wind chill. Dr Wadham, after enquiring whether I had my gloves on (as though I had any option in this torture chamber if I wanted to keep my fingers!), clambered in too, not appearing to notice the cold, with a bucket of water! After plunging my gloved hand into this, he plonked a metal bar into my hand and pulled it away from me. All the surface of the glove peeled away with it!

"There, that will teach you never to put an uncovered wet hand on metal in sub-zero temperatures." I was never likely to forget that lesson.

We had long debates about my outer layer of clothes. It was a choice between an immersion suit, extremely uncomfortable for long flights but which would keep me warm in the event of ditching; a fire-proof thick and stiff outer suit which I could hardly sit down in; or the mountaineer's survival trouser suit which doubled in size around me and looked like the Michelin tyre advertisement. I was in favour of the latter as I considered I would not survive long in the water anyway, whereas I knew a scientist had survived on the ice for a month in the insulated and lightweight mountaineering gear. The Farnborough people kitted me out with wonderful aids to survival weighing only ounces; a sleeping-bag made out of two plastic bags and a layer of man-made material; a cellophane type of cape, perhaps one ounce in weight, which kept in body warmth.

Beauforts made the lightest and neatest one-woman dinghy that I have ever seen with the fullest safety aids. They also specifically adapted a lifejacket for me, taking as much care with the fitting as if they were preparing a fabulous ball gown. Burndepts provided the latest model Sarbi survival beacon which could both bleep for forty-eight hours, or alternatively be used as a battery-run radio transmitter/receiver in water or on land. Morlands made a special sheepskin cover for the pilot's seat, which was warm in the cold air and equally comfortable in the tropics. SG Brown sent their special lightweight fantastic headset—the microphone the size of a piece of wire. All this sort of equipment was superb and donated by companies who were not only deeply interested in the flight but who helped me in every other way they could.

Late one night, Jackie Williams and I went to meet Len Roach of Goddard Space Flight Centre and Kent Martin of General Instrument Corporation who were arriving with all their black boxes for the BIP equipment at London Airport. We waited there suddenly realising that we did not have a clue what they looked like. Were they young, old, fat or what? The 'Jumbo Jet' disgorged a full load of passengers, mostly men, so as each man came through the Customs and Immigration exit we approached with outstretched hands and smiling faces. Each man reacted—all four hundred of them it seemed—with smiling acknowledgments and more. The situation became hilarious and no woman can possibly have had so many near interesting assignations in such a short space of time. We went through the lot, but still not the gentlemen we had to meet. At last I saw two enormous cartloads of crates disappearing through a customs officer's cubby hole with two gentlemen rushing after it. That had to be our men, but those crates were bigger than my aircraft! There was much unravelling of customs forms and things —and also the welcome discovery to me, the pilot, that the crates were merely protecting some incredibly miniaturised yet sophisticated equipment weighing only thirty pounds.

Len and Kent with the Oxford crew spent many a night outside with *Mythre* watching for the satellite Nimbus to emerge overhead, and show its presence by causing a green light to flash in my aircraft. My exact position would be transmitted every hundred minutes in the northern regions, although I myself would not know what my position was (except by dead reckoning!). Temperature and altitude would also be recorded. Dr Arnold Miller of Theta Sensors, California, had developed and installed a sulphur dioxide sensor to record air pollution throughout my route. This, too, would send its data direct to Goddard via my IRLS platform and could turn out to be a very valuable part of the experiment. Few mobile platforms are flying remote parts of the world as low as 10,000 feet and air pollution has become one of earth's deadly perils in this industrially technological age.

One might say I was to be permanently switched on! To complete the biomed experiment I was to wear an astronaut's biomedical harness throughout the flight which was plugged into a portable miniature electro-cardiogram recorder. The harness consisted of three fine wires with suction pads taped on to me in strategic places. After a while I did not even notice it was there except when I got caught up in the trailing wires from my middle. I looked like a puppet robot. Scientist, Joel Morris, of General Instrument Corporation invented a new black box—a kind of mental acuity test—for me which I called my monkey box! When the satellite triggered the green NASA light on my control panel, I in turn pressed a 'ready to test' button. Immediately a red code number appeared in the box. I then punched other buttons according to the simple code. How slow I was, the amount of mistakes or misses I made, would indicate my mental alertness and coupled with other clues such as change of direction, or no change of position plus altitude, readout and heart box could give me a very full picture of whether I was worried, tired or alert.

There was great merriment at Oxford airport when Wing Commander Dr Peter Whittingham, the leader of the biomedical UK team, ran ground control runs with the heart monitor. On one occasion I was actually plugged into him via the astronauts biomed harness with long streaming telephone type cord strung between our respective bits of personal electronics, and wherever I went Peter had to go too! Eating, standing, running, everything you can think of.

That same day was the first engineering flight test for the new twin-engined aircraft, so I decided to take old *Myth Too* up at the same time to bring the new aircraft luck. Peter Whittingham was still attached to me, and brave man that he is, accompanied me on the end of his telephone wire! *Myth Too*'s propeller started at the exact moment as the Aztec's—a good omen we thought. Both aircraft took off together, and we naturally expected the Aztec to show a few faults, but it flew perfectly. It was *Myth Too* who played up. Both her radios failed, and she refused to speak to the newcomer in the air even though she had wished it luck at the start. Peter Whittingham and I gave up the chase and returned her to base.

I filled in the waiting time by calling home for the numerous messages and complications. At the end of the day, Peter played my heart tapes and came up with a most interesting result. As a general rule, male pilots' heartbeats go up on take-off, and again very much so during landing—mine went up slightly at take-off, not at all during landing, but reached 140 when sitting talking about the latest paperwork problem on the telephone to my home.

Yet another technician, Walter Gabso of General Instrument Corporation from America, arrived. The original take-off day came and went unnoticed as we ran late owing to the extra projects we had taken on. The weather would no longer be as sub-zero as originally thought, but now there was the risk of adverse conditions on the ground bringing fog. In the air, the colder it is the less airframe icing hazards and the clearer the air. I was already commuting between airport and work at home and averaging four hours' sleep.

There was never a chance to really fly the aircraft except for one short test flight to Stavanger in the south of Norway with Lieutenant Commander Chris Allen of the Fleet Air Arm. Together we managed to iron out most of the snags, though I did notice the aircraft's lack of performance compared to her sister's with some suspicion. No one seemed to be able to solve this and it was put down to her weight and new shape (which in reality only lost me five knots and then only at high cruising speed).

The day came when all the aircraft bits and pieces, tanks and storage chests were finally installed and working. There was barely room for me, and Les somehow poured me into the cabin like a sardine in a can. Everything had been built around me, beautifully designed by the engineers so that I could reach it, whether astro compass or a Thermos flask, without moving from my seat (I could not move anyway!). It was an unbelievably tight squeeze. My knees were wedged up against the panel, and I wailed to poor patient Les, "Most people think poor *Myth Too* is agonising to sit in for long. She's a palace compared to this thing. I hate this new aircraft—I can't possibly sit in this for one seventeen-hour stretch, let alone sit in it around the whole world." Wise man that he is, Les took no notice of the wailing and soon got around that problem by getting a seat from *Myth Too* which was much slimmer and gave me another couple of inches to at least protect my knees!

At that moment, the late Prince William (then Chairman of British Light Aviation Centre, and an active aviator himself who had flown himself to many parts of the world) suddenly appeared on the wing. He had obviously heard all the wails of despair, and promptly gave me a special badge for luck which had been presented to him that morning. Its motto read 'Royal Flush'. We both roared with laughter for at that moment it could mean many things.

Sprigs of heather, St Christophers, a 'Ticky' from New Zealand, four-leaved clovers and even poetry had begun to appear daily in the mail, and these were stowed aboard too. There were last checks of medical and instrument rating renewals; currency to be obtained for the whole world; permissions reconfirmed; and everything going aboard to be weighed separately on my bathroom scales. Many treasures had to be discarded so the total aircraft did not exceed her permitted weight.

We had had to abandon much that I had planned to do, but the months had flown by. I must set off to the Equator by Whitsun holiday weekend, June 1st. It was now necessary to use the actual positioning flight to the Equator as a test flight to settle everything down in the aircraft! I had expected to have built up many hours in her by now. Who could imagine flying one of the most hazardous flights possible in an aircraft that one barely knew? The feeling in *Myth Too* of being one with the aircraft and that anything that happened to us together was right had been the thing that had carried me through in the past. Now everything was strange and lonely, but I tried to push aside the intuition that something was very wrong. *Mythre* looked a beautiful aircraft, and maybe she was.

10

Door bells and telephones were ringing and somebody was stumbling around my apartment in the middle of the night. I sat up with a start to be faced with a large tray of food, but my tummy turned over as I remembered this was the day that all the dreams became reality. Today I was to really fly—not just for a casual hour or two, but long glorious hours of endless sky on the way to Kenya, my startline on the Equator.

Lana St George Jeffers, my previous secretary, had with my current secretary, Fiona MacGinley, stayed up all night to finish off last-minute jobs. They rushed around in great form, as though they had just left a night club. Soon a procession of car drivers arrived to take us all to London Airport.

In spite of the early hour, a small crowd of friends waited outside Field Aviation, the handling agent's office, admiring *Mythre*, parked proudly gleaming and new in the sunlight in front of the black and silver hangar. The engineers bustled around her making the final checks, and well-wishers from my lecture tours mingled with women pilot friends and the team. Field's officers cheerfully filled in all the numerous flight documents, and produced the now traditional bathroom scales to weigh me. The aircraft and contents had already been weighed, to make sure we did not exceed the record 'class' weight together.

After doing the aircraft housekeeping chores inside the cabin I attached the fragile wires of the astronaut's harness, which I had taped on my skin the night before, to the portable electro-cardiac box slung over my shoulder. The time, temperature and many other details had to be recorded on the voice tape recorder.

Alex Torrance, chief despatcher for British Caledonian Airlines, who this morning had been lent to me as my own personal despatcher, had obtained the weather forecast and already filed my flight plan from London to Benghazi, Libya. Without his efficient help it would have been necessary to have started five hours earlier. It is one's flight despatcher liaiser who takes on the responsibility of deciding whether it is a 'go' or not, for once a flight is started it is necessary to try to keep going regardless of weather. He, too, helps in the hard preparations before the flight, and yet is the one left behind worrying until the safe arrival messages come through.

This day we expected the flight from London to Benghazi to take ten hours only. There I would remain only one hour—long enough to refuel and collect the onward weather forecast for the sixteen-hour flight over the Libyan Desert to the Sudan and Nairobi, Kenya, on the Equator.

It was good to be in the cockpit of *Mythre*, for small as it was, today it was comforting and self-contained. She still felt strange compared to my beloved *Myth Too*, but I knew she, too, would be a friend by the time we returned. My poor flesh and blood friends were still gallantly standing shivering in the cold morning air; so I gave them a last wave to put them out of their misery and quickly taxied out towards the now familiar taxiway leading to 'Runway 28 Left'. I had followed this track many times over the last six years, and Runway 28 Left at London Airport had been the start of many adventures.

Once airborne, the sky was full of traffic and the hours went by very quickly, following the air traffic controllers' directions, and coping unexpectedly with very high cylinder head temperatures every time I tried to lead the fuel off.

The thunder squalls led to a mirror of clear air which reflected numerous memories as I flew over St Tropez, and familiar scenes of the careless days of my youth before I had discovered the enchantment of flying. Tiny white sails bobbed and dipped among the waves, and great luxury yachts left streamers of froth in the clear blue Mediterranean waters. People would be eating bouillabaise and moules marinières below. It was time for lunch up here. Fiona and Lana had spent part of the night making little surprises—enough food to last two days. There would be little time for meals on the ground. As usual I found little messages and cards from the team hidden around the aircraft to cheer me on, and I remembered how they had made the flight a reality rather than a hopeless dream. The aroma of fresh coffee filled the cabin and blotted out the now pungent smell of petrol, and gradually I relaxed—confident that at last I was making progress.

The green NASA light flashed on the panel before me, signifying that the satellite, Nimbus, was interrogating the aircraft. I fumbled for the black 'ready to test' button and pressed it hard. A red number flashed its reply in the monkey box, commanding me to press the appropriate pattern of zeros and ones. I checked my other experimental jobs; the heart box recorder battery; noted the inside and outside air temperatures with the pressure altitude; wrote down the type of terrain that I was over-flying so that the researchers could compare notes with the satellite's readings at a later date; filled in my biomedical record. But unknown to me, I was flying in an area of 'noise' (electronic language for an area with much electronic activity) and while I was happily playing with my sophisticated NASA monkey toys, Goddard Space Centre's team were worriedly trying to fathom out what had gone wrong as no signals from *Mythre* could be distinguished from the surrounding build-up. Much was at stake for them and for General Instrument Corporation who had specially built and devised the extra equipment for this new type of experiment, and it was essential that we get results. A very dispirited team sat in the control room at Goddard in Maryland while an elated female pilot innocently drank another cup of coffee to celebrate, high over the Côte d'Azur of France.

I flew on down over the tip of rugged Corsica and the tiny islands of Elba and Palma and headed out towards Palermo in Sicily. Here the thunderstorms had grown to gigantic size, no doubt disturbed by the rumbling grumbles of the neighbouring volcanic Etna and her neighbours, and tossed us fiercely around. Suspiciously too, the performance of the aircraft was not as good as I expected—one hundred and thirty-five miles an hour instead of one hundred and seventy-five. I redid my fuel sums deciding I could just make Benghazi providing no more diversions came up.

Englishman John Hillier, of Libyan Arab Airlines, emerged from out of the crowd of curious Arabs to help me at Benghazi. Much paperwork and rechecking is necessary to be able to fly through trigger-happy Africa these days. Refuelling had to be done slowly so as not to burst the cabin ferry tanks as all the fuel we could take was being put aboard. *Mythre* groaned at this unaccustomed extra weight, and sank low on her wheels, tail almost touching the tarmac, and with a horrific nose-up angle.

By now it was quite dark. Curfew hours, a result of the recent emergency measures, were still in force in Libya, and the Englishmen's departure home was overdue. I must go immediately, because I, too, only had official clearance to make a technical stop for the hour's turnaround. But as I started to climb over the tin storage box and numerous wires, I suddenly felt a shiver of unexpected cold breeze on the back of my neck. The wind had completely veered in the clammy heat which meant a change of direction for take-off.

A quick restudy of the charts and the new take-off direction showed me heading immediately into the small hills. An over-weight take-off requires holding the aircraft down on the runway until there is plenty of excess flying speed, and no sharp turns or erratic manoeuvres. In the surrounding desert territory, the darkness seemed like a solid black wall and not a light showed to indicate the solid hills I knew were there. There was no way of knowing how this modified Aztec would perform in her overweight and misshapen condition. Suppose she would not climb at all? Better to delay till just before dawn when I could at least see the outlines of the solid hills.

This was a miserable decision to have to make, apart from the fact I was not supposed to remain on the airport officially. There was no alternative but to ask the airline ground crew to let me have the key of their office so that I could lock myself in for a few hours. There was nothing else I could do. They had to rush to beat the curfew, and I was certainly not allowed to leave the airport. It was complicated and hilarious enough just getting the immigration officer to allow me to stay on the ground. He seemed to think I personally, like a witch, had conjured up the changing wind and inky blackness.

I lay dozing, but shivering and cold on a stretcher in spite of the desert heat outside the office. I had a nightmare in which I took off. Every detail of the aircraft and airfield was as it really is, but it ended with us pitching and crashing to burn on the runway. It seemed to last for hours, and weirdly my dream kept telling me it was because I took off alone. Shouts and thunderous bangings on the door awoke me, and I found I had only been dozing for half an hour. The new immigration official had just come on duty. His colleague had left no instructions at all about me. After many histrionics in Arabic, like a stowaway I was once again led away across the airport to the immigration hall.

Sleeping bodies lay in odd dark corners, and but for the excitable officials nudging me along, it was like being in a ghost airport, as though a magician had waved his wand and put all things to sleep.

After many arguments, I was finally granted five hours' stay, but unceremoniously left to find my own way back. My nightmare was still very much in my mind, so it was a shock when one of the dark shadows came to life and grabbed me. An Arab had laid in wait for this unwary woman.

"Englishwoman like Arab kisses," he hissed in my face, pressing me to him. I felt his hot breath against me as I smelt him, and struggled violently, not daring to cry out as that would have woken the whole pack. In such circumstances I had learned it is no use being indignant and angry as that could provoke hurt pride or worse. I temporarily got the best of the situation and ran. Seeing the lights of the control tower, I staggered up the winding steps only to be attacked by another shadowy body, which left little to the imagination! Charming international relations be damned, I certainly needed judo training for this adventure!

Breathless but in one piece, I somehow reached the top of the dimly lit tower, where three Egyptian controllers were lazing the night away. They were charming and realised what had happened, entertained me with thick sweet coffee until at last a slight grey tinge appeared to the East instead of inky blackness. It was time to go. My friendly controllers escorted me past the suspect sleeping bodies until I was clear of the buildings. The aircraft still looked eccentric and unnatural with an even worse nose-up angle.

As the first glints of sun made white fingers in the darkened sky, I took a deep breath, staring along the runway, wondering what it would lead me to. The dream of a few hours before was still vivid. Suddenly the right aileron jerked sharply up. Startled, I looked out to a smiling English face—one of my friends of the previous night had arrived, signalling a cheery Churchillian salute. My dream was broken! I was not alone.

Lumbering and creaking, the Aztec moved slowly forward eating up more and more runway as it tried to acquire more speed. At last the needle indicated a safe one hundred and ten miles an hour, and we had left the hot dusty concrete, but within seconds all false sense of security had gone. The nose shot up into the turbulent air—elevators no longer responded to my downward pressure; the aircraft bucked like a frightened horse as the red stall warning light insistently flashed its desperate message. We were going to stall in—the nose must come down. It did, but everything went in extremes and *Mythre* porpoised over the approach lights on towards the tiny hillocks ahead looking like great mountains. Somehow the whirling propellers missed the deck by inches, again and again. Many thousands of thoughts went through my mind, but there was nothing my limbs could do except hang on tight, reacting to old training of trying to centralise the controls to make the aircraft remain straight and level. Again and again, we horrifyingly swung up and down from one crazy attitude to another. Only the daylight showing that the hollocks had gentle slopes saved us. Had I taken off in the dark the previous night I would have hit them.

Somehow I managed to get the aircraft slightly above them even though it seemed I was scraping the very scrub growing below me. The aircraft felt utterly powerless, and so was I, for at least twenty miles. Slowly, foot by foot, at only one hundred and twelve miles an hour, *Mythre* grudgingly crept to five hundred feet. By now I was way off the course I had planned for this desert leg. There were no landmarks to check against and it was many hot hours later before I managed to reach a mere thousand feet. My nightmare dream of the take-off had happened exactly in reality, except for the very end. I wondered whether the ending would have been the same if my friend had not appeared at the very last moment! It was a very sobering eerie thought.

Dust storms raged below me and particles of sand crept into everything. My eyes stung with irritation. Even at this early hour the heat was intolerable, and my shirt clung wetly to my skin but I could not let go the recalcitrant controls to remove it. No indications from any beacons were possible at this range so I was resigned to several hours of dead reckoning, until Khartoum's beam came in. Certainly I would never reach Nairobi in one hop with this slow speed, and huge fuel consumption. I would have to land at Khartoum. What could be wrong with *Mythre*?

Radio communication established that there was a two-hundred-foot dust cloud base only at Khartoum with almost nil visibility. The dreaded 'Haboob' was imminent—a violent wind and sandstorm that roars across the desert in these regions, and not to be challenged carelessly by light aircraft. The flailing sand cleared a little and I caught a glimpse of the wide Nile below me, and with more than a little relief knew I was nearly there.

Within twenty minutes of landing the airport had closed, and one could no longer see across the field. Colonel Uloth and his wife from the British Embassy were there, and despite the intense oppressive heat—a hundred and ten degrees—and stinging sand storm, helped me to shelter the aircraft while waiting the storm out. The Haboob had turned day into night.

It took three hours of paperwork battle with officialdom to finally escape after the storm had dissipated. Then later, when I neared the Sudan–Kenyan border, the daily violent belt of thunderstorms had already built up over southern Sudan. Air traffic control cleared me to fourteen thousand feet, but *Mythre* refused, and the stall warning grumbled at a mere ninety-five miles an hour, as we hung by the propellers in the thin air at a mere eleven thousand feet. The Lowdar beacon, by which one can obtain indications of where the high mountain peaks begin, was unserviceable, and visibility was nil. No amount of coaxing would make the aircraft climb any higher, but it was not possible to make it safely through the mountains on instruments without a safe altitude. The blinding downpour of furious water left no option but to turn back. The aircraft certainly would not be able to take on the world with this slow airspeed and low ceiling. There was much to improve yet—which is usually the reason for long flight tests.

Too much time had been wasted to have enough fuel to go back as far as Khartoum, and the squall line lay across my alternative—Juba. There are two or three fields on the banks of the Nile, though not with many resources, nor very hospitable to unexpected visitors, and I did not have permission to land on them. I descended to below the clouds now gathering all around me, and flew a few hundred feet over the scrubland in blinding rain back towards the swamps of the Sud. But at least there should not be any high ground to hit, and I certainly did not wish to land in the scrub among the permanently warring tribes of Southern Sudan, or even among the lions and wildebeest.

Malakar military airfield on the Nile came up but with not an aircraft on it, nor a reply on the radio from its control tower. The NASA light flicked on again as though on cue. Back at Goddard Space Flight Centre in the States, however, Jack Effner, ace Navigation Data man, had quite a hard time convincing the rest of the team that his readings were correct and that I had flown a backtrack.

However, my 'lie detector' monkey box soon backed him up. I had made a mistake while both trying to coax the stalling *Mythre* to climb a bit higher and at the same time attempting to obey the satellite commands. The altitude detector, too, indicated the unplanned low levels and the position plots showed the slow airspeed. He now had clear evidence that something was wrong aboard: my mistake proved I was concentrating on the unexpected. I should not be showing pilot fatigue at this stage. All these clues, coupled with their satellite picture of the local weather, gave the complete picture. Although it was miserable for me to be delayed yet again, my setbacks had shown the possibilities that the experiment could lead to.

As I touched down on the strange quiet airport, the heat was terrific, a hundred and twenty degrees, and only then did a voice greet me on the radio. At first the uniformed men behaved as if the airport was bristling with military aircraft; yet all that could be seen were the grazing wild animals and many excitable young children. Sweat oozed down my body making the electrode harness uncomfortable and sore on my inflamed skin. The airfield commandant suggested that I relax at the little local resthouse on the perimeter of the airport. A band of dark-skinned, long flowing robed men stared at me almost in disbelief. There were no women here in public rooms—certainly none who flew in alone. My tiny room and its thin strip of curtain at the window did little to shelter me from the prying eyes of the villagers—anything private like undressing must be in the primitive 'john' in inky blackness without any windows or lights at all.

The electrodes had been taped on me for four days now, and

with sensual relief I pulled off the Elastoplast. Buzzing mosquitoes attacked my bare skin in full force, and I hastily looked for Paludrine tablets and water purifiers. The hotel manager brought in an enormous meal of stewed meat, and rice. He was followed by the inevitable policeman who took my passport. I hoped I would see it again—it was going to be difficult enough to get away, and it would entail many more hours of formalities even if I ever succeeded in wheedling some fuel out of the airport manager.

But the airport manager suggested with pride that he should show me his town and off we drove in a very old jeep—he quite incongruously talking about the Space programme, while dark-skinned children, covered with flies, climbed on and hung to the running board. The rough road was lined by block after block of native thatched huts and gay markets. Green weed and wild hyacinths floated in the river and seemed to have netted permanently the numerous barge houseboats moored alongside.

Darkness falls early here—it was near the Equator where sunlight and darkness are nearly equal—and I prepared for bed, intending to rise two hours before daybreak. Then without warning the local Sudanese bank manager and his entire family arrived to pay me an official call. Much traditional tea had to be drunk before he agreed to change some money for me.

A mere four hours for sleep was left. I got up in the middle of the night but I was still there midday the following morning—fighting the mountains of paperwork. A small Sudanese airliner landed, flown by an Englishman; it brought a good onward weather forecast. At last a message from Khartoum came in, insistent that I land at Juba too for further customs clearance. This meant I would now fly to Nairobi via the longest route over Entebbe in Uganda and Lake Victoria.

I flew out low level, not bothering to climb over the cloud cover, following the misty outlines of the Nile, occasionally glimpsing a tribal village and large animals. There were lions and elephants here too, and the ground had become green and fresh as I left the hot eternal dust of the desert behind.

I whiled away the time with my many biomedical checks. Multivitamins, Paludine, salt tablets all taken; sleep log filled in; and liquid intake and urine output noted. Aircraft designers make beautiful little gadgets for the boys, but we women are

A TYPICAL TEAM OF HELPERS AT SHEILA'S HOME. *From the left* Freydis Sharland, a Ninety-Nine; Christine Stubbersfield, Lana St George Jeffers, Jackie Williams, Jean Duffy, who all helped with the secretarial work involved in various flights, seen here with Sheila and Lena Roach, 1972. *Bottom left inset:* Fiona MacGinley, another secretarial helper

Chief Engineer, Les Baston, discusses with Sheila the plans for winterising the new Aztec, *Mythre*, in preparation for her Polar flight

Astronaut Dr Philip Chapman
leaving the cockpit of a T-38

IN THE PLANNING ROOM
AT GODDARD SPACE
FLIGHT CENTRE. *From the left* Charles
Cote, IRLS Principal Investigator
and Programme Manager with Len
Roach, Experiment Co-ordinator
and Ground Equipment Manager;
William Seechuk, IRLS Mission
Operator; John Effner, Mission
Planner and Operator

Group Captain Peter Whittingham of the Institute of Aviation Medicine, Farnborough, explains the working of the astronaut's biomedical harness and heartbox recorder to Sheila before her Polar Flight

Commander Crawford, head of Aero Medical Branch, with communications specialist, Leroy Field, monitoring satellite downling signal at the US Naval Air Test Centre, Patuxent River, during Sheila's flight over the North Pole, 1971

Monster from Outer Space in Arctic survival wear?

Engineers Dave Brown and Reg Burden break for coffee with Sheila, Oxford Airport

reduced to using homely aids for more than one thing aboard. The obvious problem is overcome with the aid of Tupperware's pudding basin with seal proof lid. Surprisingly, perhaps, it is best not to restrict liquid intake, but drink rather more when actually flying the aircraft for long hours. A hyper-dehydrated body is far more subject to vertigo.

With so little room in the cabin—not enough space to stretch stiffened legs—it is always a problem getting the pudding basin out discreetly at the various stops, particularly as my gallant helpers always want to carry all the bags for the poor tired woman pilot. Past experience had taught me to stow it in an easily identifiable zipper bag, and never to let it out of my sight. Once on a previous African flight during the troubles, there had been just one unmarried British Consul looking after me. After reaching my room, to my horror I found the vital bag missing. I rang him up to locate it. Quite calmly he replied, "That's all right my dear, I have taken it away to put the sandwiches in it!" Somehow I got it back, but I never knew if he looked.

Over Entebbe in Uganda the skies had become once again full of the usual afternoon towering thunderstorms, and it was obvious I could no longer get through to Kenya. Needless to say I did not have permission to land in Uganda either on this new unplanned route. Fortunately Entebbe's air traffic controller was an ally, International Aeradio man, Terry Murphy, whom I had met during an earlier record attempt from London to Capetown in 1967. He greeted me by name as I flew into radio range, and promised to try to fix things for me before I landed.

After touch down at Entebbe, Ugandan Aviation Services took over the aircraft maintenance, but civilian police took over me. Even Terry could not out-talk them. Nothing less than the Commander of the ruling Ugandan military authorities (who realised my little aircraft was hardly a war plane) would do, and it took some hours of argument before Terry was allowed to drive me to the highly civilised Victoria Hotel to await their decision.

Friendly Uganda Aviation refused to take payment for their work on the aircraft, but the security men were not so generous. Only after a considerable verbal battle with a certain amount of old English vocabulary and after a furious military chief demanded an explanation of why they were holding me against

141

his orders was I allowed to depart next day. The weather deteriorated considerably as the day's arguments wore on, but thunderstorms or not, I was somehow going to get out of this inhospitable place today, across Lake Victoria to Nairobi, before someone else might change their mind. I remembered Terry's tale of being put up against the wall by trigger-happy gentlemen at a previous station, and how he was only rescued from being shot immediately without trial because an Egyptian General happened to be walking by and intervened in time. He moved to Uganda after that adventure, but I was not about to take any chances even in Uganda.

Now I flew like a tourist just above circles of grass native huts against brilliant green forestry. Giraffe, zebra, storks and wildebeest were lazily grazing below me, and beautiful birds flew up to meet me. Two and a half hours later the foothills of the familiar Aberdare mountains emerged, and there was the city of Nairobi sprawling among the game parks.

John Williams and other friends waited with Peter Whittingham, the RAF doctor who had flown ahead of me to check on his black biomedical boxes. Here the customs men just waved me aside, and the Wilken Aviation engineers (loyal friends of *Myth Too*) admired the new *Mythre*, and took her away to pamper and coax. At last after six gruelling months of preparation and uncertainty, I could rest for three glorious days of freedom and sun in one of my favourite countries, spoilt and surrounded by good fellowship and people who were well used to my sort of crazy flying themselves. For them, too, it was the only way to live—to live aware and alive.

The Washington Goddard team could now make direct contact with me via a SCAMA line in Mombasa. I started to explain to our Project Manager, Charles Cote, in the USA, all that had happened to me *en route* to Nairobi, but found that they already knew why I had made certain decisions. This was a very strange feeling, and made me realise more than anything else that I was not alone on this flight and that others would be figuring it (and me) out as I flew the route. It was as though that satellite had crept into my very brain! I was a bit uncertain whether I really liked this.

At last the long awaited and critical message came through via British Caledonian Airlines from Alex Torrance. It was time to head back for London *en route* to the Pole. The weather pattern ahead for the Arctic Region looked about right to make the attempt, but it would probably be the last chance this season. The summer thaw had started and black icing fog soon would descend.

In spite of the nagging teething troubles, good work, unbeknown to me, was already being produced by my magic black boxes and transmitted to Goddard Space Centre's computers. The SO_2 carbon dioxide sensor (Doctor Miller's experiment) had found an unexpected amount of air pollution over the Libyan Desert—from the burning of sour gases from the oil fields some distance away, to the smouldering stubble in Malakal town. At least we were proving something worked and it was now up to me to keep going to prove it around the entire world.

And so began the trek back to London—where the aircraft would be winterised overnight. It was just as bad as the journey out, with overheating engines giving insufficient performance and leading to delayed stops for further maintenance everywhere. What could still be wrong with the aircraft? The added equipment could not account for all this loss of power.

I flew across the imaginary line of the Tropic of Cancer in the Libyan Desert and knew when I next flew it (if I did) I would then have flown over the Pole, and I would be on the other side of the world over a mighty ocean, the Pacific, instead of a desert. I began to feel full of anticipation, excitement and confidence returned; somehow *Mythre* and I would make it. Les would cure *Mythre*'s problems.

But at Malta, in the RAF Mess, a message arrived stating, "Please inform Sheila Scott a few trophies have been stolen from her flat." I realised immediately that someone was trying to soften the blow and that if it was important enough to inform me while I was out here it was most likely that the whole flat had been burgled!

I continued to London full of misery both about the aircraft's chances and the sort of mess that would greet me. There obviously was no longer any question of a quick turnabout to continue to the Arctic within hours in London now. Fiona's swollen eyes told me the worst as soon as I landed, and I felt so sorry for her that I forgot my own dismay. What else in life could go wrong?

The aircraft now went back to Oxford airport to be winterised. Special muffles and blanketing devices were to be put on as well as different greases and oils for the Arctic. Two Air Registration Board test pilots were to try to solve the missing performance problems, and at least advise me on some safer operating figures.

At my home, I found everything of value had been stolen—jewellery, trophies and hundreds of little things presented to me from around the entire world. A *whole* career vanished overnight! These were the only tangible things I had had of past races, records and flights. The suitcases full of Arctic gear standing ready for the aircraft turnaround had been emptied and taken by the thieves to carry the loot in, and some of the clothes used to wrap the cups in! They had even taken the Akai video tape camera with which I was going to film the Polar regions. The loss of this film was to lose me many thousands of pounds of earnings on my return, and I never recovered financially from then on. It was too late to negotiate for another one. Without sponsorship, it is essential to have films to sell to pay for the fuel and aircraft maintenance, as well as the hire-purchase payments on the aircraft itself.

I tried to blank out the unhappiness, though I was aware that the robbery must have been done by people who knew the flat well. It was only too obvious by the things left untouched. It was a horrible thought and difficult to forgive, as I knew that their need was not greater than mine. They could not be poorer than I was at the moment. Fortunately, flying is a clean and honest thing and requires enough concentration to make it possible to forget all that is twisted and rotten elsewhere.

But four vital days went by while I dealt with the necessary formalities of this added complication as well as the aircraft. At last I thought I could escape and get the job done, but now the onward weather forecast was impossible. There were very active fronts across the North Sea and Norway, and no way for a light aircraft to get through them. Yet beyond the front, in the Polar Basin, the weather was as good as it could be at this time of year. We knew this respite of good weather up there must be the last there could be this season, because it was already unexpectedly late. It was maddening! I simply could not delay more than another twenty-four hours. I would have to abandon all hope this season if I did, and there would not be another season for *Mythre* and me. Alex Torrance finally worked out a circular flight track for me to circumvent the worst weather to reach Bodo, in northern Norway.

It was a strange day because suddenly there was nothing more I could personally do. I was lost, and knew I had not done enough preparation, but it was too late to start new work. I now hated my home and the sordidness of it all. I just wanted to escape to the Arctic Circle itself.

11

Midsummer's Eve and a Midnight Sun

MIRACULOUSLY, the new forecast predicted that the extremely bad weather in the North Sea would dissipate after midday and good weather still held in the Arctic Circle. What a joy not to have to get up in the middle of the night this time. As I lay curled up in my soft bed for a few last stolen minutes of luxury, suddenly I did not want to go. What was I doing leaving the warmth and comfort of my own bed and apartment—and actually chasing cold discomfort? I loathe mornings and enthusiastic breakfast chatterers, preferring conversation rather than talk, except when it's for flying. Even then the most beautiful flight is the one that starts in the evening sunset and continues through the night waiting for the first hint of dawn and the awakening of the sky.

I dressed leisurely, without the usual, frenetic rush on such occasions, before we drove happily in convoy to London Airport. Once there, tranquillity was short lived, for my engineers had worked through the night to change some equipment around. Anything portable had had to be moved out to make room for them to get into the aircraft. There was certainly no room for a fully grown man in the tiny space left for me in the cabin. It was so limited that things had to be stowed around me only after I had squeezed into the seat.

This time we had to repack in public the bits and pieces strewn all over the wing while all looked on and the press photographers waited. *Mythre* and I looked more like a rummage sale at the moment, and certainly did not resemble the serious Arctic explorers of earlier days. Jim Watkins soothed the customs men who looked aghast at the muddle. But at least they did not need to unpack the aircraft, for its contents were spread out for all to see! The catalytic heaters for the engine, which we had spent months trying to obtain, were now thrown out, as the temperature at Bodo would not be below freezing, and my hair rollers were stored in the nose as ballast instead. There were various passengers to be seated—Purple Cow, *Mythre*'s christening present; Saint Christopher and a Koala bear, and the most important member of my crew, Buck Tooth, my gallant toy rabbit and bedraggled co-pilot, who had started life with me here at London Airport and flown with me ever since.

It was time to give a quick round of hugs to the friends around. I looked at each one, wondering when, where or if I would see them again. Too much had gone wrong in the last few days for me to feel any over-confidence, but there was no more time left to change anything, nor did I want to, although I was far from sure exactly where I would finish this flight. The ice was breaking up further north, announcing the certain advent of black ice fog on the coast of Alaska. The last one aboard to bid me goodbye was flight despatcher Alex Torrance —kindly and trying to instil confidence.

Clearance to start up at last, with directions to follow a BEA airliner closely. The delay had certainly affected my morale and I felt utterly lost and bewildered. Suddenly, I was aware that I was more afraid than I had ever been before and became as nervous as though it was my first take-off out of a busy inter-national airport. I forgot this was the friendly London Airport, which had always given me splendid moral support in the past. Just before crossing one runway I looked over the expanse of oil-stained concrete and its glinty approach lights, to see a Jumbo Jet lumbering in. In spite of the controller's instructions, it looked too big and fast for me to make it across the wide run-way. A furious air traffic controller grumbled, "I told you to follow close behind BEA."

Duly chastised, I taxied through the concrete jungle towards a line of airliners to wait beside the BEA jet. The jet towered above me; its captain's face a blur behind the high nose and its wings like a canopy above little *Mythre*, which seems a tubby, stout aircraft compared to her light aircraft sisters and she is dwarfed against the larger commercial aircraft.

"Good luck, Sheila," an unknown captain's voice said.

"Thank you, I need it this time," I replied huskily.

"We are with you." This last message came from the pre-viously stern air traffic controller. I was to remember those words many times during the days that followed over the acres and acres of lonely desolate ice-packed sea, when it seemed that everyone else on earth had mysteriously disappeared, and that I had wandered out into space to some other planet.

The BEA giant roared off, clinging to the vast expanse of runway until it finally peeled itself away and leapt into the air. *Mythre* crept on to the wide runway feeling like an underpowered elastic-propelled toy aeroplane, as I glimpsed the other giants edging and nudging each other along the taxiways behind me. My eyes flicked around the cabin making sure no warning lights glinted, as my sticky hands pushed the throttle fully forward and the smooth modest power of *Mythre*'s engines blotted out the sound of the screaming jets. The familiar slight smell of fuel filled the cabin, and sunbeams glancing off the tarmac stretching before me dissolved all fear into an exhilarating freedom after months of strain and chores. Now only the thrill of unflown new challenges lay ahead.

Mythre hesitated but momentarily as her wheels began to roll along the hot tarmac tugged by the biting thrust of her propellers as they ate great chunks of air, rushing by at sixty miles an hour—eighty—faster still—on past her normal take-off speed—over one hundred miles an hour but still I did not ease the stick back—the bitter lesson had been learnt days before in Benghazi. The lines between the blocks of concrete got closer as speed increased. It seemed an eternity before we reached the necessary one hundred and twelve and could allow the bumping wheels finally to let go the blackened tarmac into the turbulent air left by the departing jets. Now nothing more could be done. Next time our wheels touched ground it must be in the Arctic Circle.

Multi-coloured caterpillars of traffic wove its patterns along the twisting roads of northern London; chimneys like dirty pointed fingers trailed their smoke, and pierced the leafy green patches of the temperate English countryside. Soon cumulus cloud blanked off the sight of earth below, while London Radar gave me new headings to steer up and out to Airway Amber One, the road of the sky along which I had been assigned to travel. The worst of today's flight would strangely be the north of England and the North Sea; but I still felt slightly uneasy at my lack of knowledge of the permanently frozen regions of the world through which I was about to fly. My dry throat still croaked in reply to the kindly controllers.

I switched the autopilot on. It was broken! I could not believe it. Again I had started a long-distance flight with mysterious broken equipment! The next day I was to fly the most difficult flight of my life with practically no aids, except for an astro compass for which I needed two hands as well as an uncluttered brain to be sure of making no mathematical errors. An autopilot was a physical necessity. One mathematical error from an inaccurate sight could mislead me to where I would not have enough petrol to span the icy waters. But I reasoned, of course, that the autopilot could be mended in Norway while I rested for a few hours before the Polar leg. There was no alternative except to continue on to Bodo, if I was going to make it this year. Now that the ice was breaking, even a day could make a difference. I radioed my handlers, Field Aviation, via their private company frequency in London Airport requesting them to have an engineer at Bodo to rectify the fault.

As I flew into the murky clouds, made grimy by the factories below, towards the familiar Scottish towns of Edinburgh and Aberdeen, my thoughts went back to earlier days when I visited these places, but only a quick glimpse of leaping angry spray over a desolate beach bid me farewell before the curtain of cloud finally engulfed me. Already the wings were covered with sparkling ice and the unfriendly North Sea was living up to its evil reputation. An hour and a half later I was flying over the town of Stavanger on the south-west coast of Norway. There the controller bid me a friendly good-day, wishing me luck. Occasionally through the grey sombre clouds I caught glimpses of lonely little farmhouses, nestling against grassy fir lined slopes which led to the higher forbidding crags hovering over fiords, and desolate little islands stranded in a moving surf-speckled sea.

Now the aircraft standby compass was at a drunken angle and would soon be completely erratic, hopelessly submitting to the attraction of its master, the magnetic pole—six hundred miles below my track. Its more sophisticated companion, the Sperry C 11 Compass system, would convert to a simple direction indicator to avoid the magnetic pull. Today when tested, it remained steady as a rock with not even a half degree of precession. There also remained my only Polar navigation aid, the astro compass, which needed the sun to give it life. Sometimes called a sun compass, it works vaguely on the same system as a sextant, and by sighting its shadow bar with a celestial body plus a few calculations one can obtain a true reading.

Saucy pink-edged clouds cheekily edged the gloomy overcast below; dark patches of rock and melting ice wove fantastic paisley designs over snow-capped peaks to starboard. Again, unexpectedly NASA's green light flashed reminding me that at this very time astronaut Phil Chapman would be arriving at Goddard Space Flight Centre to join my old friend, Len Roach, with Richard Ormsby, manager of Nimbus ground station and the crack locating team, Jack Effner and Bill Seechuk, as well as many others who were monitoring the various facets of the flight. Although physically alone, my green light had reminded me of the very positive friends—many latitudes lower down—who were determined that I should succeed. Indeed, I *had* to for them also, for at least one of them had staked his job against the experiment being a success. It had to work. Even if I did not actually succeed in flying the Pole, I had to get round the world.

Sixty-six degrees fifty north. I half expected actually to see the mythical line that is the border of the Arctic Circle. I had been so in awe of it for six long years, that now it had become a tangible division on the earth—an actual barrier I had to overcome—and when *Mythre* flew smoothly on without sign other than my own dead reckoning, it was an anticlimax, almost a disappointment. The border is determined by the lowest latitude, where once a year there is twenty-four hours of nightlike darkness, and six months later a twenty-four hour day of sun—Midsummer's Day—of which tonight was the eve. The higher the latitude I flew the more whole sunshine nights I would see, or alternately had it been winter, whole dark days. At the Poles there are six months of sunshine and six months of continuous night.

Midsummer's Eve is Norway's party night—when much clear firewater is drunk all night long. Twirling ribbons of smoke curled upwards from villages of gaily painted chalets, and celebration bonfires cast leaping shadows through the deep gorges of the valleys. It was time to descend below the sea's overcast to make an approach from out to sea to creep in low level between brooding isles and towering craggy mountains cut deep by fiords: herring fishing boats bobbed below me, obviously knowing every current and fathom of the Norwegian Sea. But for me—now almost as low as their masts—it was difficult both to map read and avoid the steep-sided islets and hard to believe there had ever been sun above this grim over-layer. It was not hard to imagine a Draug—the Norwegian mythical figure who foretells death to any unfortunate sailor who sees him—drifting in his half ship among the islands. But the clouds dispersed up the valley leading to Bodo's runway, and I felt I had already flown through the night. The sun was high in the sky even though it was ten-thirty p.m.

The RAF Dominie was way in the distance, waiting to escort me tomorrow to the military field of Andoya, where I would take on the full fuel load under Air Force supervision before bidding everyone goodbye to set off on my solitary journey. The RAF's Eric Stafford and Freddie French's welcoming faces appeared over the cowling with the news that we had no time to spare. Tomorrow it was forecast the weather was beginning to break across the Pole. All around us people dressed in national costume danced, drank and sang through the streets of Bodo, while most of our night was spent in last minute briefing by telephone from my mentors at Goddard Space Flight Centre or in trying to get some help and advice from England about the broken equipment. But no engineer was there. Well, I would have to fly the Pole without the autopilot. A remote and irresponsible British gentleman suggested that I return home! I indignantly refused to consider such a negative thought. We had passed the stage of getting everything perfect: if I returned, we could now spend months, years delaying and still not get things right.

Mike Hudson, autopilot specialist of CSE, probably knew how I felt when he called me next morning to give me exact instructions on how to try to get the wretched thing unstuck, and at least partly working. His considerate words of encouragement helped me more than he knew, even though I never did succeed in getting the autopilot to work.

Then came the welcome news that a new man had joined my fabulous team in America, Leroy Field, representing the US Naval Air Test Centre at Patuxent River. The Navy would be trying to communicate directly with me around the world and also the Dewline (Defence Early Warning System) would be watching my path to Alaska. For every bad thing there was at least something good to balance things up!

Finally, exhausted but unable to sleep with excitement, I lay on my bed looking at the charts of tomorrow, and retesting myself on astro compass and grid navigation. The thin curtains let in the brilliant sunshine although it was four in the morning, and the merry laughter of the revellers outside filled my room, making me feel quite unreal. I restlessly tossed and turned, half dreamily regretting my younger days when I refused to learn maths at school, preferring biology.

Meanwhile, Eric Stafford spent most of his night working out a new scheme for me. He had decided that my now proven, slower than expected, airspeed would not be sufficient to get me safely over the Pole as far as Point Barrow, Alaska, with enough fuel to spare. There was nothing to do but change plans and fly a single heading pressure pattern. This involves obtaining forecasts of all pressure levels to decide which will give the best advantage according to the wind strengths. With a pressure pattern you can fly a single heading the whole way, regardless of normal course changes—not necessarily a straight course, but a curved one according to the wind pattern. Our particular pattern would start tracking to the left and then curve towards and over the Pole, and afterwards swing back at least vaguely in the direction and safety of the Alaska coastline—though no longer necessarily direct to Barrow! If I arrived within two hundred miles of the United States coastline I should be able to pick up one of the many radio beacons to home in on, and make for the nearest field. It just meant sitting it out patiently holding course for about fifteen hours and trusting that the winds would not change too violently, until I was within range of the American navigation aids.

Originally, I had planned a direct grid course, and this new curving flight track was to give my Goddard friends some nervous moments when they saw the strange position reports that Nimbus was relaying. Although a signal was sent explaining the change of plan to a pressure pattern, they did not know what shape the pattern was supposed to be.

A fantastic Norwegian breakfast arrived which doubled for lunch, while I off-loaded all the surplus things I no longer needed (to keep the aircraft weight down) for the RAF Dominie to take home to London. There was no room for anything except bare essentials, once I left Andoya for the Pole. I needed all the stowage space possible so my ultra lightweight but bulky Arctic gear could be close at hand, and to be able to spread my numerous ready reference tables and charts.

Even though it was in the Arctic Circle, I was not very cold on the ground—just above freezing—so I did not yet need to wear all five layers of clothes. I would put those on at the last refuelling stop, Andöy. Most of these garments were made for men, as it was impossible to buy Arctic wear for women in England. They had all sorts of extra bits and pieces with beautifully built in little round bottoms. Pringle had given me a special present of an outsize but pretty cashmere trouser suit, to disguise the bundle of thick underclothes. The colour matched the aircraft livery and though I certainly looked as though I needed a diet the finished effect was vaguely feminine. One airman grumbled that I should not be flying the icy regions dressed like that! He did not know what I had on underneath, but I felt hurt that he should think I was normally that fat.

But as we collected all the data from the weather men and the computers, we could see the fog from afar about to descend amid the mountains and fiords of Bodo. We raced for our aircraft, but it was too late, the fog had already reached the sea end of the runway. I sat there absolutely devastated. I heard the radio report that it was still clear in Andoya, but it was an hour's flight away—we would never get there in time—we would have to go tomorrow. Memories of all the months of work, finance and planning that had gone towards this moment flickered through my brain. Time had run out. No! I could not go tomorrow. It must be today! The warmer it became, the worse and more frequent the icing and fog, and this could last for days at a time. Even when there were clear days, one side of the Arctic Ocean could be clear while the other side lay hidden in fog.

I studied my charts, trying to work an exact heading with the wind to fly out blindly somehow between mountain sides, and bits of rocks and islands sticking up in the sea. Suddenly, I heard the Captain of the Dominie aircraft cancel his flight plan. It was below minimums even for them. Now I had no option but to cancel out. I never knew whether he had cancelled to make sure I did not take on any more risks than I was already about to incur.

I sat dispirited in the control tower glaring at the fog as if to frighten it away. Occasionally it did lift for a few seconds, only to roll back more solidly than ever. Soon I had to give up and go back with the men into the town. Again, most of the night was spent telephoning to change all the plans once more.

Next day was brighter, and I arrived at the airport at 1500 hours ready to take off earlier, determined at least to be waiting at the jumping off place for the North Pole. Owing to the military nature of Andoya I was supposed only to refuel there and not stay the night. Hence the original reason for this overnight stop—and delay—at Bodo. A direct flight from Bodo to Barrow would only add an extra hour to the flight, but there was not sufficient fuel to spare.

The weather forecast was slightly better, at least the fog was only lasting for a few hours a day and was not expected until 1800 hours. Eric, and the Norwegians with their special computers, had checked and made yet another pressure pattern track with the welcome news that today's winds were better, which would help the critical fuel supply. Already straggly bits of grey mist crept in among the sunlit mountains, so we all hurried through our flight preparations before these spectres descended to become soul-destroying banks of rolling fog. I could not stand even one more hour of delay. I had lived for this moment since December 28th, 1970, and today it was June 23rd, 1971—two long months later than planned!

Curious Norwegians came out of the airport buildings to look at me and the aircraft. From their few remarks, it was only too obvious what they were thinking, but luckily the sight of the thickening clouds prevented me from dwelling on the foreboding gloom on their faces, as they looked at me. I did not really care. I was now determined that I was going to make it safely—providing I left today. No other day would do. It was already beginning to rain as I taxied out, but the long runway led out to sea, and patches of sunlight still glinted on the church steeple and the power lines nestling alongside green firs and mountains edging the bay.

My engine purred happily, and became a roar as my throttle hand automatically moved forward. Wheels up, and they stayed up with the yellow light gleaming steadily. No problems today, I thought, for the airspeed and climb had greatly improved in the colder air, and I soon reached my assigned altitude. Equally quickly the ice started to build up, but the de-icers and heaters seemed to be working well. The only snags seemed to be the broken autopilot and scanty aids, but by now I had got used to the idea that there was going to be little help over the next leg. Fair enough, I reasoned, for if it were any easier many thousands of light aircraft would have flown it, and I would not have had the chance of discovering a new bit of the sky for female aircraft.

The automatic direction-finding needle swung to one side, as Andoya's radar controller's voice informed me he had me on his radar screen directing me for a let-down over the sea. I descended through the solid icy cloud to my first glimpse of the Arctic Ocean, which did not appear to be the awesome, frightening thing of which I had been half in fear. Delicate cakes of ice floated lazily over dark blue-green depths; little rocks and breathtakingly beautiful mountains of green forests and caps of snow emerged alongside a runway, which led right out to the waves below me. It was easy to imagine the old graceful Viking long ships nosing out to sea, and I thought of Fridtjof Nansen, Norway's great North Polar explorer— humanitarian sailor and his ship *Fram* whose name meant 'forward'. Here too among the mountains there could well be Trolls, those old ugly giants of childhood stories. Trolls were strong and beautiful only to their own kind's eyes, but so slow it took a hundred years to get an answer when they talked. Were they perhaps outer-space robots of long ago, for it could take a hundred years to get a reply from some universes?

Down on the ground I saw the RAF's blue Dominie already was there, looking solid and comforting. Without them it would have been lonely during these last few hours of preparations before taking off into the unknown. Captain John Larsen, with other Norwegian Air Force personnel, helped me with the formalities, but the biting cold sea breeze made us hustle around to keep warm while inspecting tyres and de-icers and making sure all was well. The big fuel bowser lumbered up, and the slow hour-long refuelling of my outsize cabin tanks began.

0100 hours had been chosen as my take-off time, both for

optimum satellite interrogation hours and to enable me to get as many sun shots as possible while the sun was ahead and to the port of me. The Aztec's shallow windows and the fuel tanks covered the sun when it was in any other position. About three hours remained until 'lift-off', with the weather miraculously remaining good. The temperature at my planned pressure level of 9880 feet was not too far below freezing, but cloud would cause severe icing.

The Norwegians took us to the little fishing-town hotel, where the RAF would spend the night after I had gone. The idea was that I should take a rest for an hour, but by the time we had eaten huge Norwegian steaks, and arranged the franking and stamping of my four hundred specially issued Polar Covers, it was already time to go.

I borrowed one of the bedrooms to don my Arctic clothes, and remembered the 'john checks', for this time I was swaddled with layers of clothes. I did not see how I was going to cope easily in the aircraft and even if I did succeed, mine would be a very frozen 'sit-upon'! In fact, for this problem we had previously flight-tested a new modification—very odd-shaped spongy things. Alas, once again, they had been designed for men, and if necessary a frozen female *derrière* was almost preferable!

The pure silk long johns, vest and socks had felt luxurious and feminine, until I covered them with layers and layers of bulge-producing wool and finally my maligned outsize turquoise Pringle suit. A working, lightweight anorak, and a Himalayan survival duvet were stowed aboard ready to don in the air when needed.

Wires dangled down in front of me from the astronauts' EGT harness, which again was taped to my skin. I looked a monster from Outer Space, though no one on earth would think it was a female, except by its long blonde hair, and turquoise colour—but even that does not identify the sexes these days! I slipped on a pair of outsize comfy slippers for the take-off and carried my huge man-sized boots which had to go over three pairs of thick socks.

"You won't be needing those. It's summer on the other side," Eric said, seeing my boots. I hesitated, as they meant more weight, but something made me keep them.

"No, I'll take them. I would look silly if I did manage to land on an ice island in bedroom slippers!" I replied, though in fact my mind was channelled into one long track across the Arctic in the determination not to be dissuaded or to divert from it.

At the airport, we topped off all the fuel tanks once again so as to squeeze in even the last pint. Someone else spread anti-icing paste over every protruding bit of the aircraft, while the RAF carefully inspected every rivet. *Mythre* sat very solidly down on her main wheels, with her tail almost scraping the ground, but her nose was up like a haughty woman surveying her rivals. Her paintwork shone in the sunlight and I could see the smudges of anti-icing paste against the gleaming enamel. Small streaks of green fuel ran over her white wings, and mingled among the black oil marks of the tarmac. I looked up at the two intertwined flags of Great Britain and the United States on her rudder and was proud of her. Someone came back with a last-minute check of the weather—no change, so the flight would probably only take sixteen hours to be within range of the other coast for the 3000-mile journey.

Time to get aboard. Everyone lined up and shook me by the hand wishing me luck—some of their eyes showing that they thought it was more like goodbye—but I knew it was the luck that they were wishing me that was needed now more than skill on this journey. My heart was thumping and the heavy un-accustomed layers of clothes made me feel sticky and unwieldy, but at last the long-dreamed-of flight was reality and I was at the beginning of the most exciting thing I had ever attempted in my life.

12

I DOUBLE-CHECKED the time; three watches and the chrono-graph were in complete unison to the second. Astro compass and immersion suit were within easy reach, and all remaining loose heavy objects pulled forward to help the aircraft during her overweight take-off. I plugged myself into the heart box; re-corded the time, and noted that the gauges indicated all was wonderfully normal. We were ready.

Eric climbed up on to the wing and somehow lodged himself on top of the black storage box beside me. He carefully super-vised my last pre-flight check of setting the Sperry into its basic direction mode. Once this was done—offset by grid—I must not touch it until I landed on the other side of the Pole. His were simple checks with so much at stake, for it only meant one simple mathematical error here to put me in very inhospitable waters indeed, and almost certain death.

"For heaven's sake, turn back if there is anything wrong—anything at all. Don't press on. We shall be here all night," admonished poor Eric. It was obvious that he did not care for this job at all, but knew it was better for him to be here than leave me to go off alone. He quietly wished me luck, and as the door slammed vanished off the wing.

"Don't go yet," I wanted to say, but it was too late. The minutes were racing by now, and I would miss the sun in the right position if I did not hurry. *Mythre* groaned and creaked in protest a little as I eased the throttle forward but her nose was still high as we taxied slowly forward. I fancifully murmured, "That's right, no slouching! Let's keep our noses in the air!"

I was aware of the line of men, and the salute, but by now I was hermetically sealed in my lonely little world with *Mythre*. There was only the controller's voice to remind me I could still turn back, but we, *Mythre* and me now—for *Mythre* had now become a person to me, just like my beloved *Myth Too*—would not turn back. Just like Nansen's ship *Fram*, she must go forward. Apart from Goddard's stake, it was not only my life that was being gambled, but also that of *Myth Too*, put up as collateral against the expensive *Mythre*.

The wide expanse of concrete looked reassuringly long, and the engines sounded smooth and powerful in the cold air: I smelt the usual slight odour of petrol and heard it slapping against the steel tanks in the cabin with me. They were steadying, familiar sounds and smells. One quick glance around, as I ran the engines up against the brakes to gain precious extra feet along the runway. The brakes creakingly protested as I released them. Momentarily *Mythre* hesitated before she overcame the inertia and slowly moved forward gaining speed little by little.

The NASA green light gleamed among the multitude of dials —they were interrogating at the moment of take-off! I could not let go to do the mental acuity test, but one-handedly felt for the 'green light off' button, without taking my eyes from the airspeed dial and the runway ahead. Once again I was not to take off alone after all. It had been merely a teasing remark that I could never escape from them, but the strange thing was that the light invariably flashed when reassurance was most needed.

Lift-off at 0113 GMT on June 25th! We were skimming through spiralling smoke from wooden chalets over fir trees and fishing boat masts, slowly headed upwards, delicately—imperceptibly, turning through a few degrees to get on to track for if the direction indicator gyro precessed we were lost for ever. There was one last glimpse of the wooded land—the last trees I would see for days—before the cloud dipped down, caught us, let us go and teased with its tentacles to envelope us finally in its icy grey heart.

"Watch that speed. Do not climb so fast, the de-icers will do their job," I bullied myself. "Above all hold that heading of 341 degrees—you are half a degree out!" Would I be able to hold it for possibly seventeen hours without an autopilot?

At first it had been *Mythre* who was roaring to go and trying to climb up quicker than we should, but now it was I who pushed, and coaxed. At six thousand feet, still in cloud, I urged and begged her to keep climbing, but she stubbornly refused more than a foot or two at a time! The wing de-icers were working well, but the antenna on top were probably stacked with ice. Aeons later, at seven thousand feet, I was still cajolling her up at a mere twenty feet a minute, only to fall back to seven thousand feet every time I relaxed on the wheel.

The red stall warning light angrily flickered—*Mythre* gave one drunken lurch—I nearly lost her. It was no good—she was too heavy as yet to climb any higher. Still I had to make nearly ten thousand feet to be able to fly the planned pressure pattern safely and accurately. Well, it was no use turning back, for wherever I went I would find this same problem. Luckily the clouds were thinning into layers and I could keep between them until I lost my enemy the ice and its excess weight.

The sun peeped between cloud gaps, so it was time to set up the astro compass. My engineers had rigged up a portable sliding bar across the front of the instrument panel so I could move the astro compass across it. Even so, the occasions when I could actually shoot a sun sight were limited, for once the sun was behind the wing it was of no use to me. We had worked out the sun positions as it would be by eye in relation to the aircraft and time of day, but this was really basic and far too slap happy for real navigation.

At 0238, I managed to get one sun reading but needed three more at four-minute intervals to start my plot. The sun played fast and loose and quickly hid behind a cloud long before the fourth minute was up. Ten minutes later it was back and I started all over again. The resultant plot indicated I was two degrees off my desired grid heading, but as I was now flying a different system from our original plans I held my course, using the sun compass today as a backing check.

I had raised no one recently on HF, though by switching the frequencies I heard others, sometimes in a very strange language. Arctic radio blackout is quite normal, and varies from day to day and at different positions. It is caused by the high magnetic activity in these areas. But now I heard one controller talking to another—possibly Nord again—about GAYTO, and commenting that the aircraft had too little airspeed out of Norway.

"Jeepers, not a woman out there on her own!" came out among some more garbled conversation. I smiled and as I could not answer him back said to Buck Tooth, the rabbit, and *Mythre*, "Oh, that old argument, and we are not alone. We've got each other. Though I must confess I don't know for sure where we are, and somehow *Mythre*, you have to curb your drinking until I do."

She was gobbling up fuel. I exercised the propellers to prevent the prop oil freezing solid, then leaned the fuel off again. The left engine spat with fury at being robbed of its life blood; it needed the fuel, but I hoped the fuel flow gauge was over-reading, as it often did! I was using sixty-five per cent power to stay in the air, yet the airspeed was a mere 130 mph (113 knots)—not even enough to reach Barrow with this high fuel consumption.

At last I had managed to coax *Mythre* up to the necessary nine and a half thousand feet, and hoped we were somewhere in the vicinity of my pressure pattern track. The higher altitude gave the radio more range, and my speaker gurgled with a conversation which clearly included the remark, "She's heading for Russia!"

I tried to make contact, but no one replied. I reasoned that remark did not necessarily mean me—aircraft are called 'she' too. Nevertheless, I one-handedly tried to open up a contact chart to see where else, according to airspeed and time, I could possibly be heading if I were not on my chosen course. To try to spread a chart the size of a tablecloth in my overcrowded cockpit is quite a feat even with two hands. Was it possible that I was flying in a circle—that I had fallen into the time-honoured trap of all polar venturers, whether they be earthbound on the Cap or in the air? If I were heading for Russia there would have had to have been an enormous wind shift. I looked down, trying to get a clue, but the low sunlight was dazzling over the rolling silver expanse of cloud.

Even though the sun was radiant, I was very cold. I dare not use the aircraft heater, for fear of wasting even a gallon of precious fuel. My electric gloves and socks became so hot within seconds and the smell of burning rubber made me decide not to try again until there was imminent danger of frost-bitten extremities. The arrangement of HF radio or heated socks had become too complicated without an autopilot to relieve me because of all the re-tuning of stations that had to go with each change. Instead, I pulled on yet another pair of my progressively larger socks. A knitted shawl swaddled my head, and my many layers of gloves made my fingers so fat I could hardly turn the knobs. I tried to warm my toes by wiggling them.

But as I warmed up my arms and legs made themselves known, and began to complain. My fingers were sore, where I had cut them trying to get the cabin fuel tank selector on. Because of lack of space, the selector was in a narrow gap behind me among the tank wires, and probably as a result of the sand storms I had flown through in Africa, had tightened up. Sand seeps into everything far worse than water. My nails were torn and jagged, and even my jaw ached. I had been clenching my teeth with tension without realising it.

"Time to loosen up and hold that stick gently," I bullied myself, "you've only been airborne for seven hours." I hitched a small cushion beneath me to change position slightly, and did some isometric neck and jaw stretching exercises to ease the tense aches.

I could smell the fruit that someone had put aboard, but where? So much had been loaded forward on the storage box I could not get at anything. The immersion suit lay there, ready to put on quickly should the need arise, though heaven knew how I could stretch my legs far enough to get it on in this over-crowded space. I grinned as I remembered the dress rehearsals with this particular garment at home sitting on a stool, as though I were in the aircraft. It is like a stiff boiler suit with feet, and practically stands up by itself, and of course it, too, was designed for men. Somehow you had to get your head through a tight rubber banded neck, and your legs into the lower part, then bend over and pull a zip down your back, and up through your legs. We had smeared the zip with Vaseline to make it easier, but you still had to be a weight lifter as well as an acrobatic contortionist to make it!

Time to try to make contact on the radio again, and this time I tried to tune the radio compass to T3, the Naval Scientific camp, based on a floating ice island 270 miles below the Pole (and unfortunately 270 miles to the port side of my track). Unbelievably, the needles showed interest but to *starboard*, which meant I had to be flying backwards. It could not be right so I tried again, and with difficulty read the Morse signal VD. That was the Russian scientific team's ice island beacon and who knows where that is, except almost certainly to the right of my planned flight track over the Pole.

Floating ice islands are used by the Americans and the

Russians for scientific purposes in preference to ships which cannot stay for long periods, and anyway cannot get through to the high Arctic. The islands are massive glacier floes which gradually move around the Pole over many years. They are stable enough to build huts on, instal special experimental equipment and sometimes even a rough runway. The life, of course, is incredibly hard for the men stationed there, in spite of supplies flown to them from the Naval Arctic Research Laboratory in Barrow. There have been several American ones, and the Russians still have several today with light aircraft permanently stationed on them!

There are many four-footed beasts on the floes, too, and many Arctic tales. A favourite one is of Roscoe, the Arctic fox who stealthily followed the local polar bear to dine off the bear's leftover meals of seal. The bear began to explore, and became too familiar around the huts so the men had to get rid of him. Lazy foxy Roscoe was left without his easy food supply but he unwittingly got his revenge on the men by developing a love for insulating cable; everything from telephone wires to electric installations was nibbled. As fast as the men mended one piece of cable, foxy Roscoe chased back to the piece they had just mended, and eagerly devoured the freshest cable. All winter he drove the men mad, and still they could not catch him, until finally another polar bear arrived and Roscoe happily reverted to his old lazy habits. This time the men left the polar bear to his own devices. It was simpler avoiding him than repairing the wires!

Eight hours airborne, and if my pre-flight plan had been correct I should have been near the Pole, but my airspeed strangely had still not improved with less weight. There was something really wrong. As I looked at the outside mirror mounted on the port engine, I seemed to see a piece of fuselage hanging down! Shocked I looked harder. It was half a wheel. The nose wheel had partly emerged from its casing, and the door was hanging down. There was my loss of airspeed! I recycled the gear mechanism to try to retract it. It worked, except the amber light signifying 'gear up and locked' only blinked at me and then went out again. I tried again and the light only blinked again, but as far as I could see in the mirror the gear was up. Poor *Mythre*. This must have been what had been wrong with her all the time. Maybe the wheel doors had always been slightly ajar. This could account for most of our earlier unsolved problems.

I sadly remembered how often I had murmured, "Are we sure it's not the wheels?" I had had to fly to almost the top of the world to prove it—hundreds of miles from a landing strip or a human being, and not even a ship to circle over. It meant serious trouble if the wheel would not stay up. Somehow I had to get more airspeed. Unless a fantastic tailwind appeared— which was highly unlikely, as there is a prevailing headwind in this direction, I would run out of fuel some miles off the Alaskan coast—if it was Alaska I was still heading for.

The ice below was rough, far too rough to land an aircraft safely because of the currents of the ocean below it, but I knew it was much smoother on the Alaskan side and that little aircraft certainly landed there to collect scientific data. Several had force landed there and escaped. But below me Wally Herbert and his team had crossed by foot over the Pole—it was incredible how they had traversed this ghastly terrain by only their own physical efforts.

No more radio communication was possible and now the clouds had vanished the sun was behind me. To have returned to Andoya at this stage could spell equal disaster, as I was no longer sure of my position. I merely knew that whatever my position was, I almost certainly could not stretch the fuel to Alaska either. The very beauty of the scene dispelled gloomy thoughts and euphorically I watched the deeply shadowed, green streaked, glittering land of ice. I almost felt content, for I was doing what I had chosen to do.

Glistening snow ahead caught my attention. The clouds were dissipating and I saw the ragged surface of shadows caused by roughed-up ice—the pack ice. Now I knew for sure I had left behind Spitzbergen and all its notorious bad weather; but it was a slender clue for such an expanse of ice. More than 5,000,000 square miles of it covered this ocean—and I had 2000 of them ahead of me, without a living soul except an occasional polar bear and the seals below the ice.

Navy blue puddles of melted water oozed up between milky snow, embedded with green rocks and miniature glaciers. If I had been below a high cloud level, I might have found my clue to what lay ahead from the atlas of the sky, from the shades reflected upon it: open ocean makes black patches on the clouds but solid ice reflects as grey. Bush pilots in polar regions learn to read many signs from sky reflections. Once a couple of them were forced down off course with little hope of rescue from the ice without radio communication. One of them thought of flashing the strong torch they had aboard at an angle to the clouds, knowing it might reflect hundreds of miles ahead. It did, and soon a flashing Morse light came back establishing communications, and eventually rescue.

The beastly wheel came down. I recycled it yet again, but the airspeed continued suspiciously low, indicating the undercarriage doors were not completely shut. Puffy, green tinged clouds lay to the port of me, and teasingly solid ones built up behind, looking like far-off glaciers, austere and sheer. Clouds? Surely those were mountains! Mirages are frequent in the Arctic regions, but I was wary of this possible manifestation.

Where was I? Had I been flying in circles? Was it St Joseph Land? No. Those mountains looked 10,000 feet high. Nothing on the charts seemed to fit them and yet they looked suspiciously like the films I had seen of Greenland. That was where I should be if I were making a true track of my pressure pattern path, but the earlier chat overhead on the radio had not indicated that I was following course! I did not know what to believe now. The only station beacon for hundreds of miles up here was Nord in North Greenland, but one radio compass needle pointed to port, and the other to starboard. No recognisable Morse signals. It could not be Greenland.

"GAYTO to any station," I called on the HF frequency. I was currently tuned into the same one on which I had heard voices earlier in the morning, even though earlier they obviously had not received the position reports I had blindly transmitted.

"Nord here, Tango Oscar," most surprisingly replied a deep-down voice. "Where have you been? The whole world is looking for you!"

"I have been here all the time but nobody answered me." There was nothing else I could say.

"Tango Oscar, where are you?" What could I answer? I hesitated, and finally honestly replied,

"I'm estimating, repeat, estimating, 84 North at flight level nine zero, but it is only an estimation. I was unable to pick up Bear Island and Spitzbergen beacons earlier today but now I can see glaciers to port of me."

"That's not surprising, as those island beacons are usually overcome by a stronger Norwegian one. Where do you really think you are now?" said Nord. "Have you got my beacon. Try . . ."

"I am already tuned to your frequency, but one needle points one way and the other another way! Do you have very high snow-covered mountains—about 10,000 feet with low cloud below them, where you are, Nord?"

"It's all snow here! We have mountains, but clear skies. It's lovely sunshine here! You must come to Nord. There's nowhere else for you to go up here. Everyone is worried about you. Where is your radio compass pointing to now?" That was the trouble: according to the conflicting dials, I could be heading south between Greenland and Iceland, to Siberia or almost anywhere. The normal compass had long since given up its unequal fight against the overpowering northern magnetic forces up here, and the sight of it only made me distrust my direction indicator. It was better not to look!

"I have two and they are pointing in opposite directions," I repeated once again.

"Are you up there alone? Jesus Christ!"

"Affirmative."

"Then you *must* come to Nord. You will just have to choose one needle to follow and trust it."

Silence, while I decided to trust the port-seeking needle for the far-off mountains were there too. I made a private deal with the Almighty about my fate for if it were not Greenland it could be somewhere not very welcoming—or worse, it could be a mirage!

I flew on over low clouds which shadowed the dazzling green ice floes of fantastic colours—a medley of jewels—of emeralds, turquoise and aquamarines laced by glittering silver against jet black shadows. Ahead lay a crown of icebergs and beyond a blanket of snow leading to the blue and white sheer glaciers. This was no mirage. Occasional glints of light, like a hard, sparkling diamond, caught my attention, but it was just the Arctic phenomenon I had noticed earlier. Vainly I chased dark shadows, resembling igloos, and even some graceful Arctic sea-gulls, but there was nothing to indicate that man had ever been there.

"Where do you think you are now, Sheila? You pronounce it Sheila, don't you?" said the voice from Nord.

There was absolutely no sign of anything like a hut or a puff of smoke let alone an airfield, yet now there was a strong Morse aural signal from Nord's beacon. I studied the chart again; it could be the other side of the glaciers of this indented coast. Again the NASA green light came on in the strange way that it so often did when least expected. I gleefully punched all the test buttons. At least somebody would eventually know which land I had ended up in but to me it was truly 'No man's land'.

"Nord, I could be at 82 North 14 West. I am going to fly out to sea again and round this mountain range and hope to see you on the other side." I certainly did not want to try and fly over the mountains and get lost unable to make sufficient height among the glaciers beyond, until I knew exactly where I was. Without roads and rivers, towns or land marks, and no com-pass, it could be a hopeless quest among the uncharted glaciers.

"My name is Pierre," continued the heavily accented voice. I decided the voice sounded French. "And there are twenty-seven men here, all waiting to meet you. You must find us. You must land. It is lovely here, and we will give you food and petrol. We have nine thousand feet of runway."

It must be a good-sized airfield. I looked for a village, think-ing he meant twenty-seven men on the field, and that there must be an Eskimo community at least nearby, as well as the complex of buildings that normally go with such a field. I recalled pic-tures of runways like tunnels between tall snow banks, and realised that even if I found it, I still had problems, particularly as my wheels could be damaged. There were no skis on my air-craft nor had I ever made an ice runway landing.

At last I turned the corner, but again it all looked the same. I chased every long dark shadow and looked for a village in the direction that one of the needles was pointing. Nothing for it but to stick to the needle I had chosen, and follow it towards the mountains. As they got closer I saw a long dark slope—it could be a runway—but where were the houses? Then I saw a tall mast—a beacon? There were a few low huts. It must be

Nord. It had to be! It was! I was lost no longer. There among a glittery snow patchwork quilt of brilliant colours was a runway of swept gravel. Huge snow banks either side of it certainly made it a tunnel. There was not enough fuel to continue to Alaska but still too much aboard to land with a possible undercarriage problem. I explained that I must circle to burn up fuel remaining in the tip tanks, particularly as there was a strong crosswind on the runway.

"All right," said Pierre, "as long as you really are going to land here. We are all waiting to meet you."

"I have not got permission to land here. Can you arrange it?"

"That's all right. The Station Manager is expecting you. We are looking forward to seeing you. What colour hair do you have? Fly down low Sheila, all twenty-seven of us want to see you."

"Will do," I said. "I'm blonde, but I am a great age, so don't get excited."

"Oh, we know all about you and what you look like, we already have pictures of you here, but in black and white!"

I descended lower and could see the men waving from snow-covered buildings, some perched on the roof watching the air-craft through binoculars! I circled over magnificent scenery such as I had never imagined.

Next Pierre informed me NASA had made contact with them through Thule Air Base and wanted to know how I was physically? I thought they must mean what shape was the air-craft in, as the computers must have passed on data about my low airspeed. I replied that at least one wheel was partly down, but I was burning up the fuel and thought we would get down all right.

"No, no," said Pierre. "They want to know how you yourself are! Are you all right physically? They think you must be exhausted."

"Tell them I am fine, I'm having a cup of coffee at last!"

"They would like you to try radio frequency 17909. Thule Air Base wants to talk to you, to try and link you with Goddard."

I duly changed to that frequency, but could not think how Goddard could possibly talk to me from Maryland on my little radio, even relaying through Thule. Leroy Field, of the US Navy, was now using the ultra strong naval transmitter in

Washington, but today the air was too full of static interruption to make contact. Although I never did reach him, he often heard my airborne reports all round the world, and relayed them to Len Roach, in the Navigation Data department at Goddard. What remarkable people they were! Despite all their valuable equipment aboard, and other considerations, their first concern was whether I personally was all right. It was very moving, the deep trust that had grown between these American men, most of whom I had never met, and myself in Britain.

When the aircraft was light enough to land and after much pumping and pushing, lights showed the landing gear safely down. As I descended to land banks of *sastrugi*—high ridges of hard solid snow caused by wind, up to several feet high—met my startled eyes. It was far from flat snow. Roofs laden with men towered above the tunnel of snow banks. A group of blond-haired, sun-burnt people dressed in fur-edged parkas waited at the far end. Bearded Morgens Lund, Station Manager, looking like a handsome Viking, welcomed me to Nord with typical Arctic hospitality. No worry with official papers here. Hot coffee and food were waiting. A Land-Rover with huge snow tyres was ready to drive us to the wooden mess-hall hut. Around me lay a jungle, but of sculptured ice, not trees.

There were radio masts and cables instead of trees, and rolls of wire netting to keep the polar bears away! Little puffs of fog rose up from the track in front of us like the pipe smoke of a friendly giant, yet I could clearly see the pink-edged, green ice-bergs further out. Music streamed from the gaily curtained huts and mingled with the cries of the husky dogs outside the mess hall.

There was one other guest here—Count Eigel Knuth, an archaeologist who was here to collect his mail and await an air lift home. It could take months to get the lift. He lives quite alone in Peary Land, and is Nord's only neighbour. The nearest so-called civilisation is many hundred of miles away though there is a village, Danmarkshaun, 560 kilometres away, with a grand total of twelve inhabitants to man its radio weather station. No ship, or car, can ever reach Nord. The occasional Air Force aircraft, which accounts for the beautifully kept run-way, is their only means of survival.

Nord is a weather station, built in 1952 with the aid of the

USAF, completely staffed by Danes. The Greenlanders, whose land it is, will not take the job, as they say it is too tough! The men here usually remain for two or three years without leave or seeing other people. All are weather scientists or personnel running the station. There were no aviation engineers but there was plenty of fuel and the station electrician was eager to help me, if we could somehow make contact with the outside world for advice.

The men regaled me with wonderful stories of how they lived, and how the temperature varied according to who was looking at the thermometer, a pessimist or an optimist. It is a completely dark world for twenty-four hours a day from October to March, and the temperature can fall to minus fifty degrees. The storms sometimes become so bad the men cannot even move from one hut to another—a mere stone's throw away, for two or three days at a time. Each hut has a telephone, and every time a man leaves a hut in the winter he must telephone back to say he has arrived safely. One meteorologist walked outside in a gale to take his weather readings and was literally blown away. His body was found thirty miles distant months later.

Younge Helge, a radio operator, grew bored one stormy day, and broke the rules and left his hut to go to his work in the radio hut, a few yards away. He vanished and was missing for two days. It took a whole expedition and chain of men to find him among the huts. He was lucky, for he had stumbled upon the food warehouse door unlocked and enough food for the station for a year. He was a very frozen and thirsty young man, but he was not hungry for a long time. No one ventures from the camp alone, even in the summer, without a rifle; not the least danger being polar bears, which in spite of their enormous size, are among the quickest animals on earth.

Morgens allotted me to a hut. Each hut had about a dozen rooms in it, with a tiny shower room. Clogs and anoraks hung in the entrance. We went then to the radio hut, which was also brightly furnished, with beds and kitchen attached, for the dark days when they could not get back to their own huts—a mere stone's throw—for days at a time. That day messages were pouring in from Thule, as radio reception was fairly good, but not a word from England. We sent off messages home and replied to Goddard that I was determined to go on over the Pole from here, and head for Barrow as soon as I could get the wheel problem patched up. I believed that after a few hours' sleep I would be off.

The Telex system is an old hand type and the radios are dependent on weather conditions. So Telexes took days, not minutes, at Nord and messages intercrossed and were scrambled together. It was obvious that the answers to my queries from England were not going to be received today. I snuggled under my coverlet to sleep, with sunlight streaming in as though it were midday. I had been awake nearly forty hours without realising it, because of the continuous sunshine. Up here there are no set hours for sleeping in the Arctic summer—you just sleep in the sunlight when you feel like it. No one ever gets ill here either, for there are few disease-causing bacteria. I awoke a few hours later and found still no answers had come through. I tried to set up a new grid course and plans on the few charts I had. Nord had not been planned as a possible alternate originally, and I only had charts for Canada and Alaska. I rejected all thoughts of moving along to Canada, or of going down to Thule. As far as I was concerned, it was the North Pole or nothing and somehow I must nurse *Mythre* to Barrow via the Pole. For that there would be no second chance.

Morgens picked me up for breakfast across in the mess hall. Instead of traditional breakfast mail and newspapers, we collected our news from the radio room. Still no word from England, but Thule's generous Air Force Base Commander planned to fly an aircraft up here, with oil and spares, to see if I was all right. I was horrified at the thought of the cost of the huge transport plane, and knew I must prevent that, until I knew for certain that I was really stuck. We sent more messages, and I prepared to wait some more. Were it not for finishing the last leg of the Polar attempt, I would have been content to stay here for months; there were so many new experiences to enjoy, and so much to learn.

Over coffee and delicious Danish pastries, Count Eigel Knuth amused me with tales of his lonely research work and his house—surely one of the most remote habitations on earth. He had discovered evidence of fireplaces and cooking utensils showing that people lived up here four thousand years ago, and an old boat, proving that people were still here as recently as the fourteenth century, when they appeared to have died out. We discussed the misnomers of Greenland and Iceland, for Greenland is infinitely more icily forbidding.

We returned to the radio station, but no news at all came through. Above me floated a sonde weather balloon, the size of a car; an aviator meeting one of these in the air might well believe it was a UFO. Everywhere I looked was dazzling white full of coloured shafts. The brilliance of the scene was painful and it was necessary to wear sunglasses even inside the huts. The horizon was a line of icebergs, as the camp looked straight out over the Arctic Ocean. There was animal life—several birds and many lemmings (a rat-like fur-coated animal), and an occasional seal moving among the navy blue puddles, its throaty voice mingling with the sharp cracks of breaking ice and the muffled creaks of overladen icebergs.

The electrician had finished his normal station duties, and we piled into the truck to drive roughshod over the pebbly, gritty earth tracks among the snow drifts to refuel the lonely *Mythre* at least partly. The hydraulic bottle seemed to be still half full and was not, apparently, the cause of the wheel trouble but there was a shortage of oil and de-icing fluid. Another day went by, tinkering with the aircraft as though it was a normal day back home in Oxfordshire. It is always bad to be delayed unexpectedly on the ground during any endurance attempt—one becomes soft again and enjoys too much the luxury of regular food and of not having to discipline oneself to concentrate solidly on what one is doing. Doubts creep in where there were none before. Again I felt my confidence ebbing away as I fell asleep.

A loud pounding soon woke me up. Draping the downy cover around me, I struggled sleepily to the door for the message. But it contained advice I had already tried—recycling—and gave further suggestions about oil and hydraulic fluid, none of which we had! I was advised that a new take-off time would be following: hours of day-like night went by and still no further messages. I very quickly became accustomed to the timeless way of life and realised how wonderful it was compared to the rush and bustle back home. I could understand how people at Nord were able to take the hardship—the timelessness outbalanced that and so did the feeling of being out of the rat race, with time to laugh and time to talk and to think.

Flight Lieutenant Eric Stafford instructs Sheila on grid navigation at RAF Manby's School of Air Warfare

Flight Liaiser Alexander Torrance briefs Sheila before the last Atlantic flight, while the Girls Venture Corps look on, and the newly presented Ford Capri is used as a plotting table. Biggin Hill Air Fair, 1972

Above: Mythre's control panel, in contrast to NASA's ordinary-looking black box (*below*) which held the miniaturised IRLS equipment

Sheila, perched on the most
northern land on earth, Nord

Greetings at Point Barrow,
Alaska

The most northern hotel in the world, Point Barrow

The Lufthansa's crew, Captain Heinrich Auger and his co-pilot, who transmitted the weather they could see ahead so that Sheila could make a homemade weather chart while she was at Nord

Later that day airliner 'Lufthansa 650' made contact with
the radio station, and asked if I was there. The German Captain
sent greetings, and said they would like to make a date to meet
me to celebrate in Anchorage. We quickly asked them to transmit the weather they were seeing, as long as they were in contact, which would enable me to make my own home-made
brand of weather chart. Even though the weather is very
different at 35,000 feet, at least I now had an idea of the type
and amount of cloud cover.

Off went another Telex to Goddard, this time suggesting
replies via airliners over-flying Greenland might be quicker. By
now we were all hilarious—me probably from the champagne
air—and signed the Telex 'With love from me and twenty-seven
men thousands of miles from nowhere without a chart.'

Saturday night was special, and all the men dressed up in
their best clothes, though all I could find was some make-up.
I had to make do with straight hair, but they treated me as
though I were a princess in a ball gown. We toasted each other
in beer and schnapps, ate and sang, just like a Saturday night
anywhere in the world—except that our night sky was full of
sunshine and the view was of icebergs.

Next morning Nord's operators could not keep up with the
deluge of Telexes that descended on us, mostly addressed to
'Santa's Workshop'! The first one gave a take-off time ten hours
before it even got to us! A very formal one from England
followed, giving exactly the same information. The outside
world did not seem to realise that the earth rotates very slowly
on top! We replied to all, as 'twenty seven Danish Santa
Clauses and one Mother Christmas'—a name which stuck to me
further on, as far as the Goddard Gang were concerned.

More and more Telexes poured in, all one day late, one reading "We'll have you in our stocking any time," signed Goddard
Gang, and finally another instructing me to revert to "normal
test theatre", signed "we will be watching, bon voyage". Phil
Chapman and the Goddard Gang with Lee Field of the Naval
Air Test Centre, Patuxent, were working as hard to re-establish
communication, as if I were returning from the other side of the
moon—and were equally determined that I should continue
over the Pole. There was to be no aborting of this mission, and I
was glad that this time I could not escape from them.

13

June 28th. 0100 hours.

THE Telexes had caught up in time to plan for an eleven-thirty departure later that morning. I hastily rechecked my new grid calculations, with a little sadness, for it was doubtful if I would ever return to Nord again. It's not the sort of place for a week-end visit, however sophisticated your transport may be! I had grown used to the good fellowship of these men, who did not make me feel alone among them, and the clear pollution-free air which had made me healthier than I had felt for years. Here life without frills promotes a direct honesty and real friendship straight from the heart, enhanced by the stark beauty surrounding us.

It took hours to fill my inside cabin fuel tanks, for it all had to be done by hand pump from barrels. I was going to be late for my first interrogation today, and Nimbus would find me still on the ground. I knew the satellite had been specially fed with data today to ensure as many position readings as possible over the Pole. Hurriedly collecting Thermos flasks of coffee and delicious specially baked Danish pastries—Nord's culinary speciality—I hugged my bearded friends goodbye, each one of them in turn giving *Mythre* a little caressing pat too.

Mythre's head was up in the air again, her tail weighed down by fuel and once more she looked like a gull ready to soar high into the sky. I knew she must be restrained even though the minutes ticked by towards our planned 'lift-off' time, urging me on. Madame Fate would not condone anything forgotten today. I carefully checked and set the direction indicator very aware that my life was at stake on a single dial, and this, my final check. The Telex message had read the weather could not be better, so the only thing now left to chance was the changing wind and its effect on my course. But the fiery ball of orange sun above the horizon would verify my heading on the astro compass.

One last wave before I headed along the grit-covered runway

through tunnel banks of snow, with the sound of engines thriving in the sharp cold air—their roar somehow exaggerated by the tranquillity of the scenery.

"We have lift-off for the Pole," I murmured with relief, as *Mythre* climbed confidently over billowing snow drifts towards sharp peaks of icebergs like soaring glass castles. A firm tug at the undercarriage and amber lights signalled the wheels smoothly up. The first hurdle had been cleared—today our wheels were safely tucked away. Smooth air cushioned our wings rather like a springboard helping us aloft. High cirrus clouds scurried way over to port but ahead the way was clear; the icebergs behind me became pink with distance, backed by glacier shafts of silver reaching to the sky. Below me, the navy blue puddles of Arctic Ocean seeped between emerald ice. Certainly, if this were the gates of heaven and my last glimpse of earth, it would have been the most impressive sight of my life. No words of mine could possibly describe the emotions aroused by the spectacle of this wondrous wilderness of beautiful shapes and colours—the very essence of primeval glory.

The calm air enabled me to return to the more mundane chores in the cabin, like testing the heart tape box, and inspecting the bouquet of wires sprouting out of my tummy. Today would be an important test biomedically, for whatever the outcome it could not fail to be the most exciting challenge of my life—enough to promote any amount of adrenalin, whether in triumph or failure.

Now I had left the most northern piece of land on earth behind me, yet I would be heading south when I landed, although I was to fly an almost straight line. Almost imperceptibly, a blue horizon line had developed indicating fog ahead, and the navy blue water had become floating wedding cakes of ice. In spite of the eternally grinding ice, everything seemed to be silently waiting.

It was as though I had flown straight off the top of the earth to a planet far out into Space. Perhaps this remoteness was heightened, because I was now totally removed from my normal life in the cooped-up apartment in London with its daily battle of paperwork. My only contact with the earth seemed to be my little green NASA light. I distinctly felt the Space Centre's influence; I was very aware of the collective positive thought of the men studying my flight path. I had the unreal feeling that I was two people—one the observer, the other the doer.

Looking around I found there was one link left with earth. The radio compass was actually giving a back bearing off Nord, and so far indicated I was on course, if my grid calculations were correct. Soon the sun would be in the right position for me to get a sunshot. At 1306 it would be ahead and directly over the North Pole. I tried calling Nord on the radio, and today they answered immediately loud and clear.

"Operations normal, and a lovely day it is," I reported, but no further reply came back from Nord and thick clouds appeared from nowhere far ahead. To port a great mass of damp air nosed forward. I hoped it would not reach as far as the Pole.

I looked back into the cabin and saw that the yellow light for the wheels was out again. Recycle the gear. It flicked on and then off again. Recycle—light on—light off. Recycle and so it went on, with a mere airspeed indication of one hundred and thirty. It was going to be an exhausting trip but at least today there was fuel to spare, providing the headwind was still only ten knots.

At 1415, the time I should originally have been in the vicinity of the Pole, I was scheduled to attempt to call Nord, as 'November Hotel Kilo Three', the Navy's strong transmitter. in Washington, DC was attempting to relay HF messages through them today. My dead reckoning told me that the slow speed and delayed half-hour on take-off meant I could only be in the vicinity of about eighty-seven degrees fifty minutes north.

Today we were to try a new plan to solve my communications difficulties; as so often air traffic control could not hear my messages, and yet occasionally I could hear theirs. But invariably the people sending messages to me spoke at such length and so fast, it was impossible to get even the gist of the message against the static. This time, we decided that if I deliberately failed all the mental acuity tests, it meant I could hear the radio loud and clear if they would only speak slowly. Now once again nothing answered my call, except crackling static from the speaker, and the radio compass had given up the struggle. The famous Arctic blackout again, and my earthly ties had gone!

Grey tentacles of cloud clawed at the wing tips; little rivulets of frosting framed the windscreen, and slowly crept over it like

an army of white ants. Time to put on the heated windscreen—
a small panel of heated double glass—to make a small clear
patch to peer through the frost.

At 9000 feet the temperature was only minus 9°C, 'warm'
enough to be conducive to severe icing. I watched the ice
slowly cover the black rubber boots edging the white metal
wing, longing to switch the de-icers on immediately, but it was
essential to wait a few more minutes. The ice must be allowed
to build up so that the pulsating boots could break it cleanly off.
If I switched on too early the boots would be unable to do their
job. The HF static aerial, which was strung from the aircraft
tail to the far port tip of the wing, turned from copper to a
glittering rope of ice, and twanged and quivered like a taut bow.
An ugly thud echoed round the cabin as a lump of ice freed
itself and hit us underneath. It had probably formed on the
loose wheel door. I apprehensively watched the boots pulsate
the wing ice, breaking it off in chunks leaving bare patches of
black rubber. Now as soon as the automatic pulsating stopped,
the ice built up at horrifying speed. Time to get down out of
this. It seemed to take for ever. Below was worse, and the only
way out of ice was higher still, but I could no longer climb.
I was obviously in the expected Polar inversions near the Pole
itself, where the air is much colder lower down when it meets
the permanently super-cooled surface. In my pre-planning I
had hoped to escape severe icing here by crossing on a clear day
well out of cloud. But it was too late—the weather had broken
at last.

Now I was meeting the ice ogre face to face. Somehow I must
get the wheels to stay up, for I needed all the airspeed I could
get to fight him off. Recycling had no effect any more, but the
emergency pump for use in an electrical failure still worked.
I pumped and pumped with my right hand, hanging on to the
stick with my left, trying to hold the aircraft straight and level.
The wing leveller could not hold course in the increasing
turbulence, it merely levelled the wings every time they dipped.
My arm ached until I thought I could not go on. One final hard
pull made a reassuring click, and the yellow light gleamed. A
tiny bit of comfort for a few minutes in a grey ghostly world.

The HF aerial now whipped and pulled so hard at its restraining nuts that I knew soon it must break. It would not necessarily

hurt the tail but the drag would be considerable, and heaven knows how much drag had already built up over my head where the special antennae were. They could be covered with inches, or even feet of ice! The patter of sound on the windscreen now heralded the hail and rain.

Freezing rain is the worst kind of icing to get into, as it flows back over the whole aircraft, wrapping it in a cocoon of ice. Very afraid, I manually switched the boots on and off to make them work quicker—even the defroster did not seem to work. How much could the pressure have changed and caused my altimeter to over-read? How far could I descend, and how much fuel would I waste getting up again if it did not work?

At last I got through the worst of the storm cloud and *Mythre* stopped bucking. There was silence, except the homely noise of the engines, but the light was still grey and eerie between ragged layers of cloud. Chunks of ice flew off the wings, but sticky little bits remained, like plankton on a whale, riding up and down on the boots. The windscreen army of ice crystals slowly retreated. The vibrating HF aerial spat dirty little strands of frozen water.

Now it was bitterly cold in the cabin. I was freezing. Wires festooned me, and made me awkward. Three wires sprouted out of my middle to the heart box; another from my ear-plug to the panel; wires from both arms and legs to the electrics; another wire to the tape recorder, plus headset, shoulder and lap harness. I had never noticed so much wire before, and disgruntled, complained to *Mythre* and Buck Tooth, as there was no one else to groan to.

Perhaps the greyness had imperceptibly lightened—or was it the flash of intuition one sometimes finds in the air that told me things were better. Almost immediately the grey mist broke into tattered gaps, to show a great white carpet—a continent of ice. A wide lead like a black river appeared, and the carpet became a smashed-up sea of giant floating, broken china—huge floes of ice unendingly grinding and colliding. A rainbow seemed to dance and glint amidst the confusion of ragged ridges which no longer looked motionless. One could almost see the sound of noise and chaos! In fact, the ice moves at the rate of three miles a day—twenty miles in stormy weather—in a crazy ever-circling pattern.

I consulted my air almanac to precalculate my sun position

ahead of time, for the sun might yet escape through to indicate my true heading. I was now holding a grid course of 022 degrees to make sure I really went to the Pole, and did not curve inward and miss it. Without the sun or radio compass any more, there was simply no way of knowing where I was truly heading. I had only my watches to tell me roughly how many miles I might have travelled. There is no landmark that signifies the Pole. If one were found, within weeks it would no longer be the Pole. The landmark would lazily drift off over the clockwise currents and around the Pole centre. At last the sun thrust its beams through the overcast and I chased it with the shadow bar of the astro compass, but elusively it fled again long before I got my sight. The time was 1530 hours.

"Pole minus twenty minutes and still counting," I said to a lonely sky and to Nimbus, the satellite orbiting in clear outer Space somewhere above the earthly murk. The North Pole must be very near now if my course had been correct. Doubt tried to creep in, but I pushed it aside. I must believe I was heading for the Pole, come what may when the time was up. This was not the place for doubts. It was too late to change anything.

The outside temperature had incredibly risen to —2°C and it was almost warm again for a while in the cabin. Only the desolate but magnificent sight below was cold and forbidding, yet so strangely compelling. Even if it meant landing on an ice floe, I would not have missed this scene. The fever of the Arctic caught me, like those before me who had discovered its glories and were to return again and again to its isolation that is like insulation, until it finally claimed them for ever. I will never forget it.

The fragments of cloud below the brooding mass parted to frame a tiny perfect hill of snow among the tumbled ice. The time was right for Ninety North. I was on top of the world. *Mythre* and I were at the Pole! I was sure I was—it had to be. This was the piece of the Pole that I was going to stake as mine!

The cruel icy slipstream rushed in with a deafening roar, and bit my cheeks as I opened the storm window, but the sheer exhilaration of the moment made me uncaring. I unfurled my tiny Union Jack, and found my paper 'Snoopy' from my American NASA friends, and stretched a gloved arm through the icy blast to let them go. Both whipped past the window towards the tail, as the icy blast cut into my cheeks and made me gasp with shock.

"We're here—I'm on Top of the World." I felt irresponsible and had hilariously touched the mike button.

"Say again," incredibly came a loud and clear reply! It was Nord, and one of those fantastic freaks of skip that happen with HF.

"I am on Top of the World. Operations normal. Tango Oscar is at Ninety North." I dutifully made the correct report now but there was no reply.

I obediently transmitted again and again in formal language, not really expecting anyone to hear because I was much too far out in my own little uninhabited world. What if I were not yet at the Pole? How awful if I turned too soon! Was I even near it? There was no way of telling—no beacon worked out here. Even as I uselessly peered the air became sullen and broody again—yet I still tingled with excitement. Suppose it was the Pole, and I had truly made it, but I must continue on, in a straight line for another twenty minutes, to make absolutely sure. Again ice crystals skittered across the windscreen, as the deep slanting cloud wrapped round us, and within a moment my triumph was gone. Now it was a fight for survival as I struggled free of camera straps and wires—the turbulence making all movements clumsy.

The mirror showed the wheel again—no matter how hard I pumped—five minutes' respite was all it would allow me before it fell down again. Once more I tried, and felt a shuddering stop. The handle seemed to disintegrate in my hand, to become limp and useless. This was serious. The wheel was down for good. What had seemed a short flight leg of thirteen hours would now become perhaps seventeen, and it would be necessary to conserve fuel as never before.

Every nerve in my body yelled in panic, as ice built up at a horrendous rate; I wanted to get out—turn away. But I could not, I had to make sure it was the Pole I had over-flown. There was only one way and that led straight ahead through this bumping hell. Fate was testing all my resources now and making me pay for those relaxing moments of pride and triumph.

Each second became an eternity as the heartless hands crept round the chronometer dial and almost seemed to stop. Twenty minutes akin to twenty hours went by before I dared to turn slowly through the forty degrees to port that would hopefully lead me to Alaska. Endless foggy vapour still lay ahead, destroying all my earlier elation. I was sure I had missed my target, and now there would never be a second chance. It was too late to change anything—how could you restart or even finish, if you did not know where you were anyway? If the sun did not come through this sticky veil of icy moisture soon, it would be too late to ever know, for although at this time of year it hung for ever just above the horizon, soon it would be behind me in its own circling quest.

As though to cheer me, a glancing sunbeam struggled through to make two dancing arcs around the propeller tips. But the sun god was merely taunting and disappeared the moment the astro compass was set. By now the astro compass had to be at such an angle, my head was jammed against the bumping windscreen to read the shadow bar. Already it was too late.

1750 hours . . . The NASA light flashed. In my delight at the fact that *something* worked I did my mental acuity test too quickly. I had to get the next sequence right—the segments of interrogation usually followed every few seconds—to signify I was hearing the radio loud and clear or they would think I had failed the whole test deliberately. Apart from the eternal static and echoing ice on the fuselage, it seemed I had not heard a sound for days.

I was very aware of the Goddard team and pictured the control room in which they now sat. It was as if they were in the aircraft with me, I was very conscious of their being somewhere near though they were thousands of miles away. The feeling of sheer responsibility, the determination not to let them down had driven me on many times now but more than that, a great bond of affection and complete understanding had grown among us all. The flight was all of us, and no longer just my personal whim. I prayed I had at least been vaguely near the ninetieth parallel, for they would feel as bad as I would if I had completely missed it.

My feet and hands were freezing, my eyes were burning and my back was aching from being unable to move. I had now been airborne for thirteen hours—the time we had originally thought I might do it in, but so far there had been no hint of radio communication, nor flicker on the radio compass dials. Where could I be? Was it the United States ahead, or Canada, even Russia? I idly tried even the beacons way down in the Bering Strait. One needle showed interest, but commonsense prevailed. I knew it was a freak of distance—a trap. Its bearing showed me far south—much faster than I could fly. Now the spectre of a ditching joined me in my solitary reverie.

Being alone, for me, does not mean I am necessarily lonely, for it is only in solitude that I really find true clarity. Up here, even though my body is still, my mind does not run down like a dead battery: it goes on working, I have no excuse to deviate from its path of real self truth. Adventure, challenge and national pride are forgotten, as I learn a little about who I am.

There have to be more reasons than mere fame or fortune for those of us who venture frequently. Habitual gambles with one's life are the stakes which make one take more care, and so in fact one's life becomes more valuable. Our ventures are not the submerged death-wish some critics would have us think. One becomes more dedicated to striving for perfection, which is never found, and so one has to try again. Efficiency increases with added knowledge, and develops a higher level of consciousness. There are few physical limits, if the spirit is strong enough: you can learn to conquer discomfort and use it to advantage. I have learnt to do this in the air, but alas not yet on the ground; there, I still love soft pillows and long lazy mornings in bed, scent and silky baths.

More static crackles than usual interrupt my thoughts again. It's time to try and make constructive contact with earth once more. This time a deep French-Canadian voice answered my call, but instead of taking my position report, promptly asked me to change frequencies as someone wished to speak to me.

I dutifully changed frequencies only to get the same request. I did this no less than four times with four different frequencies. Needless to say, all had disappeared by the time I returned back to any of them, but the radio compass had picked up a Northern Canadian frequency, which appeared to be abeam to port. This boded well, although without turning the aircraft it was impossible to tell how far away it was. It was a case of sitting it out.

Hours later firm contact was made on HF radio and I gave

an estimate of where I thought I was. By now I could hear unknown voices enquiring of others how I was getting on! I wished I knew myself.

"The winds have got her and she's still way up north," an operator reported. Well, that gave me a good clue! I readjusted my dead reckoning accordingly, as someone appeared to know where I was. Obviously I must be heading for at least the right continent. The radio compass hitched firmly on to an Alaskan Beacon, just as I finally received an urgent direct message telling me to head for Barter Island as the weather was better there. Barrow, my intended landfall, was completely in the stormy murk.

The winds had already drifted me way off in this very direction, so that plan suited me. I saw a rocky coastline way in the distance and flew on towards it. I tried to align it with a chart, but it did not get any closer. I decided there must be a terrible headwind and I must be standing still in the air. Then, for no reason, the land was no longer there! What on earth happened to it, and where did it or I go? Disappointedly, I realised it must be a mirage, or my own wishful thinking. Mirages are frequent in the Arctic and caused by bending light rays as a result of warmer air lying over very cold surface air.

I was utterly weary and a little cross, which is unusual in the air. It was nature's warning that I needed oxygen, but now my limbs were so weary that even untightening the oxygen cylinder was a chore. The smell of oxygen is like winter hazel, quite different from normal air, and was refreshing in spite of the rubber mask smell mixed with it.

High in the sky, white horse tails of cirrus hung over pale violet-tipped ice floes—like coloured crazy paving. Ahead lay sun-tinged cloud chariots and again I was aware of the hugeness of the stark ocean, with not a ship or a human being within hundreds of miles. A dark line emerged from the purple haze ahead—too flat to be land. It was a great black lead—of water. That meant the coastline must be near.

Barter Isle replied to my call on extended VHF, but their report was far from welcoming—they were having the worst weather of the season! The airport's one dirt strip had a strong crosswind in a blinding snow storm.

"We have been told to spread foam on the runway for an

emergency landing. Are you sure you can land your aircraft with a crosswind in a snow storm with a four-hundred-foot base and a damaged undercarriage?" The operator's voice sounded vaguely annoyed.

"Those are the instructions I have been given," I replied and, as he obviously did not want me there, went on, "but I would appreciate any advice about a field with a better forecast."

He disappeared off the air, and came back with winds but no weather. Barter Island beacon responded strongly now but so did the snow and cloud. There was no mistaking where I was but how did I get down? In came another report that the weather was clearing rapidly further west towards Point Barrow, my original planned landing place. I worked out my fuel state. There was just enough to get to Barrow. Here there were Dewline stations, to divert into if necessary all along the coast. NASA was interrogating, and again I was caught in my spider's web of wires, as I tried irritably to hold and circle in the snow storm, answer Barter Island's requests and do my tests all at the same time. Reaction was setting in. I longed to get down. The problem of the wheels remained. Could I successfully shoot them all down or would they collapse. The nose wheel had been dangling now for many hours, and could be damaged even more! The main wheels were out of sight but I suspected the worst.

I was back in civilisation but nothing looked beautiful any more; the air was full of turbulence just like civilisation itself, I grumbled. But the weather improved the further west I flew, and so did the friendliness of each Dewline station I called. A desolate land of ice-topped tundra lay below me edged with tumbled piles of icebergs, but the voices were human and warm, and soon I was flying into sunshine again.

"This is Barrow. We are expecting you."

What wonderful words! I was nearly there. I had made my landfall. I had flown the Arctic Ocean! It was unbelievable and my heart jumped again with excitement and happiness. I even forgot the wheels, but Barrow had not, and were preparing to spread the foam. I begged them not to, until I reached the field, and could try shooting the remainder of the gear down.

Point Barrow coastline curved away as the northernmost tip of America—so far north it was once considered foreign ground

—but there was no sign of an airfield. I thought of the great Wiley Post who flew a seaplane with Will Rogers to Barrow to give an airshow to the Eskimos. Mistaken information that the village was on the tip—it is in fact ten miles below—had misled them in extremely bad weather, and after emergency landing near another Eskimo camp, they had crashed into the nearby lake after take-off. I steered more south and found the weather was perfect after the storm. The icing fog had rolled away less than an hour before, allowing me through almost as though it was expecting me. A strange kind of shanty town emerged from the tundra. Could this collection of iron roof shacks and piles of rubbish be an Eskimo village? I think I had expected igloos. A Cessna aircraft informed the Barrow radio that he would inspect my wheels, but against the tundra we could not see each other, and soon I was over the airport.

"Circle low so we can see the damage," instructed the tower.

I could see tidy rows of quonset huts, radio masts and huge trucks against a red earth and snow-speckled ground. Many birds flew before me as I descended, and people crowded on to the edge of the runway.

"Your main left wheel and nose wheel are hanging down but the right one seems to be still retracted," came the report. That was not good, and I might yet need the foam if I caught a tip tank on a one-sided landing. I was thankful that most of my fuel was burnt up; it could make all the difference.

I had one chance left: the cylinder bomb which could shoot the wheels down only once—though it was designed to shoot all three down together. I throttled back to get the airspeed to below 100 mph. Carefully, I held the aircraft straight and level—I could shoot some of the innards of the aircraft away too if this operation was not done right—and with one hand gripped the emergency loop under my seat, which would activate the cylinder, and I pulled gently. Whoosh—something had happened all right and the first light in the cabin triumphantly gleamed. It seemed an eternity before three green signals showed that all three wheels were safely locked down!

Slowly and steadily, *Mythre* and I lined up on the runway far out to make sure I did not have to 'go around'. Her wheels kissed the runway smoothly. We were down and it was the metal runway that made the terrific din—not us—as we finished our landing roll, though *Mythre* seemed to give a swerve at the end of it.

"Remain where you are," said the radio. All triumphant thoughts had gone, and I leapt out of the cockpit, wires trailing behind to look at *Mythre*'s legs. All I could think of was whether she was too hurt to go on, and I was quite bewildered as I was pulled to my feet from beneath her by dozens of people slapping me on the back, shaking my hand, taking pictures and all chattering at once. I had almost forgotten the Pole!

I had been airborne for seventeen hours, and I thanked them for staying up so late, or getting up so early—I was not quite sure which—then realised it was only I who had been through a day and a night, and it was only late afternoon here. I had forgotten the Alaskan local time is thirteen hours behind Greenwich Mean Time.

Someone presented me with a huge mug of champagne while gaily dressed people whirled before me, happy and welcoming, but my ears were deaf and still singing with the sounds of the aircraft. I did not know whether I had been near the Pole, but it was exciting to be here with good warm people. They were insistent that a message had come through verifying I had been over the Pole, and that I truly could celebrate. I simply did not believe them. But soon the radio phone rang and I heard far-off voices from Goddard, interrupted by constant static, and Phil Chapman say, "You went right over the Top! How do you feel?"

"Top of the World," I replied laughing and crying in disbelief. "But are you really sure I actually flew over the Pole? No kidding, you are not trying to make me feel good?"

His voice came and went, so did the noise of the party interrupting with the static. How I longed for the team to be here! There was so much I wanted to tell them—they had grown so close, and I had become dependent upon them. There had been few I could really trust, and the strange thing was, I had never even met most of them. It was a relationship I had never really known before.

Barrow is probably one of the most mixed-up places in the world. Utterly exhausted and with ears still full of engine noises, the sheer exhilaration of seeing so many entirely new things kept me from a bed. I was delighted when the engineers said

Mythre could not be fixed overnight; it meant an extra day for exploration.

The blue-and-gold-painted modern Naval Arctic Research Laboratory resembling a sprawling prefab is a complete surprise after the rugged huts. It sits on stilts. It is impossible to build normal buildings here, the permafrost reaches to several hundred feet below the ground. Windows are of triple glass, and door knobs plastic to prevent hands freezing on ice-cold metal! Nearly a hundred researchers can live here in more comfortable and attractive surroundings than in many a hotel; yet the windows look out on to a desolate wilderness of prairie snow where caribou, lemmings and wondrous birds can be seen.

I joined the laboratory's human inmates in the kitchen, gossiping and drinking coffee, while we all washed our clothes in four huge washing machines! There and then, I stripped off my turquoise cashmere trouser suit, which was now very much the worse for wear with dirt, oil and my inevitable coffee stains, and dropped it in too. I was quite respectable as I had my 'long johns' undies on, but where else but here could I do a public strip act with mixed sexes whom I had only met half an hour before? This is one of the great things of Arctic life. Sophisticated scientific work is being done, and the elements are of the hardest and toughest in the world to fight, but life is completely natural —the way life should be but rarely is in softer elements.

After rescuing my pants next morning I visited *Mythre* in the great covered, heated hangar, where she sat in comfort with a new friend, the laboratory's huge C47, which is a self-contained laboratory in itself and has landed on many an ice floe. The engineers showed me what they had found in poor *Mythre's* belly. Pools of fluid lay beneath her; the aileron cable had sliced a hole in her hydraulic pipe. How fortunate that aileron cables are stronger than hydraulic pipes. I recalled the weather over the Pole, and also reflected what would have happened if I had not landed at Nord; for up in these northern regions I had already learnt how easily trained men (or women) can just disappear without trace. No human can exist except with very strict observance of survival aids and Arctic rules. Perhaps this is what is so intriguing here—the rigid discipline coupled with complete freedom to be a human being and yourself!

The village of Utevik (Eskimo language for Barrow and

meaning 'Place of Retreat') has to be seen to be believed. A complete hodge-podge of a shanty town, peopled by the traditional and the modern, jostling side by side. It lies on the coast and partial skeletons of whales, tin cans and skin boats litter the beach. Just a few homes are the traditional igloo and the others are tumbledown wooden shacks surrounded by empty fifty-gallon tin oil barrels (for these are valuable in these regions). Rubbish does not disintegrate in such cold, and anything buried in the winter comes to light with the summer thaw—including the cemetery!

Few homes use seal oil lamps any more. Electricity recently arrived, but more important, Barrow sits on a natural gas supply. It has its own private gas operation (perhaps the only private one in the world). Snowmobiles jostle with dog sleds. The supermarket is packed with deep-frozen foods from the south, and yet the housewife's home refrigerator is still an old-style cache outside in the frozen ground. No one ever steals his neighbour's cache of food—a tradition which dates back from quite recent days when survival literally depended on how much food they could hunt.

Barrow is only one generation away from isolation and although there are now modern schools for the youngsters, there is still no high school, so the children have to go south to further their higher education. This means they return with dual values; full of modern ideas but having to fall back on old ways for survival. Major supplies can still only be shipped once a year, when the ice breaks in August only. All other supplies are flown in. Delightfully, it is still possible to pay the store in skins and whalemeat, for commercial survival is mainly still by whaling and seal hunting.

In winter water is sold by the foot. A block of ice from the freshwater lake costs thirty-five cents a foot, and in summer a fifty-gallon can of water costs three dollars. There are no sewage works.

The Eskimo here wears the traditional parka, fur lined and enchantingly embroidered. Their life is of the toughest in the world and yet they retain a sweet childlike quality. Their whole life is still based on sharing in true Arctic tradition, even to the point of wife swapping on occasions! Superstitions abound—the belief for example that illness is caused by an enemy; the afflicted one cures himself by changing his name to fool the evil one! They also believe that they are nearer to heaven than any other man on earth! Indeed the atmosphere here is half that of the Equator—where it is approximately ten miles thick. One wonders from where they derived so much knowledge many generations ago when such things had not been discovered elsewhere?

The Naval Arctic Research Laboratory has brought many assets to the Eskimo village, and provided some people with work. It operates a whole network of field stations, as well as very complete research facilities in all aspects of Arctic research in its own laboratory. The Naval Camp was originally a Naval Oil Exploration camp; in 1947 seven Arctic researchers leased one of the naval huts, and from this has grown the far-reaching laboratory of today which has been responsible for the activities of thousands of scientists. One of the most interesting things it does is to establish and operate bases on the famous floating ice islands. The biggest one today is T3.

It operates several aircraft, both for research and rescue work. Apart from the obvious studies in oceanology, and weather, it researches Arctic survival and environment, and the study of Arctic animals. The latter has more use than might be generally thought, and some of the results were used in the Space programme. For example, an experiment on snow blindness and the discovery of why an animal does not suffer like a man from it could be of future value to men in the glittering light of space.

14

THE next morning, without her monstrous fuel load, *Mythre* became as a young girl, bounding for joy off Barrow's metal runway. Once free in the sky she changed yet again into a magical bird—legs tucked safely under—made at ease and upheld by the keen air. Below us, a myriad of tiny pools and lakelets—the flat tundra prairie of the north—reflected back at us. Wondrous birds led the way to the frontier of everyday earth. Our boundary line was the Brooks Range: the division between the High Arctic, my personal pinnacle, and routine life. Like a curtain roughly pulled aside, the weather quickly changes here and heralded our return with growling thunderstorms and flashes of fiery temper. Sulky, ice-bearing clouds closed round us covering *Mythre*'s aerials with their excretion. The HF aerial, as though unable to bear returning, gave a final twanging quiver of utter weariness and snapped—broke away, leaving a thick cord of dragging ice behind us.

Glimpses of deep canyons cleaving snow-capped mountains of misshapen stumps—outposts leading to more graceful verdant sisters—grew more frequent as our latitude decreased. A river led to the leafy basin that surrounds the gold pioneer city of Fairbanks. I looked at a fantasy land again. Everything was green. Even the sky seemed green after the brilliance of the higher latitudes. I was dreaming. Nothing was real. I was still back there over the frosty wastes of my other planet. It was a shock when kindly Ed Eisle, NASA manager of the Stadan station, warmly greeted me, large as life! Although I had often talked to him over the previous months of preparations, I had never met him in the flesh. Our meetings had been via satellite communications between London and Alaska. It was his Stadan station that was collecting the data from my interrogating satellite, Nimbus. I was still between dream and reality—not truly believing I had already been to the North Pole, and yet not accepting my present rural surroundings either.

Anchorage, in its bowl of scenic mountains and glaciers, came next, and with it many friendly faces organised by Airforce officer, Colin Bell. Even my German airborne 'date' of the North Polar region waited there, Lufthansa's Captain Heinrich Auguer, the man who had radioed the weather to me when I was stuck at Nord. Here, too, I met the first of the Ninety-Nines I had yet discovered on this trip. Ninety-Nines are an international group of women pilots. Amelia Earhart as first president in 1929 named them thus—because ninety-nine licensed women pilots attended that first meeting held in the back of a hangar on Long Island.

When I left, a walrus tusk, Billiken—the 'God of Things as They Ought to be'—a keepsake from Alaskan Ninety-Nines, sat beside Buck Tooth. I am supposed to rub his tummy when in trouble, but that day I rubbed it in affection, as I flew out over the crown of the Pacific—the Alaskan Gulf—leading to the coastline of Canada and the great North-West scenery of America. Reality started to come back, as the West Coast air traffic controllers led me down through the splendours of the Rockies under a canopy of gilt-edged clouds. I had become used to the silver brilliance of the ever-circling sun of the Arctic summer and my own physical loneliness. I had forgotten the richer colours of the sky's spectrum and also the richness that can come with the warm humanity of people welcoming you back. This is what flying was all about. Where else but in a light aircraft can you find such incredible and differing beauty, meet so many friends, in fact learn so much in such a short time—not so short that you cannot absorb it nor long enough to be bored. No airliner or boat can give you all this, and certainly no earth-bound chariot!

I see the dawn first, and earlier than those asleep below me, but my day lasts longer, for I also see the setting sun long after it has left those below. I have more time than most to think, to almost touch the world that lies around the earth, and to see for myself the glorious thing that earth could be. On days like this, all the shatteringly terrifying moments of the storms, or the miseries of the brick-lined petty cage at home are like birth pains. They are forgotten and overshadowed by the magnificence of the present.

Recently I had seen only the pale moon in the summer Arctic sky to remind me of the planets above, but now the stars had returned to my sky. I looked especially for Polaris, the North Star and Venus, my own birth planet. Soon I would not see them again as I flew into the Southern Hemisphere until I was heading north again towards England. The moonlight scene was a constant moving twinkle of blue diamond-like stars above the warm house lights below. Dark silhouettes of mountains loomed beside me. Although my now unaccustomed night eyes wanted this glorious scene to continue, I still apprehensively looked at my transponder to make sure the controllers were still interrogating me and knew where I was heading. I had even become unused to the more sophisticated aids of airways flying.

The relationship between controllers and pilots demonstrates how trust can take place among all men of all nationalities. Early in instrument training you learn to trust both the controllers and your instruments far more than yourself. To survive you must trust them for your physical reactions can lead you completely astray when visual aids are no longer there. Yet there have been times, when not in contact with others, I have found an intuition or some sort of help I did not know I had (undoubtedly stimulated by something outside myself, and of the sky), which has led me out of danger.

At last the shimmering lights became almost a sheet of light, as San Francisco and its multitude of suburbs emerged ahead. It was time to leave this airborne fairyland and follow the approach lights over the water leading to the solid dark tarmac of the runway.

Ruth Rueckert, another member of Ninety-Nines, was there to smooth my passage, and Butler Aviation to inspect *Mythre*. But there was to be yet another delay, for this was the July 4th holiday weekend. San Francisco, my last outpost of the States, was where the autopilot control was to be replaced. I had flown almost half the world without it, but now there was no excuse to take unnecessary risks. I would have to wait.

Checking into the Airport Hilton Hotel was an unbelievable experience. Even in slacks, I stuck out as something over-dressed and really square. The place was full of hippies! Long flowing garments, or practically nothing at all, tinkling bells and jangling jewellery, pipe-smoking women, pigtailed men with garlands of flowers greeted me. Right beside me at the check-in point in the lobby sat a Yogi in a trance! San Francisco had indeed changed since I last saw it. I had read about the West Coast hippies but thought that they were just a small section of the population as in London. Here everyone was hip, from the very aged to the babes in arms! It was not until the next day that I discovered these were members of the Science Fiction Writers' Association Convention and that all of San Francisco was not like this!

Astronaut Phil Chapman, with his T-38 jet, flew up from Goddard, Washington, to bring me news of their story of my Polar flight. Doctor Arnold Miller, inventor of the aircraft's Theta Sensor, also visited. He told me that his sensor had detected air pollution actually around the North Pole itself. So *Mythre* had earned her keep in spite of her wobbly wheels.

Here, too, Elgin Long visited us. He was interested in the set-up of my aircraft as he was going to borrow the larger Piper Navajo to attempt to fly both Poles, which he did in November 1971, but my mind was already switched on towards the rest of the world. I had yet to fly the Pacific Ocean to Australia and then to start another record attempt back home over Asia.

Mist shrouded the San Francisco Gap, my gateway to the other half of the earth, and the glorious Pacific. I was exhilarated. Inevitably there would be many more experiences and adventures to enjoy before the final home stretch. I had found great happiness on earlier flights among the islands and atolls of this mighty ocean.

That day's journey to Honolulu would take about fifteen hours and my little green light would not be such a frequent diversion now. I was nearing the Equator and Nimbus, my satellite, was in Polar orbit and could not reach me in all its orbits. But already streamers of vapour trails intertwined in the sky, and below, cargo boats made paths of bubbling surf.

How marvellous it was to have the luxury of a working auto-pilot now and to be able to indulge in as much black coffee as I liked to keep alert. I was certainly not lonely, as the US Coast Guard were keeping a careful watch over me over the entire Pacific all the way to Australia.

Speedbird, Qantas, United, a whole host of airlines talked to me the whole way across, and when they were near, suggested I try and recognise their vapour trails. A slight hesitation as to exactly where you are encourages a host of fascinating conversations. It is a great way to make friends. This morning it was like having a safety rope right across the sky! The ocean weather ship, twelve hundred miles out, as always, gave me excellent bearings, and my groundspeed. After I had left the weather ship far behind, I could see the hurricane to the left of my track blowing out the usual sky debris of angry cloud.

Soon the commercial radio stations of lovely, volcanic Hawaii led me with music to the 'Sandwich Isles'. So named by Captain Cook who discovered the Hawaiian Isles, after his benefactor, the Earl of Sandwich. The Earl, a great gambler and sponsor of adventures and therefore a man after my own heart, refused to leave the gambling tables for food; thus the sandwich was invented. I wonder if Captain Cook named them with a sense of humour, for the old Hawaiian settlers were a great betting people. They would stake even their wives on a surf race.

Koko and Diamond Head, well-known landmarks now, came up and familiar controllers' voices timed me over Honolulu field. A sprinkling of rain lessened the heat, which I took as a good omen for my onward flight. Here rain means good luck and happiness, and is much desired for weddings and funerals.

Lindy Boyes with Betty Miller (the first woman to fly the Pacific) headed up the Ninety-Nines contingent here greeting me with sweet smelling *leis* of welcome. The Airport Holiday Inn provided a super suite for me, and Air Services a resting place for *Mythre*. Irene Rogers, up-and-coming woman aerobatic pilot, helped me to explore Honolulu, while I waited out the hurricane which had now moved into my proposed flight path.

Hawaii, legendary 'Island of the Gods' said to have been formed by the children of the gods dropped into the sea. Next came the people, the Polynesians, who emigrated from the Southern Pacific Isles and atolls hundreds of years ago, in seventy-foot canoes which held a hundred people. Two canoes lashed together, with a platform between them, supported both a grass thatched hut for the women and children to live in, and fires, built in a mound of earth, to cook on. Pigs, chickens and dogs and plant life travelled with them too. They navigated by the stars and with the aid of shell charts (plaited twigs and shells representing islands they had heard of) and also by following the passage of migrating birds. Their sails were made of thin plaited grass mats.

They were a superstitious race, and were governed by strict Chiefs—those men who could prove closest association to the gods. Women's Lib would have been incensed in those days, for the women were not allowed to eat with men, nor were women allowed to eat certain foods. By the nineteenth century, the Chiefs ruled by a system of fines. Adultery could cost thirty dollars, or shouting and singing in the streets on Sundays one dollar. The missionaries had discovered them. There are still parts of Hawaii where you can imagine all of this happening, but much of its beauty has been lost as a result of the land developers, and trails of discotheque bars and supermarkets.

15

THE hurricane was dissipating, and time to make the twelve-hour flight to Canton Isle, just below the Equator. Here I would be able finally to claim a 'First Flight' from Equator to Equator via a Pole. Hardly a fast record thanks to the problematic wheels, nevertheless it *was* a first, so perhaps it did not matter.

Soon I had left behind the white-spray-lashed black lava rocks of the gods and the long flight began—with time to think. There were no airliners on this route to talk to, and no reefs or atolls to navigate by. Fourteen hundred miles ahead lay Canton Isle. Somewhere in this desolate ocean the Navy was preparing, and moving in for Apollo 15 which was to lift off in a few days' time, and hopefully splash down in the Pacific after its moon shot.

The intertropical Convergence Zone, the weather front which constantly moves up and down and around the Equator, lay at about latitude 10 North. I had hoped it would allow me through smoothly today, but the hurricane had really made it angry, and Zeus grumbled and, with indignation, spat fire at me through the silky clouds. Sometimes the clouds are like dimpled faces with sunny smiles and only gently tease, then suddenly change into a sombre, serious and vengeful mood. Openings like spiders' webs beckon you into the trap as you think you see a clear spot, but the cloud tentacles close behind you, and giant hands hurl you up and down with frightening cracks of a whip. You hastily tighten your seat belt while throttling back, keeping a careful watch on your airspeed and kid yourself that you are relaxed.

Today the thunderstorms were too violent to be taken on lightly. Again and again I had to turn out of the blinding pouring rain, as the airspeed went off the clock, and the altimeter wound up and down like a yo-yo. I edged more and more to starboard, and let down lower over the disturbed sea. It, too, had turned black with rage and a green waterfall had built up over my windscreen. Streams of frothing bubbling water built up between the double-paned heated panel. It looked as if I were swimming under water.

The flight seemed an eternity, almost as long as the Polar leg. Perhaps it was because I was again in sight of my goal—the Equator—and the major aim of the flight was almost made. One gets to know every nut and bolt in the aircraft. Each scratch on the gleaming paint becomes an intimate thing; one longs to clean off the dried grease on the de-icer boots outside on the wings; the sand, dust and smears on the glass of the instruments inside remind one of the sandstorms on the other side of the world in the Libyan desert; the rivulets of oil from the engine cowling are still there from way back, but the coffee stains on the flight bag are new and will get worse as the flight advances.

Today there was a mixed aroma of bananas, coffee and stale cigarettes. Sometimes it is a modern sophisticated smell of some fragrance, but that usually means something has leaked in my Arden mini make-up case. The dri-towel for cleaning my hands, or the instrument dials, is an old-fashioned smell of Eau de Cologne.

Daylight switches from one extreme to the other—undiluted vivid and bright, or dark as pitch in the storms—far darker than they appear on the ground. Colours are more noticeable and you see every pastel hue as well as the dramatic, glorious deep colours of a sunset.

There are comforts, almost sensual, appreciated so much more up here. Such taken-for-granted luxuries on the ground as the comforting sheepskin seat cover; the longed-for mug of coffee bathing a parched throat; eye drops that soothe hot stinging eyes, and the snuggling feel of soft cashmere on chilly nights; the surprise gift that someone hid in the cabin, or an unexpected message from one's team at home tucked in a chart.

On the other side of the world in my birthplace, England, it was midnight and many people would be asleep. Here, in the middle of the vast Pacific, it was early afternoon. Time. What a strange unsolved thing it still is. In England, preparing for the flight, time had fled far too quickly; yet in the High Arctic it had been timeless, and quite unimportant; here, alone in the countless miles of the Pacific, it now appeared to move again, though slowly. Undoubtedly, it would quicken again the nearer

I got to Europe, until finally I would be once more trapped on the ground in our relentless rat race.

The green light of my NASA IRLS package gleamed, abruptly turning my thoughts to pressing the right buttons to show my mental acuity state. These 'housekeeping duties' turned my random thoughts to Space, and I wondered when and what would cause the ultimate break-through to other planets. If this earth solves the problem and there are intelligent beings on other far-off planets, there is every reason to suppose that some of them might be far advanced in comparison to ourselves. For them to have survived the great scientific power that advanced knowledge must bring, they must have become ultra-sophisticated beings to have governed their planet in universal peace. And peace it must have been, for any war, run on advanced knowledge, must have shattered their planet long before they reached a higher form of civilisation. Their philosophies must have become more civilised, and developed in unison with their scientific discoveries, whereas our scientific achievements seem to have out-stripped our thinking. Will they accept Man and his uncivilised ways? Will they try to teach Man or will they destroy him just as we ourselves try to isolate and destroy an infection?

It was time soon to worry about my own isolation in the Pacific and find Canton Isle, itself once a space-tracking atoll. I was weary. The clouds had become scattered, casting island-like shadows on the water, but I knew my atoll would lie under one of them.

The radio crackled with a friendly American voice, and the familiar unmistakable crescent shape of Canton soon appeared. Three hundred and seventy military men were stationed here, and not a female on the island. The odds were getting better! Last time I had visited here there had been just fifty-one men— the entire population—to greet me. I wished I could have got out with freshly shampooed hair and a feminine skirt, but that was too difficult to arrange in my overcrowded cockpit. Luckily today I managed to clamber out without damaging the strategic spots!

A megaphone boomed a welcoming speech, and a microphone was thrust in my hands to reply. I cannot remember what I said, for half my brain was still flying up in the sky, but it did not seem to matter for these kindly American men cheered and applauded as though I had done something great.

Canton had once been a seaplane base for the clipper runs between Auckland and Honolulu, and during the Second World War housed many military men. A grounded troopship can still be seen out on the reef. The Space Agency leased it in the sixties to aid tracking in the early projects Mercury and Gemini and the first manned space flights. Southside, the British side of the atoll across the lagoon was now deserted though the huts remained. I regretted there was not time for this lone Britisher to stake a claim on it.

The Commanding Officer, Major Blair, escorted me to the Base Supports manager, Ben Moore, and his abode where I could refresh before continuing. There a super party had been laid on with all the food in the shape of flowers! Once again, as previously in the all-male Arctic camps, I was made to feel one of them, absolutely natural, and quite at home. It was just like being in one great family.

Next morning, there was much to explore and see and many people to talk to. It was becoming an overwhelming experience realising how many people outside Britain had joined in this flight, both to help and to wish it well. How can any woman say it is a man's world? For me, outside Britain, it is a woman's world made possible by men!

Coffee and doughnuts heralded mid-morning already and long past take-off time for Fiji and Melanesia. I dipped *Mythre's* wings in salute to my gallant gentlemen of Canton before setting course, and soon the tiny atoll was out of sight, even though I could still hear their voices and music on their private radio station, until finally I was alone with my 'monkey-box' and my thoughts again.

The bad weather was now behind me. *Mythre* changed back into a gliding bird instead of a frightened bucking animal. Royal blue ribbons and emerald depths melted together into frothy white lacy collars rolling up to the minute beaches of the reefs ahead. Deep down, the coral gave hints of orange, blue and red in clear, ever-changing, translucent depths.

Tranquil and happy, I tried to analyse why I had always found so much peace on this side of the world. On this, my return flight one year later to the Pacific, with all the Arctic memories added to my experiences, I wondered, "How can what I have learned be expressed in mere words?"

In the air, beauty is of greater impact and more concentrated; colours are brighter, clearer and yet more delicate. Sensations are intensified and yet the body remains still, with feet and hands on the controls. Fear is almost a cleanser in the air. One feels the physical stab momentarily and then comes a great calmness in spite of the shaking hands and shivering knees. You are afraid, but you find a power inside yourself which you did not know you had, and you are able to conquer the animal, anguished panic.

For me personally, it is flying and a small aircraft which show me the signs of a mighty overall power or pattern. The solo long-distance flyer finds a freedom and yet, although free, is made aware of an overall, magnificent influence which gives him a sense of humility at his inability even to imagine the vastness of this power, while lifting him beyond the barrier of earthbound thoughts to glimpse the future that is Space.

Today I was returning to my islands beyond the Dateline from a different direction, and tomorrow had become today. Suddenly, as always in the tropics, the blazing dusk became a dark curtain, the stars met the fluorescent waves over the reefs. Leaping flames of brilliant fires were below me, and I realised this must be the burning of sugar-cane leaves in preparation for new harvesting in Fiji. The bobbing light of a lantern showed clearly the bullock carts, and the fiery bonfires outlined dark purple-black silhouettes of the Nasouri Highland Mountains.

A gentle boom from the tank behind me reminded me that it was from near here I had acquired one of my most treasured possessions—the *Tabua*—the tooth of a giant sperm whale, which had been presented to me and *Myth Too* in Fiji last year. Just before leaving for the Pole, I had received a message that my Fijians particularly wanted me to carry it with me on this flight in her sister aircraft *Mythre*. It was now swinging against the fuel tank behind my head.

The last glimpse I had had of Fiji had been at dawn, and it was almost symbolic that I should be returning with it at sunset as though I had just been away for a day. Then a Fijian chief and his followers had risen during the night and driven to the airport to bid *Myth Too* farewell by ceremoniously presenting us with the *Tabua*, predicting that it would bring us back to Fiji. At the time there was little hope of my return. Certainly not for years. In eight short months here I was back in Fiji! The *Tabua* had performed its magic, but unlike its fellow *Tabua*, ours had now also crossed the snowy wastes of the Arctic and the North Pole.

Today, landing at Fiji's international airport in the balmy warm air was like a comforting homecoming, and '*Bula*' was the first word I heard—Fijian for welcome! Old friends, Bill Schutt, Manager of Qantas Airline, and John Besant of the Fijian Hotel, and Hank Curth, broadcaster and author, were there to meet me, and drive me to the hospitality of new Travelodge. The same Qantas engineers who had looked after *Myth Too* took over and admired the new *Mythre*. More minor spares were needed, which would have to be obtained from Sydney. However, it was a welcome enforced wait here in one of my favourite parts of the world, and I did not have to chase any records until I reached Darwin in Australia. I was delighted to find time had become timeless again.

Fiji seems far more civilised than the other side of the world even though the last cannibal known here was as recent as 1935. There is not a great deal of money here, and yet all look chubby and well nourished—though not from recent cannibalism! One never seems to see a lonely old lady or starving child here. The whole village looks after its own, not just the family, and although it is often close communal living, it is a life of privacy too, because of the courtesy rules. When you visit the thatched-roofed, hibiscus-surrounded, grass and bamboo *bures* of the tidy green-pathed villages, you never stand directly in front of the open door, but stand to one side and knock softly on the wall. You take your shoes off before entering and wait with slightly bowed head just inside the threshold until your host asks you to the centre of the room, where you sit cross-legged on the plaited, mat-covered floor. Here all races manage to live happily and peacefully together. Why? Have they learnt so much in such a short time and remembered what we have forgotten?

The land developers have moved in here too, but fortunately the major part of the islands remain in their gracious state. Once again I found the hibiscus flower left by my washbasin to wear in my hair. The maids offered to massage my aching back, and refused to take personal payment. They explain it's something they have been taught to do since children. They certainly seem to have healing hands. It was once believed that individuals had certain healing powers for illness and if one man's powers did not work on that particular disease, you changed to another healing man until you found the cure.

I was so carefree and happy to be here that I cleaned my teeth in cleansing cream by mistake! The cracking voices of the yellow-beaked, white-tailed myna birds grumbled at me for more food from my plate of paw-paw and pineapple. They had already cheekily pinched it all from under my very nose. Lizards darted across the floors, and toads (specially imported to keep the insects down) lay in wait in the bushes.

The Fijians told me their stories of the old missionary days. It was no wonder their ancestors preferred to eat missionaries rather than listen to them, for they introduced many strict new laws—and said sex was wicked (except in one position—and this has been called the missionary position ever since!). Here, when the girls were told that they must be properly covered, the girls took the missionaries' shirts and wore them as necklaces. They taught that it was wicked to trade on Sundays so the artful traders built on the Dateline which then ran through Fiji. On Sundays customers would use the back door which opened on to Monday, and the front door during the rest of the week. Simple!

I returned to the beautiful Fijian Hotel and it was in a village near here that Ratu Meli now arranged a special Yagona Ceremony to celebrate my crossing of the Pole. He went to a great deal of trouble days before to make sure the ceremony was prepared in the traditional way with all the genuine ingredients. No tourist ceremony this. No Europeans were allowed to be present, except for John Besant, and it was an unforgettable scene of the real thing.

Sunlight streamed through the open doors of the thatched *bure*, as the gentle Trade Wind carried the scent from outside of tropical flowers. Quiet noises greeted me, for this part of the ceremony was a serious affair. The men of the village were dressed as in olden times; adorned in skirts, green leaves and anklets of vine, and sat cross-legged behind the huge *Tanoa*—a wooden bowl—waiting for me to arrive. I removed my shoes outside and entered, waiting for the Chief to assign me to my place in the centre of the room, where I, too, sat cross-legged on the floor.

Amid chanting and sounds from a drum of hollow bark the Yagona root was prepared. Many times it was pounded with water until it was of the approved consistency. At a sign an assistant, dressed in brightly coloured dyed leaves, strained the liquid with a brush-like wad of paper-mulberry tree.

The drinking cup, *Bilo*—a half coconut shell—is attached by a sennett rope hung with shells to the Tanau. Once it was an insult to step over this rope and punishable by death! The Yagona was offered to me first as guest of honour, and I drank it back in one after clapping three times, and chanting 'Bula' as I had been taught. The assistant then squatted in front of me and clapped three times while I said my '*Vinaka*'—thanks, and so the bowl was passed around the room.

I drank many bowls, and although it is non-alcoholic and numbs one's mouth, it is certainly euphoric. The ceremony over, the wives all came to sit beside me, and shake my hand. The serious chanting turned to gay and naughty songs and soon we were all dancing together Fijian fashion.

There followed a feast in another village of breadfruit, small potatoes, turtle flesh, chicken and prawns, yams and all imaginable tropical fruits which we ate with our fingers, and drank a delicious kind of shrimp soup out of coconut shells.

Another night I also visited an Indian Ceremony of healing by walking on fire which only takes place once a year—a most impressive ceremony. This night there were twenty-three volunteers (as they must wish to do this themselves and must not be persuaded by others), six of them women and several young boys of about fourteen years, who believed that the Fire God Goinda could cure them of their troubles.

The people go to the simple thatched-roof temple two weeks before the ceremony and must not eat meat, smoke, or drink alcohol nor leave its vicinity during that time except to go to the river to bathe. They must leave all earthly thoughts out and concentrate wholly on their own God for any religion can join in this training.

Two days before the chosen date, a flower is placed on the fire idol's head, as the priest's praying becomes more intense. Only when the idol's head nods (and I have met people who have really seen this happen) and the flower falls forward, and if the petals fall into the priest's hands, may the ceremony take place. If the god's head does not nod it means there are bad elements around and the ceremony must not go on or the supplicants will be burnt by the fire! The bad elements have to be found and removed before preparation for another ceremony.

That night all had gone well and the god had signified his approval. The chanting and music could be heard far away. We drove up a rough winding path into the Masouri mountains, where crowds were gathered round the temple's enclosure. Burning embers glowed red, like an oriental carpet about eighteen by ten feet. The supplicants could not cheat—they had to step in the embers several times to get across!

The priest led the supplicants, dressed in flowing robes, the widows in white, other women with a red dot on their forehead signifying they were married, round the pit and into the temple many times. One young boy was obviously in a euphoric trance, and danced wildly and with complete abandon (though when I spoke to him later there was no trace of trance or drug in his behaviour which was that of a normal youngster). Finally, to a crescendo of praying and chanting the priest led them slowly through the fire again and again. The flowing garments did not have a single mark on them, and some even knelt in the fire, others picked up the burning embers and threw them over themselves. They showed no fear at all.

Later at the feast given to the watching public, I talked to the people who had walked through the fire, and examined their hands and feet. There was no trace of a burn, not even a reddened mark remained; their skin had remained supple and smooth! They were obviously happy and gay and told me they felt nothing on their feet except a little heat around their body when they were in the fire. Some had been through before— though they are only allowed to do it once every three years— and affirmed that their sickness had been cured! They also told me that if they went near the fire now that the ceremony was over they would get burnt just like anyone else.

Again and again they told me that if I had sufficient faith in the things that I believed in—not necessarily religious—and meditated on these things in the temple, I, or anyone else could walk through unharmed and even beneficially. The power of

The runway at Tarawa atoll, Pacific Ocean. The runway is the same width as the land

A Pacific-style bath   A precarious-looking loo

Sheila in Ratu Meli's village, Fiji, after a special celebration of her crossing of the North Pole

Nakabuta village, Fiji

Shopping in Savu
market, Fiji

The Far East Fleet
knew Sheila was coming
and baked a cake!
Singapore, 1971

Diagram showing how the satellite Nimbus worked in the IRLS experiment with
Mythre in the North Polar flight. See Appendix III

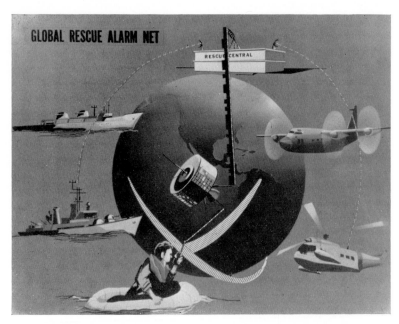

Diagram of the US Navy's GRAN experiment. See Appendix V

positive thought cannot be denied, though the fact that the supplicants had always believed unquestioningly what they had been taught since birth may well have been partly responsible for their thoughts being more positive than mine. My thoughts were not so undivided, nor so sure as theirs. I had been taught traditional beliefs which I had grown to query and found in practice something quite different—certainly an overall power but as an actual force, more a scientific thing—could we but learn to communicate via another dimension of intellect.

16

THE aircraft spares arrived by Qantas airline from Sydney, Australia, and after my new flying 'canoe', *Mythre*, had saluted the friendly Fijian villages, it was almost time to leave the South Pacific. I had yet to make several landings before I reached Darwin in Northern Australia, to start my attempt to break the Australia to England record. This was still held by New Zealander Jean Batten, the great woman pilot of the thirties. She broke this solo record in a Percival Gull aircraft in 1937, and still held it now, thirty-four years later. She had made it in five and a half days, and I hoped to lop another two days off it.

Take-off day from Nandi for Townsville of Queensland, Australia, was a calm, silky day. The golden red and sepia hills of Fiji were left behind as the sunshine glistened and reflected from spectacular coral reefs encircling the tiny silver beaches of sporadic islands, until the dark green foreboding mountains of New Caledonia emerged from the horizon mist. Here the weather sharply changed its mood and a line of heavy squalls quarrelled among themselves across the Coral Sea leading to Australia. Now once again the air ahead was full of tumult and darkness, and long before we reached landfall, the aircraft defied the buffeting air with a fury of its own. It was better to land at Noumea, capital of New Caledonia, to wait this out for there was no record to break today, and it was unnecessary to flirt deliberately with such disgusting weather.

The same welcoming faces of the French tower operator, the engineers and refuellers of previous flights were here smiling, "No landing fees for an old friend," and the free ride into town with an air traffic controller was most gratefully accepted, for this can be one of the most expensive stops in the Pacific.

Arrival at Townsville, Queensland, Australia, was very different. It was the Aero Club's barbecue night and Harry Taylor, its chairman, hesitantly supposed I would not want to go. Of course I wanted to go to it, but when I got there it seemed that they themselves were all rather formal, and not at all like the Australia I had grown to love. Aviation songs, known the world over, began but sounded oddly different, and very straight-laced.

"Funny—I don't remember my flying instructor using exactly those lyrics!" I finally commented; giving chief flying instructor, Bill Kiernam, a quizzical look, absolutely sure this show of propriety was being put on for my benefit! Great roars of laughter and sighs of relief broke out all round, and from then on all became more normal (and Rabelaisian) and I began to feel I was with a flying fraternity again. Obviously the infamous side of my reputation had gone before me and they later confessed they had not known what to expect, except the worst, from the confused reports of the ill-fated (for me!) England to Australia Race! I retorted that I was not sure what kind of people they were themselves at first with their formal unbending attitude. How often that happens with flyers I have never met. Thank heavens I occasionally get the opportunity to stay and get to know them and invariably find quite a few of my critics become my very good friends, and are far from puritanical.

The Great Dividing Range Mountains shelter the idyllic coastal climate of Queensland but also literally divide the weather and the environment. Beyond them lies the Great Out-Back, where people accept little aircraft and HF radio as necessities of life for often these are their only fast means of transport or communication. No 'over the fence gossip' for the woman here. She chats by radio to her neighbours hundreds of miles away. Her child learns his school lessons from the School of the Air and maybe he will be a pioneer in his own way for the day is approaching when there may well be Universe schools via satellite.

Were it not for the heat, it would be like approaching the tree-line of the Arctic, for the trees become more misshapen and stunted the further inland you fly, and the ribbons of riverlets spread out until they become lost in an arid desert. Somehow people manage to live there, as the Aborigines did for centuries without ever leaving it.

All hints of the sunny Pacific behind me, I flew on over the desolate Northern Territory of Australia to Darwin in readiness to start the trek back to England. Occasionally the red smoke of great bush fires made more pollution for my 'Theta sensor' to digest, and send its discoveries of the earth's environment back to the computers in America. Few roads and no human beings were to be seen below me; buffalo and sometimes dingoes and kangaroos stood near the sparse waterholes. Nearing Darwin, the land became green and trees upright again, and I saw the termite 'cemeteries'—great slabs of mud built by thousands of termites—towering up to the height of a one-storey building!

The friendly US Coast Guard and US Navy were left behind in the Pacific, and now the British Royal Navy would be liaising the stops between Australia and the UK. I was hoping to do without sleep and fly almost non-stop from Australia to London with only five technical landings for fuel.

Peter Denholm and women pilots Christine and Kathy Henderson helped me organise the coming record attempt as well as to explore the Northern Territory. Together we visited the Aborigines, chased across country to watch the animals and great variety of birds in flocks of thousands—more than I have ever seen anywhere before. I also deposited some precious sleeping hours into my 'sleep bank', so as to be able to stay awake and alert for several days. One hoards sleep before the event, rather than getting used to doing without it. The reasoning being that one's endurance halves week by week rather than increasing with practice.

The Australia to England route had to be planned to over-fly Indonesia and yet get in and out of Singapore, avoiding the height of the tiger thunderstorms at both places without too much delay. It was only just midnight in England when I started off from Darwin. But here it was already next day's lunch time! I was chasing time again.

The Timor Sea shimmered with heat waves leading to the volcanoes and islands of Indonesia. I remembered 1966, the first time I flew it from the other direction, one of the most satisfying moments of my life, for I never dreamt that I would be flying myself there—for becoming a pilot had not been one of my younger day-dreams. Three years later in 1969 there had been that other day, one of forlorn hope, when I had been but a few feet over the sea with a thirty-foot cloud base, no forward visibility and sabotaged radio aids—quite hopelessly lost and beaten. Then, too, one of my '*Myth* Miracles' occurred as so often happens, and I remained alive even though nothing had been quite so uncaring after.

The green undulating jungle hills of Timor Island under a golden sun made it difficult to imagine the web of wet clawing cloud that had clothed it before when four human beings in two tiny aircraft had desperately tried to find a visible landfall. Night brought down a merciful warmth of darkness as I passed Makassar, which by being there had saved my life in 1969. The memories of that day were frightened things, and the start of a deep depression and sense of failure. There, high up in the skies, I saw the lights of another aircraft, like a passing friend giving me an affectionate hand, just as the glimpse of an aircraft's lights had caught my attention that other time.

Firework displays flashed far ahead in the sky, signifying the thunderstorms, gathered around Singapore, seeming to dip and meet the dancing shadows of the bonfires below in Borneo. The radio compass needle jerked under its dial in fear and panic, not knowing which electrical master to obey, and the HF radio hissed its furious sympathy. Now which side of the storms should I fly? The galaxy of the sky's theatrical lighting was so vast there was no advantage either way tonight.

My landing lights picked up the familiar uniforms of the British Far East Fleet, waiting near Singapore Aero Club. Efficiently, they got on with the ground jobs, and I was surrounded with laughter and happiness again. A beautiful iced cake was produced in *Mythre*'s honour, baked by a Navy chef. I longed to cut a piece there and then, but I was supposed to take it back to the UK with me. How, without breaking it? Finally we solved the problem by stuffing it with a roll of toilet paper!

A misty veil of dawn disguised Malaya, as I flew out over the Straits of Malacca, talking to the Naval ships below by HF radio. Eleven hours later, the exotic tropical forest-covered mountains and sparkling white beaches of Southern India lay ahead of me. Ravens and eagles greeted me by playfully dive-bombing my wings. A very green city, cleft by the Cooum River, graceful temples and shrines soothed my sun-strained eyes for Madras is a city of the arts, scholarship and reverence. Most of the population is Hindu, but Saint Thomas the Apostle was said to have been martyred near here in AD 53 accounting for the many shrines and holy buildings all confusingly named after him! Sixteen centuries later, the town was founded as a result of the English East India Trading Company building a fort, around which a community gathered, and so eventually the great seaport of Madras grew.

Crowds of elegant Indian people surrounded me at the airport, for even the poorest give an impression of gracefulness and beauty in these countries. The women in flowing colourful saris, one or two stood out with lacy veiling thrown over tunic dresses covering harem balloon trousers, stood back from the turbaned men in the traditional jodhpurs and jubba coats, in contrast to the emaciated and ragged holy man sitting with his bowl nearby. In comparison to my journeys, his was a very hard way to follow for undoubtedly he had travelled many thousands of miles by foot.

It was like being in a more leisurely age, for here every member of the family, no matter how slender the relationship, must courteously be introduced to any new distraction. All are so charming in Southern India that rather than disappoint one in anything, they will give one the wrong answer which can have very disconcerting results.

Flying on through the night, as I hit the edges of the grey monsoons around Bombay and circumvented the turbulent showers, it became increasingly difficult to work out my true course from the false readings I was receiving from my once again frightened radio compass dials. Today it was not one of my beautiful fresh dawns and it was sulky and very petulant. I was still at the stage where my whole body ached. Each individual muscle and bone made itself felt. I was unutterably tired. Neither stronger coffee nor my super Dextrose glucose tablets helped. I longed to land and just sleep and not bother with a record. Whatever was I doing it for? Even NASA seemed to have become remote, and I seemed to have lost the point of what we were doing. Down here the satellite could only interrogate twice a day, and I missed its friendly twinkle.

Over the border of Pakistan, the controller held several conversations with me, as to my whereabouts, and gave me very exact instructions to follow. The only trouble was that he changed shifts without bothering to repeat his own instructions to his successor. His successor only too obviously did not notice where I was, in spite of repeated position reports. It is rare that a civilian air traffic controller deliberately makes a fool of a pilot in the air, but this one certainly did, almost to a point of danger. He had a most appreciative male audience and simply could not resist it. Frankly, I wished that each male participant would just once fly themselves alone for several days without sleep. It would have been my pleasure to control them!

Commander Henry Bains, a Naval aviator himself, and British Naval Attaché in Karachi, waited patiently with Indian engineer Kasim Dada, at five in the morning, until I was eventually allowed to land by this stubborn controller. Henry was much concerned anyway about my safety and would not allow me to wander, for all of Pakistan was on the point of boiling up, with the devastating results for many thousands of innocent people involved in the war a short while later. This probably accounted for the controller's difficult mood.

Eventually the airport guards allowed us past to the airport restaurant for bacon and eggs before I jadedly flew out towards the Persian Gulf and Bahrein, another seven flying hours later. Gradually my physical aches disappeared, though this was not necessarily a good thing for the dry breathless heat of the day was unbearable. Only the extreme turbulence prevented my swollen eyelids, now sunken in my cheeks with exhaustion, from involuntarily closing altogether! I longed to stretch my hurting arms and legs, but there was no space. No amount of coffee helped now. Stinging cologne on my eyelids helped a little, followed by soothing eye drops. Sometimes it is helpful to have physical discomfort to overcome. You can use it to your own advantage; that day it helped in keeping me awake and alert. I had so little physical strength left that it was almost impossible to turn the oxygen cylinder's cap. Ten minutes of oxygen revived me and as my tunnel vision rescinded, I felt ready to fly on for days. The colours of the deep aquamarine sea contrasted once again against the pale sapphire sky.

A cheery English voice greeted me and woke my dreaming brain, way out from Sharjah control tower. It belonged to another of my old but never seen friends of past flights. There is little traffic here, and the few words of merriment probably woke him up as much as me on this sizzling afternoon.

The old pearl-fishing island of Bahrein lay ahead, its pearls now forsaken for the great oil rigs that lay out to sea around it, with an occasional romantic dhow moored among the workaday tankers and sleek Naval craft. This barren island, thirty by eight miles long, has thousands of inhabitants, but a bare three miles of cultivation to feed them. Here, too, lay the ruins of the Bronze Age and the largest prehistoric burial ground on earth dating back to 3000 BC.

Almost before the propellers stopped, HMS *Jufair*'s Naval men were climbing all over the aircraft to refuel and replenish her. Moslem men in long robes and those headdresses silently watched, some from camels and white Bahrein donkeys. I saw no women this day, but many are still in *purdah*! The ruling Sheik had sent a representative to meet me who took me inside out of the unbelievable heat oozing in from the desert. There I found a stretcher for me to sleep on—but alas, again there was no time to use it—there was a record to be won, and I had to fly.

The golden curtain of the night sky overture cast its long shadows, and in the distance, the red flames of an oiling ship lit up the sultry waves of the Persian Gulf. A last military transport aircraft seemed to be almost motionless above, as it came in to land with its undercarriage and spoilers down, looking as a great illuminated eagle hovering with its claws ready for the swift dive of attack. But the little bird, *Mythre*, had already soared off the runway before it.

As though someone touched a light switch, the golden sky disappeared to suddenly become a blue-black canopy studded with crystal star brilliants over the pit of blackness that was the desert. There would be no radio interruptions now for hours. The aches of my muscles were left behind, allowing my thoughts to become clearer in the cool of the night.

My thoughts wander from Outer Space to olden times over the Saudi Arabian desert as I approach Old Testament country; on over the ancient fertile valleys of the Euphrates and Orontes rivers, once the scene of the great caravan routes of ancient Roman times carrying goods from as far afield as China, India and Persia. Somewhere to starboard in the desert of Mesopotamia, now called Iraq, had once been King Nebuchadnezzar's famous 'Hanging Gardens of Babylon', six hundred years before the birth of Christ.

Biblical Damascus was already in modern radio range, but tonight, just like olden times, the air was full of problems as the Syrian controller forbade me to fly over the tip of Jordan for fear of arousing the wrath of a military night fighter jet. My own current problems with air routes and their diversions reminded me of how so many people think, teach their religion and revere their god as something and someone still existing now exactly the same as in centuries ago, ignoring present and future development in ways of living. Nowadays, the god must be a god of the future to have sufficient influence over the world as it is now. Could it be that there once were many visitations in various parts of the earth from somewhere teaching a higher thought, who either abandoned this earth because we were, as yet, unteachable, or were forced to leave us for a stranger reason? Certainly the five major religions of the earth all denoting different teachings indicate several visitations from several different beings. All these religions are exhorting man to improve himself, and to do this he had to be given an example —a parable—to follow, as normal vocabulary is not extensive enough. Thus followed many different told stories from many men—or physical beings from another world.

It is easy to have high-minded, remote, beautiful thoughts when your surroundings are compatible, but it is obviously not enough just to meditate in isolation. One must be able to relate one's philosophies to reality and to modern conditions to make them have any valuable meaning. On the few occasions that I am able to do this, it is indeed like rediscovering that lost sense —a sense that at first is frightening because you fear that others will think you have lost, rather than gained a sense. In fact, you gain a power that enables you to smoothly move through problems to almost another layer like the smoother air higher up! Such are my thoughts when I am flying over the deserts and great oceans, and there is nothing to distract me from them.

Now below me lay a busy city—Beirut—and the Lebanon. Its garish neon lights competed with the soft glow of moonlight, and cars like glow worms crept over its winding hills. It was but a short stretch of water to the islands of Cyprus, followed by Rhodes sheltering under the craggy outlines of Turkey. I began to feel rather ill, perhaps all the more so because it was at that hour when it is neither morning nor night, the coldest time of the day, the time when everything seems blacker before the first hint of a lightening of the dark sky appears to give sign of a new day beginning. My stomach was objecting violently to this non-stop sleepless life now in its third day, making me short-tempered with the many necessary air traffic control messages of the busy network of airways leading to Europe.

As I approached the seat of the ancient philosophers, Athens, I flew over the island of Patmos, where twelve centuries before, St John in exile there heard a voice say, "What thou seest, write!" and so in a cold desolate cave the great book of Revelations was written. To port was Crete, where even as recently as 1826 miracles were reputed to happen and the fourth-century martyr, St Minias, is said to have reappeared mounted on a white charger, and to have held off alone an army of Turkish invaders from the unsuspecting Easter-day congregation worshipping in the cathedral.

Indeed, this part of the world is steeped in the Western World's history, some of it without doubt mythical, but much of it with a basis of truth. At that very moment the men of spaceship Apollo 15 were actually walking and riding on the moon above me; and might we not have dismissed this event as a myth had anyone predicted this seriously even in my early lifetime? Who would have believed the sight of the new lunar-roving vehicle being used for the first time this very night had it been sketched for us many years ago? Thousands of miles up there was my namesake, astronaut David Scott, making modern history while below him I flew a tiny unsophisticated earth-roving aircraft over the temples of the ancients! Even two hundred years ago we both would have been branded devil and witch! Time made some of the ancient beliefs appear mythical, but are they so strange any more?

Three days and nights had passed since I left my bed in the motel in Darwin almost half a world away, but days and date meant little now. Once out of the aircraft and on the ground at the modern airport of Athens, physically I was near collapse, and everything hurt again. The weather forecast was bad and I almost grabbed at the excuse to give up. I sat like a limp rag-doll on the bare stone floor while trying to analyse whether I could really get through if I tried hard enough. The cold stone gave me no encouragement. Of course I must go. What had got into me? It was still 'go' until I made London but I must fly at some lower altitudes. My endurance was at a very low level now, made worse by the inevitable dysentery of such a monster flight. I went to the rest room to try and splash myself with cold water but it was too public as dozens of gossiping women were squeezed in a small space. I bullied my lifeless limbs to walk to official office after office to sign this and that. I knew I must get back into the air fast before someone offered me the luxury of a soft seat.

Finally airborne, the authorities had already forgotten my request for a lower altitude, and no amount of argument would allow my flight plan to be changed to one below the airway in spite of the clear visibility. It was ridiculous, for the only high ground was miles away. There had been no time to refill the oxygen cylinder and the gauge indications were ominously low, not enough for the whole flight.

Somehow I struggled through the day over the toe of Italy, and on through the Mediterranean skies towards France. Now even the sun seemed to irritate me. Had there been one more leg to fly after landing in London, I doubt I could have remained airborne even long enough to get to London. The knowledge that tonight I could sleep and stretch out in a soft large bed helped me to somehow produce some extra energy to move my wretched limbs efficiently. I observed my reactions as though I were a second person. They were so slow. Now everything I did, I checked three times for safety, whether it were radio frequencies or altitude.

Other than the vitamin injection at Singapore two days before, and a continuous diet of coffee, I had used no stimulants up to now fearing the let-down that would follow such a recourse. But now, worried by my lethargic brain, I took an emergency amphetamine tablet. It seemed to have little effect on how I actually felt, and the tablet certainly did not produce a happier or more confident sensation though I no longer wanted to sleep either.

Clouds disguised Paris and the English Channel but I caught a glimpse of the 'White Cliffs' of Dover telling me I was home after circling the earth. So many times over the past few years those cliffs and London Air Traffic Control had welcomed me back. In spite of my weariness, my little enclosed cockpit gave me a feeling of security. Its windows had reflected the whole world. I knew I had been doing what I had been made for, and now I wanted to turn back—back to Paris, Athens—anywhere except the end of the flight. I wished I could just have a good sleep and then fly on again up to the Arctic, and down to the Pacific all over again.

Over Kent, southern England, the weather gave me one last dose of icing and turbulence and one of my prop de-icers failed for good measure! Someone's tyre had fallen off on the runway at London Airport, causing a landing delay. I went tiredly round and round a holding pattern over Biggin Hill beacon, wearily longing for the flight to be over. At last the record was broken. We had made it. Dear *Mythre*, in spite of her troubles, had brought me back safely, just as *Myth Too* had always done. I gave her a kiss and Piper Champagne Company drenched her as well as me with bubbling magnums. For a few minutes I felt surrounded by warmth, as an old friend, Geoffrey Edwards, had generously given a reception at the airport for my friends to greet me. Two thousand sweet people from the general public gathered on a roof to wave a warm welcome. Later, when I entered my darkened apartment and saw its avalanche of paper, it was as though the beauty of the Arctic was a figment of my imagination. Any slight pride or triumph I might have felt had gone. It was over.

The very next day I was back in my same old life trying to earn enough to pay for the fuel; the spark plugs; the unexpected repairs on a new aircraft; the mistakes in others' accounting and so on. Nobody wanted my story—I did not have any moving film to sell, the burglars had taken my video camera! I had flown full circle, it seemed, and now I was back twelve years but with no aim left. My sheer exhaustion made me forget the wonderful things—the only difference from then seemed to be that I had now reached my century—one hundred world-class records. One hundred bits of worthless cardboard—the only things not mortgaged or stolen!

But there was a bigger difference than just the cardboard pages and when I had time to think, I had no regrets about having continued with the 'impossible flight'. It was more important that I had somehow kept my word, thanks to Les, and counselling of the engineers so many months before in the darkened hangar. I had done what I wanted to do for me, and had learned a little more about the unseen influences on earth that I am sure are there. At the same time my flight had not been completely selfish. Some worthwhile experimenting had been done, although I did not know to what extent it would be used, but however remotely, it had been accomplished via the American space programme. A programme to which I longed to belong but alas I was far too old to get out there. Women will be there in the future, for Space does not bar woman, providing she can do the job as well as a man and holds a doctorate as well as the necessary flying experience.

Were it not for my age, even now I would return to a college and study for a scientific degree. But it is too late. I shall have to be satisfied with having seen the mythical stories of my childhood of the man in the moon become reality when an earthman actually sets foot on it. I remain one of the thousands of space enthusiasts clamouring for the space programme to continue for the good of all on earth, but unlike so many of them, at least I had been able to lightly touch the programme. Mine, too, had been a window on the whole earth, but still too narrow in comparison with the heavenly panorama of the astronauts. I knew at first hand just how the satellites that have helped to guide men into space could also help those countries I had flown over, and bring all men together. For when I meet people face to face, they become quite different from what I have imagined, and I like them. Imagine how many people—people who have never even heard of each other—the satellite can reach. The friendships that could be made this way by actually seeing and hearing the people of a country; the universal education; the discovery of the most fertile land; and the medical relief of diseases —to quote but a few of a satellite's advantages. By the planning and the experiments involved in sending man way out into Space, already we have found ways to produce food and oxygen in a small space. These are essential products that will be desperately needed in centuries to come, particularly if multiplying man survives his war-like impulses, for he is fast using up the earth's natural resources.

EPILOGUE

Unfinished Symphony
1972–1973

17

ONE would expect to sleep for days after not seeing a bed for four and a half days. Seven hours was all I could manage that first night, but what a sensuous joy it was to stretch my limbs the length and width of my soft downy six-by-six-foot bed. But I had forgotten how to sleep, and as the nights went by, the hours of rest got shorter and shorter. I felt ghastly, swinging from one extreme emotion to another—mere moments of feverish elation followed by long nights of forlorn retrospection. The only thing I was sure of was that, more than ever, I wanted to see the Antarctic now. So it became just as it had always been before. I was not willing to settle for my recent flight really being my last long-distance attempt and was already planning the next, though I did not know when it could be!

I still wanted to go on even though there were times when I wondered if it had been truly worth it, as I struggled to pay the sums of mortgage. But why did I have to fly to find happiness? I think it is because in the sky I am able to stretch my brain rather than my legs, and find motivation to satisfy my insatiable curiosity, to experience things myself, to be able to understand them, thus I find meaning and a sense of man's superconscious. I must fly over every horizon to see what it is like on the other side! To me there are many horizons which open up new perceptions.

Flying also gives me a spirit of adventure—which I believe is a necessary thing for future progress both individually and internationally. Soon computers will instil a great deal of knowledge into all men's mental progresses in a very short space of time, much quicker than the old fourteen to eighteen years' learning period. But unless man has individuality and some responsibility for his own actions, he will become as a computer himself, until there is nothing further to learn. Now the satellites can help the whole earth to eat, to learn more quickly and extensively, and above all, can promote earthly peace as people learn more about each other. But all of these advantages would be useless if man lost his adventuring quest for first-hand knowledge.

To me, the mere piece of paper that is my flying licence is more than a permit to fly an aircraft. It is the licence—the vehicle for me—that has led to consciousness of an energy much stronger than myself. Obviously I fly for myself, but I am learning that sometimes when one loses superficially one evolves more rapidly. I have learned too that one should do as much as one is able, and then push it a bit further. It's quite surprising how this works, and seemingly impossible things can be done.

To me, flying has been like one of my Arctic icebergs full of glittering peaks among dark submerged depths. Not merely the depths of preparation and dedication needed, but the mistakes one makes, the uncertainties and fear, all of which one must go through as a sort of springboard to the peak moments. There is no doubt that my creative energies are most pronounced after critical situations or danger, both in the air and on the ground. Undoubtedly this is due to the pure focussing—divorced from casual distractions—necessary to bring all one's energies to one point. In other words I am thinking purely—wholeheartedly—in one direction. This 'organised type of thinking' continues after the event that caused it, and it is then I get a sense of meaning—evolving.

My personal self-evolvement, my flights and what they are teaching me cannot be totally selfish for I am meeting more and more people—in other spheres of life—who think and are striving as I am. Together our experiences may only be particles towards renewed discoveries of the superconscious but I believe these are of value to man's higher development. Occasionally I just want to switch on my personal autopilot and sit back, for modern life is increasingly automatic, but then I find I am bored, negative and become self-destructive. Fortunately another unexpected idea soon arises and once I have put it into words, I am chasing again, thinking of nothing else until it's done. I must live for the idea totally, completely involved, and know that it is what I have been born for. It is always a flight path of the sky that I am following, but it is not an escape, for often it is painfully disapproved of and it would be easier not to go. It is a search, but a search neither for fame, nor riches. My flights cost far more money than I ever have!

Many of us are actively aware of an extra-sensory perception. I think people have become more aware of this in this age than in earlier times, possibly because of our rapid leap forward in scientific discoveries. Flying has heightened this for me and I know there are few coincidental happenings in my life. Once I thought I took up flying by accident but too many miraculous things have happened for them to be mere chance, and I have remained alive too many times when there was no chance. Why or how, I do not know. I still have much to study—for even now in my mid-life I still mentally feel I am only at the beginning of following a flight route, which has no charts but seems to have controllers.

There are times in my life when everything I do or say happens with another like event literally simultaneously, or within seconds. It can happen as simply as making a remark as I turn on the television set, and when the sound comes on, the voice will be almost repeating my remark. Friends have been furious with me when I finish all their sentences midway. The telephone has rung, or letters are dropped through my mail box from various parts of the earth just after I have mentioned a friend I have not spoken about nor even thought about for years. This kind of thing now happens to me so many times a day, every day, I no longer notice it. It is normality! Providing I never purposely try to make it happen. If I do—it vanishes for days, weeks. Perhaps it is nature's safeguard against misuse. Yet this awareness has always been there when I desperately needed its help.

I was undoubtedly picking up extra-sensory influences during my Polar flight for how else could I have flown right over it without any normal aids at all in, at that time, a very sickly aircraft and with little hope of even making a landfall? I am certainly not a brilliant pilot so my navigation guidance did not come from within, though the concentrated thought of those monitoring the flight in Goddard Space Centre may have accomplished it for me—or was it something even stranger? Perhaps the answer is so simple but we have lost the sense that makes us aware of it—a sort of mental wave like a radio wave.

To catch these perceptions one must be in a sensitively receptive mood. This, however, can open one's mind to many other influences too, some corroding and negative. Perhaps this is why I personally find it easier to find these perceptions associated with the sky. The sky represents complete honesty to me; it is inflexible and no man can yet change it on any vast scale—except locally. Everyone has their own special think-tank which they sometime in their life refer to. Some climb mountains, or settle in far-off lands such as the Arctic, some potter quietly thinking in their gardens and others retire to a monastery. I am obviously not a Christian in the orthodox sense because I cannot accept that any one religion contains the whole truth, nor the wars and violence religions sometimes cause—though I want to try to behave in a Christian manner. I often visit a beautiful church or temple alone, when there is no crowd of people, to be able to think and to appreciate, but the sky is more awe-inspiring than the greatest cathedral, and full of even more wondrous things.

Of course, these experiences can equally happen on the ground. Falling in love, for example, is a sort of reverberation of sound, of voice, smell, touch, all far more significant than the images the eye is reflecting to the brain. The physical act of making love to its peak can be an escape to another world. Could it not be a recapturing of a hidden primeval sense which, over the centuries, we have deliberately submerged in self-defence, and no longer know how to find? For one can get caught by the love of the wrong one—a mere temporary sexual desire—worse then than a brain-washing cage. It is then that another can get inside one's thoughts and destroy one by making one feel unsure, insecure and completely wrong in one's beliefs. At such times I become afraid to relax enough and too negative to follow my own inward maze of thoughts. Wrongly I temporarily submerge the positive wonderful moments when, fleetingly, I have met others with the same awareness of an elusive magical force—strangers I have never met before who gravitate towards me across a cocktail party and within one minute are discussing it; or others who teach me scientific facts which become deep philosophies during the conversation.

Now after my Polar flight, temporarily, or was it for ever this time, I was caught in my brick-lined cage in London. Desperately I was trying to find a solution to keeping the aircraft that had made so many things possible. *Mythre* had become another necessary extension of myself, just like *Myth Too*; I owed her much for she had flown me safely over the North Pole around the world. But beloved *Myth Too* had to be looked after as well, pending the decision between the two aircraft. So it was little single-engined *Myth Too* who lived in the warm hangar while poor *Mythre* was left out in the cold with only her poor pilot taking pride in what she had done.

There was still my dream of an adventure and South Polar filming flight to be accomplished. It was not to be chasing records though obviously I wanted to make certain aspects of it a first! It was to be an attempt to show what a world of things a little aircraft can lead one to, as well as deliberately looking for all the adventure to be found throughout South America, and the remote Pacific Islands I love so much, to contrast with Antarctica.

It was essential to retain an aircraft, as bitter experience had taught me no sponsor will produce a whole aircraft, though this time I knew there were great possibilities of some help. So even without knowing it, the decision had been made for me. It was *Mythre* that had to be retained as the single-engined Comanche was not approved for such icy conditions. The strange thing was that this very choice, long before I owned *Mythre*, had been predicted by Maurice Woodruff, the famous clairvoyant. I had not believed him, but five of the six things he predicted have come true, and all would have seemed impossible at the time. The sixth was that I would get married again quite rapidly one February to someone with a not completely English accent! He had also predicted, unknown to me until after it was planned, that a woman with the initials S.S. or S.C. would set a new world record in 1971. My full initials are S.C.S. and I flew the North Pole in 1971!

Normally I do not believe in ordinary fortune telling, but I do believe some people are able to see more clearly and as time is not definable, they are able to see future and past. We have proved the validity of present and immediate future extrasensory perception, so why not long-term forward vision? The trouble is too many have been frauds and it is often difficult to believe in any as a result.

It had become a standard joke for the gossip columns to revive yearly the news that with all my flying licences I had still managed to fail my driving test three times! This year at just the right moment, Roy Spicer, the *Sunday Mirror*'s driving correspondent, called me with the news that he had just passed his driving instructor's course and would I become his first guinea pig? I was bored and ground-logged, so why not indeed? But I was not allowed to do it the easy way. No automatic gear-change car for us. We had to do it the hard way!

Roy was the greatest fun but, nevertheless, sat ready to jump every time we turned a corner, for to me those pedals were aircraft rudders and the steering wheel an elevator as well as ailerons! Every time we went right, my foot stepped on the accelerator pedal and every time we turned left, we changed gear. I shall never forget his hypnotised look of utter surprise the day I put my foot down and we reversed at racing driver speed heading for the largest tree in sight!

The British School of Motoring, who had lent us the car, now sent their most high-powered gentlemen to join our circus, and soon the car was full of experts all discovering new and better ways to teach idiots like me. No one can ever say I did not have the best of driving education after this experience, and meanwhile, all England was being treated to my school reports! Wherever we drove, people grinned, and waited for the screech of my gear change and the sight of my kangaroo starts; some very unkind gentlemen dilly-dallied behind me trying to put me off with simply wicked winks via the rear mirror!

No manufacturer had ever offered me an aircraft during my flying career, but now the car manufacturers were vying with each other to provide me with a car. Letters and telephone calls poured in offering me cars, trucks, caravans, more free lessons and even a chance of a ride in the forthcoming tough Round Britain Car Rally.

"The country has gone crazy," I said to Roy. "I could fly all day if someone gave me an aeroplane, but I'll never make a racing driver!"

"Oh, that's not all," he replied. "Now you have been offered a motorbike if you will drive to the test in it!"

By now the cartoonists had already gone to work on my driving and I could just imagine what they would make of that idea! The evil day of the test arrived far too quickly, and I was greeted by a crowd of grinning press photographers. It was like being at a party instead of the expected funeral wake of my thwarted hopes for a licence, for the examiner was bound to fail me when he saw this lot! To my surprise, the examiner ogre was a nice friendly gentleman, who firmly forbade the men to follow and said they could do what they liked with me after it was all over! Never can anyone have been so scared and I doubt I would even have got the car started if it had not been for the patience of this kindly man. As we drew into the kerb, he laughed and said, "Well, you've passed in spite of the fact that I have never seen any woman's left leg shake so much!"

In spite of all the proffered help in other worlds, there was still none in flying, and the final day came when I knew I could not earn enough to pay the delayed payments on *Mythre* without selling the equally beloved *Myth Too*. I felt utterly disloyal to *Myth Too* for she had done so very much for me, and made me what I am today. Luckily the word went around and I did not physically have to advertise her. Various people made offers and I hated them all!

One day a couple of possible buyers arrived at the airport and I made Les show them *Myth Too*, but I followed them into her hangar and heard the soft words, "She is a beautiful aircraft!" I looked at the man with interest for he obviously loved aircraft for their own sake and not just for what they could do for him. This was Max Coote (a model aircraft distributor as well as pilot), spokesman for the Lodge Flying Group at Elstree (the airfield where I had had my first trial flying lesson). This was to be the beginning of what became a very loyal friendship, but that day I quickly walked away. The tears had almost started, for she not only was the most beautiful aircraft, she was my closest friend. Nothing but the legal trap I was now in would have made me part with her. Undoubtedly no aviator in history could have had a better aircraft, for she had flown everywhere for me except the extreme Poles. If I did not sell now she would be forcibly taken by the banks against the Aztec. I bitterly thought of the robbers of my few possessions and the movie camera. They had taken from me so much more than the things they had stolen.

It was the Lodge Flying Group's offer that I finally accepted for they allowed me to become a member of their group, and also undertook not to resell *Myth Too* without giving me or a museum the first offer. They, in fact, look after her better than I am able to afford myself, and, although I did not recognise it then, it was the happiest solution that even I could have planned! She had to be converted back to a six-seater aircraft with ferry tanks removed. I took her on a final test flight; she seemed to be reproaching me by flying superbly in perfect trim as though she were still a gay young thing, and made me feel guilty about letting her go.

At first I did not want to visit *Myth Too* at her new abode, for I thought it would hurt too much, even though I could not afford even the fuel to fly *Mythre*, the Aztec, so that she too was almost not a living thing in my mind any more. The day came when one of our usual strikes in England, transport this time, looked like preventing me from getting to one of my speaking engagements. These were paying for the past flight, so the only way to get there was in *Myth Too*. Dear Max, how I under-estimated him and his kindly relaxed manner. The sun occasion-ally danced among the clouds and like it, I realised I was happy again with someone else flying the precious *Myth Too*. Later, for he insisted on attending the all-women meeting, I found he was telling them the truth behind my flying attempts. The Lodge Flying Group somehow led me back to meeting with real friendship, the sort of pilots I had once learned to fly with and I found I was relaxed with them. *Myth Too* was still promoting happiness for me.

Life began to get busy again with lecture bookings, radio and television and even expenses-paid appearances in *Mythre*! I began to love her as we did little jobs like landing in the middle of a race course to give away the prizes, or flew smoothly up to the north of England to film in an hour instead of my usual stint of five hours there and five hours back on a shaking train. I was broke, but becoming rich in happiness again, and absolutely sure now that the 'Adventure Flight' would take place, sponsored sufficiently to enable me to make the flying film.

Then I was invited to take *Mythre* to Transpo '72 in Washing-ton, DC. British Petroleum provided the fuel, and Iceland a completely expenseless landing, to help me on my way, while I planned at long last to meet all the wonderful people who had been such a close part of my last flight, and at the same time start the preparations for the next. Already there was a possi-bility on this very trip of continuing back up to Barrow, scene of my landing after the North Pole, to do some filming for the future documentary.

After a mad scramble to get ready, I undertook to take off on the final day of the Biggin Hill Air Fair, May 21st. By chance it was the anniversaries of both Lindbergh's and Amelia Earhart's Atlantic crossings. Separately they had been the first man and first woman to cross the Atlantic. There were many surprises for me that day. The Girls' Venture Corps (would-be junior pilots) were smartly lined up guarding *Mythre* and *Myth Too*, whose new owners brought her there to see us off. Then a beautiful scale model of *Myth Too*, complete with the reproduced autographs from the world flights, was presented to me by air model champion Mick Charles.

Beside *Mythre* was the most beautiful psychedelic green Ford Capri. How thrilled I was to be given it! Me, the woman who hated cars, now longed to drive it. A year ago my engineers had refused to allow me to have a green aircraft in the hangar, but now I did not notice any lack of offers to look after my new shiny green possession in the hangar while I was away!

A few moments before take-off, Vincent Mulchrone, former fighter pilot and now aviation correspondent for the *Daily Mail*, insisted on an urgent interview. We sat in my new car while he told me Fleet Street was buzzing with the idea that I was dreading this short flight over the Atlantic more than any other in my career. As I stared up at *Mythre*, starting to answer, as though on cue, I saw a Tiger Moth fall out of the air behind her. I leaped out of the car, but was assured that it was merely part of the act (which in fact it was not, although they did not let me know as I was the next act off). I turned to Victor, and finished my remark:

"Anything that happens to me in the sky is fair enough and my life is worth losing for it if necessary, but it's the ground I fear!" Some of those words were only too quickly to come true, and very shortly, fate was taking me on, for it was the roughest flight of my career, and even the birds were not flying that day over Newfoundland. *Mythre*'s rig along with many electronics was broken and one of my ribs. However, somehow we arrived safely in Washington, even if bruised and prideless!

After Transpo, I delivered *Mythre* to the Piper aircraft factory for some much-needed cosseting, and spent my own time making glorious visits to Goddard Space Flight Centre to meet the men I knew so well and yet had never met before. It was an incredible experience for me, for almost every man told me how close to me they had felt during my fateful days over the Arctic. So it had worked for them, too, the incredible feeling of a close-knit team of people all willing the same thing. I played like a child with the incredible computers; noughts and crosses with one, but the wretched thing always won; another serenaded me with croaky voice, and yet another produced a drawing.

There followed an equally exciting visit to Patuxent River and the Naval Air Test Centre to visit Dr Crawford and Lee Field who had so splendidly arranged world communications for me. The Old Crows (electronic experts!) were convening there, too, and I found by some strange Naval metamorphosis I had become an old crow instead of the gentle English dove I had imagined myself to be!

One of the worst hurricanes in North American history was wreaking its vengeance from one end of the United States to the other. As it hit the New York area, I worriedly tried to call and get to the factory in Pennsylvania to *Mythre*, but all lines were taken over by the emergency. Everyone assured me that the storm had already passed, and in any case, the plane would have been flown out of danger. There was nothing for it but to believe them, and wait for normal communications to recommence. Meanwhile I uneasily returned to Washington, to attend a long planned party at Goddard, celebrating the anniversary date of the start of our Arctic flight with a beautiful *Mythre* cake. Television showed us the pictures of the devastation of the hurricane that night but not a hint of any devastation where the plane was. The cameras had not ventured so far up the valley. Indeed though we did not know it, my friends there were without houses, food and medical supplies until the helicopters arrived to help them out.

I actually left a meeting of a leading glossy magazine group, having captured their interest in the future flight, only to be told at the hotel that I no longer had an aircraft. The utter desolation and despair at now perhaps having lost both aircraft in one year was indescribable. I was completely helpless. I could not even get to *Mythre*. The weather eased, and Frank Marshall of the local airport, Manhasset, was able to fly me up to the Piper field. Mist, made brown by the red flood waters below, still swirled over the Appalachians and a devastating sight awaited us as we slid down alongside the hills. The happy busy little town of Lockhaven had become desolation. Broken wooden houses lay like overturned dolls' houses kicked aside by an angry child, but the child had been a fully grown Hurricane Agnes. Women and children were stooped digging up solitary possessions; muddy, stained clothes and strips of bed linen flapped in the breeze, among the piles of debris. The grey asphalt runway was a straight line of red mud, and idle puddles of evil-smelling water, carelessly left behind by Agnes now she had worked her temper to a halt, reflected the desolation of twisted metal, torn paper and debris, and great empty spaces where once living aircraft had stood.

Silently I left my friends to walk across the barren field towards a stack of grounded flying things. Momentarily the sun won its struggle with the tiresome mist, and like a great spotlight lit up a gay moth pictured on the tail of a turquoise blue aircraft. Above it shimmered two small flags, that of Great Britain and the United States. *Mythre* even then bravely beckoned me on.

"She lives—she's escaped!" I stopped, stood silently but ecstatically grateful. Her turquoise livery was stained with battle-weary stains, but we had looked worse than that on some of our flights together and a good wash-down could make her look pretty again. For many moments I stood, a kaleidoscope of all the things we had seen and done together passing through my mind, with the things we still could do. A few days before we had celebrated the anniversary of the start of one of those adventures, and although I did not remember at this moment, I later found that this, the moment I stood and watched her, was the hour and the day one year later that together we had made our first contact with earth again after flying over hundreds of miles of glittering, awe-inspiring peopleless ice— like nothing else on earth—the land of the Arctic and the North Pole. Then we had experienced in one short flight everything an earthling with wings could dream. Beauty and colour; sound and silence; peace and fear; striving to survive and yet complete acceptance if we did not; a pride that perhaps we had been the first to circumvent the top of the world on the wings of a light aircraft, coupled with a humility at the magnitude of the things we were seeing and experiencing. We had survived together against what the critics had said were irresponsible odds. Why, unless to fly on together to the ends of the earth to try and catch a little more magic and to learn.

I caught the brushwood and the rags with my hands to tear them from her aerials. The key turned easily in the lock. Long before my eyes focussed on the true horror, the indescribable smell of decay undid my dreams in a mere milli-second. With dumb numb horror I saw a red carpet of slime where once the throttles, the very heart of *Mythre*, had throbbed with powerful beats of assurance. It was as though her very lifeblood had been spilt. Time stopped.

A gentle voice said, "She's a total, Sheila," and led me to the stranger's aircraft which flew me away into the dusk leaving all my heart behind me. Why? Why? Why not together? I had no life that I wanted any part of without a *Myth*. The utter senseless irony of it. During that flight a year ago, *Mythre* had been the first light aircraft to be used in the early experiments of the new programme GRAN (Global Rescue Alarm Net), but now it seemed no one could save her.

Weeks of battling for her repair followed. I listened to the bank's demand that she be totalled and written off, and was forced to do this, for no one would advise that she would ever be safe again however thoroughly she was rebuilt. Then finally having steeled myself to do this, the assessors for the insurance company overrode us all and insisted on a rebuild, or rather a patch-up, which was the worst answer of all! Now my fight had really begun, for as far as I was concerned she had to be completely inspected down to the last nut and bolt and all electronics and engines replaced. The utter futility of one pilot trying to fight the battle alone with an ocean between me, and the banks and insurance companies almost defeated me. It was eight long weeks before I finally got her into specialists' hands, men who would rebuild her as she once was, and maybe even better.

There were times when I did not want to live, for it seemed I was to be given back a sort of a Bath-chair *Mythre*, on whom I owed thousands of dollars, and through no fault of my own I would not be able to earn them, not even by selling her, for who in England would buy a drowned aircraft? Miraculously

I found old Buck Tooth, my bedraggled rabbit, somehow caught and saved by the restraining wires of the ferry tanks (all else that was loose had floated down the Susquehanna River). Buck Tooth became a tangible thing to hold on to. It was all I had, although I again and again tried to believe that fate had let this happen for a reason. That is the way it had always been in the past—a kind of deliberate pattern but never coincidence. But it was empty this time and I could not think straight.

The little Gralyn Hotel in Washington and the kind people around me tried to help but none of them could give me a reason for wanting to live a 'ground-caught' caged life. I knew I was a hopeless person without the sky to support me. The nights were nightmares but I learned to live the days by refusing to accept a yesterday, or a tomorrow. The traffic aircraft, a Piper and its companion helicopter, seemed to make deliberate nightly patrols circling over the area where I was staying and drove me mad as their insistent lights stabbed the darkness, and their engines angrily buzzed looking for prey. Then the engine noise started to become a friendly sound encouraging me and seemed determined not to leave me alone until I started fighting again. The South Pole could still be done, and why not have faith in *Mythre* sorting out her own problems?

I started visiting the Smithsonian Museum in Washington, DC. It records the history of many a hopeless quest which became successful. One of the curators invited me to a Bald Eagles lunch, where I had to say a few words, but I could not talk too much yet about the memories and just told them simply why I had flown. G. V. Glines, aviation author, understood what I was saying and as a result of his kindly telephone call, I found myself meeting Eleanor Friede, of the Macmillan Publishing Company, and editor of Richard Bach's book, *Jonathan Livingston Seagull*—the story of a seagull who wanted to fly. Here was someone who did not need to be sold the sky. She was a pilot. Hesitantly, I handed over my sheaf of papers which vaguely resembled a skeleton book. Within eight days it had been accepted.

Back to England to sort out *Mythre*'s problems. First my English publishers, Hodder and Stoughton, accepted this manuscript too. I could eat. But as fast as this was settled, *Mythre* was in trouble again. The mortgage bank called a halt to their agreement, and insisted on *Mythre* being totalled even though she was partly mended. For me it was too late—I had seen her start to live again. I refused to be a party to re-killing her off, even if it meant I could not own her in the future. It was up to me to do my utmost to see she flew safely again. She had not let me down when I nearly lost out over the Pole. As I finish this manuscript *Mythre* and I are still together but belonging to each other only and to no one else—as yet both in a hundred bits—but cleaner bits—*Mythre*'s across a hangar floor. Somehow *Mythre*'s bits will be put together again, and she will fly safely again. After all, I have met all my aircraft for the first time in pieces on a hangar floor and watched them grow into flying things. All three must fly, even though I may not have the chance again.

Perhaps I may have to start my life all over again, and maybe do it right next time! It is what I believe in anyway. That there are different levels of existence, and even if one goes back it is never quite to the same level. It could be to a higher or a lower layer.

Now, as I wait for *Mythre*'s wings to mend, I see the sky as a universe of mirrors reflecting good enough memories still to lead me on, even if it is not physically in the sky as we see it.

I have now known in a small way what it is to be alone—seemingly completely alone in the accepted sense—in my aircraft hundreds of miles from sight of human eyes, or sound of human voice. I had to discover for myself what this was like, but in fact by doing this very thing I learnt it was but an infinitesimal part of understanding. Previously I had been fighting mythical giants and devils, but I had always used the same vehicle—my aircraft. But even the aircraft itself is subject to many influences which in turn influence me, and so however dedicated, and even by using the same vehicle to learn more about your personal aims, you can be greatly misled.

I am just beginning to understand that there can be many other areas and vehicles in oneself. One can always go on discovering more and it possibly requires far more discipline and courage to do it in this more simple way. Discipline to prevent your imagination going wild and to stick to the aims you have set yourself; courage is required in all kinds of ways, sometimes even in homely ways such as when and whether you should be leaving your room or deserting your studies to please others, or equally whether in reality you are learning from these associations too, or whether your mutual negative emotions make both you and them worse. It requires courage to keep yourself on the accepted sane path, for if you let your imagination run wild, insanity will be said to have crept in. I do not believe that those who recognise and are truly striving to understand inexplicable chances and happenings are peculiar. For thousands of years there has been evidence both in man and animal that there is much to discover from a sort of 'mental commuting'—though it is not quite as simple as this—for it is in reality around us as well as in the mind.

Here in my room, sometimes all is clear and happy just as it was in the sky, but much of my time here too is like being 'on instruments' as in the aircraft. My brain and body work to read the instruments of everyday life and follow their directions from books, people, events and so on. Just like the pilot, somehow, I struggle through, and find a landfall, though not necessarily the piece of land that I was aiming for, nevertheless smooth enough to get down on and often find an unexpected experience—and so I refuel and take off once again to continue with my quest.

APPENDICES

APPENDIX I

Afterword by Dr Philip K. Chapman, former astronaut

In 1970, I went to the annual convention of the Ninety-Nines in White Mountains, New Hampshire, to give a talk as a representative of NASA. It was an interesting meeting, although I naturally found myself having to explain why there are no female astronauts in the US Space Programme, a difficult task because I fully agreed that there is no reason why women should not play an equal part with men in Space. I was particularly delighted at the opportunity to meet Sheila Scott, whose name was of course quite familiar to me, as it is to pilots everywhere, and I was impressed to find that this graceful and very feminine blonde had just flown in for the meeting from Fiji, in her Piper Comanche, *Myth Too*.

A week later, Sheila was in Houston, and spent a few days with us at our house near the Manned Spacecraft Centre. My wife Pam and I both come from families which have been involved in aviation in Australia since the pioneering days, so it is not surprising that we found we had a great deal in common. I remember sitting by the pool one night in a long rambling happy discussion of flying and philosophy, listening to the incredible tale of Sheila's adventures earlier that year in the great London-to-Sydney air race which was held in commemoration of the bi-centenary of the discovery of New South Wales by James Cook. This was particularly interesting to me because Rusty Schweickart and I had tried hard to enter this race (in a LearJet), until we were finally refused permission by NASA on the grounds that it was an unnecessary hazard for two astronauts to undertake.

Sheila also told us that night of her plans to fly over the North Pole. Having had some experience of flying under Arctic conditions (in Antarctica, during the International Geophysical Year), I must admit that I had doubts about the project—I was particularly concerned about the difficulty of search and rescue, of finding her if she were forced down. I was not then fully aware of her remarkable tenacity in pursuit of her goals.

At the time that Sheila was preparing for her Polar flight, I was working as Mission Scientist for Apollo 14, and I invited Sheila to the launch at Cape Kennedy, in January 1971. She made many friends there, among NASA people as well as the other Space enthusiasts who congregate at the Cape for every manned launch, and it was there that the suggestion arose that the Nimbus weather satellite could be used to track Sheila over the Pole. I believe this idea was originally due to Dick Hoagland, who was then with CBS.

Once it became clear that it would be possible to get a position fix on Sheila's aeroplane during every Nimbus pass (every ninety minutes in the Arctic, and less frequently at lower latitudes), my reservations about her flight vanished, and I became an enthusiastic supporter. During that spring, however, I was deeply involved in collating the scientific results of Apollo 14, and so had to remain only a peripheral participant in the preparations for her flight. I did arrange to borrow an Apollo biomedical harness to telemeter her pulse, respiration and heartbeat back to the Nimbus Ground Station at Goddard Space Flight Centre in Maryland, each time the satellite interrogated the IRLS transponder aboard her aeroplane, so as to keep track of her physiological condition. When it turned out that the output from the Apollo harness could not be made compatible with the IRLS telemetry format, these data were eventually recorded on tape aboard her aircraft, to allow later evaluation of how she responded to the stresses of the flight.

The first six months of 1971 were not an easy time for Sheila and I remain amazed that she managed to get ready in time, before the Arctic summer was over. Given the difficulties she met, most people would have abandoned the project, but she just kept going, overcoming failures of people and equipment only because of her remarkable will to succeed. Finally the day came when she was off the ground at Nairobi, and I went up to Goddard to be on hand during the Arctic leg.

All the credit for the successful use of the Nimbus satellite to track Sheila's lonely little aeroplane across the Arctic Ocean must go to the dedicated NASA people at Goddard, and to the equally dedicated people at General Instrument on Long Island, New York, who manufactured the IRLS equipment and installed it in the aircraft. I was there because I was fascinated with what Sheila was doing, because I was a pilot with personal experience of the sort of weather she might encounter, and because, as an astronaut, I could probably get quicker access than most to the necessary people if anything should go wrong.

Those long days and nights at Goddard were some of the most memorable experiences of my life. From the first IRLS fix, which happened to come during her take-off roll in Norway (as we could tell because we had a read-out of her altitude and airspeed), the 'Goddard Gang' rode with her every mile of the way. About three hours out, it became clear that she was not making her expected groundspeed, and that she was also veering off course to the west. We tried to get in radio contact with her by every means available (including asking a Pan American pilot over the North Atlantic to act as a relay), but to no avail. It was soon apparent that she would have insufficient fuel to reach Alaska, so we started broadcasting in the blind, advising her to make for Nord, in northern Greenland. We were very relieved when the fixes showed that she was heading north along the Greenland coast, although we found later that she had not received our messages and had wisely decided on her own to go to Nord.

Once she was safely on the ground at that Danish weather station, our next problem was to get through to her, to find out what had gone wrong. Communications throughout the Arctic happened to be very poor at the time, but we finally established a teletype link with Thule Air Force Base in Greenland, and the Thule operator could get through to Nord intermittently, in Morse. By this means, we learned of the trouble she had had with the aeroplane, and we started feeding her information about how to correct the problems, obtained from the Piper plant in Pennsylvania, as well as weather forecasts and other flight planning data.

The navigational problem faced by Sheila at Nord was much more difficult than in her original plan of flying directly across the Pole, from Norway to Alaska. The navigation equipment available to her was rudimentary, consisting only of a sun compass and a directional gyro, an instrument which can be relied on for a heading only for short periods without an update, because of its inherent drift. The flight plan was necessarily based on dead reckoning, which is notoriously unreliable even under normal circumstances, where a fix may usually be had occasionally from recognisable landmarks and where, in any case, an estimate of groundspeed may be obtained from watching terrain features go by. Even over the open ocean, at lower latitudes a magnetic compass may be used for heading and wind speed and direction may be estimated from observing wavetops. The Arctic Ocean is a featureless waste of ice and snow, with no islands nor anything else which can be charted, and a magnetic compass is naturally useless, so close to the magnetic pole. If Sheila found herself under cloud cover, she would not be able to use her sun compass, and there would probably be too little contrast in the snow features below even to estimate drift and groundspeed: the probability of a fine day was decreasing steadily with every day she spent at Nord, as the short northern summer waned, and the available weather forecasts for her route were known to be inaccurate, because there are few weather stations in the Arctic. Furthermore, it would no longer suffice merely to maintain a good heading, as she would have to fly up to the Pole and make almost a ninety-degree left-turn there, on course for Alaska. With no good way to determine groundspeed, it would not be easy for her to estimate when she was over the Pole, and an error there could place her many miles off her desired track at her destination. At Goddard, we would know where she was every forty minutes, but the satellite system was not designed to give her a readout of position in the cockpit, and there was little expectation that communications would improve enough for us to help her in real time.

Faced with these problems, there was some talk of persuading Sheila to abandon the attempt, but those of us who knew her were well aware that nothing would make her quit while there was any reasonable chance of success, so we just gave her the best information and advice we could and wished her Godspeed. The first few IRLS fixes after she was airborne showed that she was making a surprising good track due north for the Pole, although again at a lower groundspeed than was desirable. We were receiving no communications from her, but Lee Field had arranged for us to have the use of the US Navy transmitter at Patuxent River, Md, which is the most powerful in the world, so that we had some hope that she could hear us. When we estimated from the fixes that she was over the Pole, we took it in turns to broadcast congratulations to her and advised her to turn immediately for Alaska. The next fix, about an hour after Pole passage, showed that she had turned, although she seemed somewhat off course, an impression which was confirmed by the next Nimbus pass: she was heading down a meridian of longitude which was about thirty degrees away from the one which passes through her destination, Point Barrow. Fortunately, the error was to the east, so that she was heading for Canada, not Siberia.

We did not know, of course, that our fears had come true, that she was under an overcast, and hence was reduced to her directional gyro as her only navigational instrument, nor that she was again having trouble with the hydraulic systems in her aeroplane, so that her landing gear would not retract fully and she could not maintain her design airspeed. We kept calculating and broadcasting heading corrections designed to bring her to Point Barrow, but the IRLS fixes showed her steady on course for Canada, so we had to assume she could not hear us. To confirm this, we asked her deliberately to fail the mental acuity test on the next Nimbus pass, but she turned in her usual fine performance, so we started looking for landing fields in northern Canada too. The fixes of course gave us a very good indication of where she would cross the Alaskan coast, so we phoned the nearest Dewline radar station, at Barter Island, asked the duty officer there to watch for her on radar and gave him her operating frequencies so that he could contact her. There is a gravel landing strip at Barter Island, but it is short and was snow-covered, and the weather there was approaching minimums in blowing snow.

There was nothing more that we could do, except wait. Barter Island informed us that she had circled there and then elected to fly along the coast to Point Barrow, six hundred miles and some four hours away. It was not until we talked to her after she had landed there that we found that this was not just because of the weather conditions, but because her hydraulic system problems prevented a safe down-and-locked indication from her landing gear. After all the troubles she had encountered and the stresses of the flight, this last leg must have been particularly nerve-wracking, culminating in a dramatic landing at Point Barrow, with the runway foamed and the crash trucks out. It was a delight to hear her voice, although she naturally sounded exhausted, and after we had talked to her we sat around at Goddard, looking at each other, too relieved even to celebrate, just very thankful that we had not had to fulfil our principal function, that of telling search-and-rescue where she was if she had been forced down.

There was one other result of that time at Goddard which is worth noting. Before I went there, Dave Scott had asked me if I could suggest some simple little experiment which he could carry out on the Moon during Apollo 15, something which would be understandable by high-school science students and which would demonstrate the unique characteristics of the lunar environment. I discussed this with Dick Hoagland late one night, while we were waiting to get in touch with Sheila at Nord, and the outcome of that conversation was the Galileo experiment which Dave tried just before the end of his last excursion on the lunar surface, dropping a falcon's feather and a hammer together to show that all objects fall with the same acceleration in a gravitational field. The television record of this experiment is now the most convincing demonstration available for science students of this fundamental property of gravitation.

After the Piper agency in Fairbanks, Alaska, had repaired *Mythre*, Sheila flew down to San Francisco. I went out there to meet her in a NASA T-38, and saw her off on the next leg of her epic journey, across the Pacific to Australia and back to London. After the Arctic, those flights, which were impressive feats of endurance and navigational skill, must have seemed almost routine: they certainly did not get the publicity they deserved.

Philip K. Chapman

INTERROGATION, RECORDING AND LOCATION SYSTEM (IRLS)

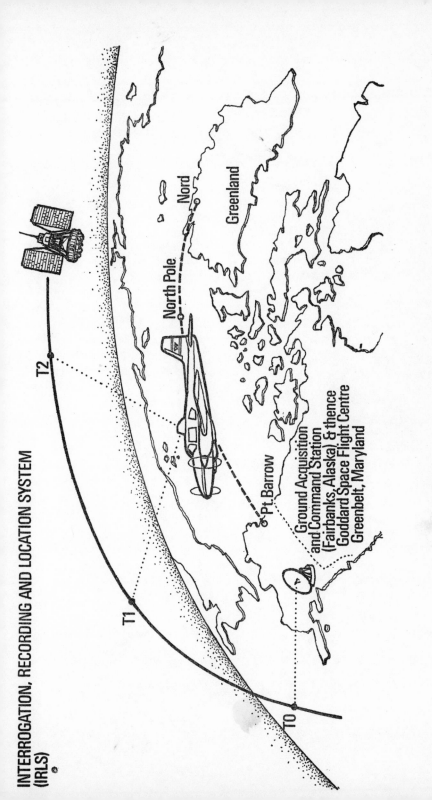

North Pole

Nord

Greenland

Pt. Barrow

Ground Acquisition
and Command Station
(Fairbanks, Alaska) & thence
Goddard Space Flight Centre
Greenbelt, Maryland

T2

T1

T0

APPENDIX II

National Aeronautics and Space Administration with Institute of Aviation Medicine Teams

NASA Headquarters, Washington, DC

Bruton B. Schardt, Nimbus Programme Manager
George Tennyson, Nimbus Programme Manager

Goddard Space Flight Centre, Maryland

Charles Cote, IRLS Project Manager
Len Roach, IRLS Technical Manager
Gene Gilbert, IRLS Electronic Technician
Phil Chapman, Astronaut
Ralph Shapiro, NASA Manager Nimbus Ground Station
Dick Ormsby, NASA Assistant Manager Nimbus Ground Station
Ben Palmer, General Electric Operations Manager, Nimbus Ground Station
Jack Effner, IRLS Operations Planner
Bill Seechuk, IRLS Operations Planner
Ed Eisle, NASA Manager of Fairbanks Stadun Station

General Instrument Corporation

Ernest La Froscia, Liaison Project Director with Goddard
Kent Martin, Special Engineer
Walter Gabso, Engineering Associate
Joel Morris, Design Engineer—inventor (Mental Acuity Box)

Naval Air Test Centre, Patuxent River

Cd W. R. Crawford, MC USN Head of Aero Medical Branch
Leroy Field, Communications Specialist

Scama Facilities, UK

Larry de Hayes, Manager

UK GPO Staff
Dr James Williamson, Clarendon Laboratories, Oxford

Institute of Aviation Medicine
Group Captain Peter Whittingham
Dr Wadham

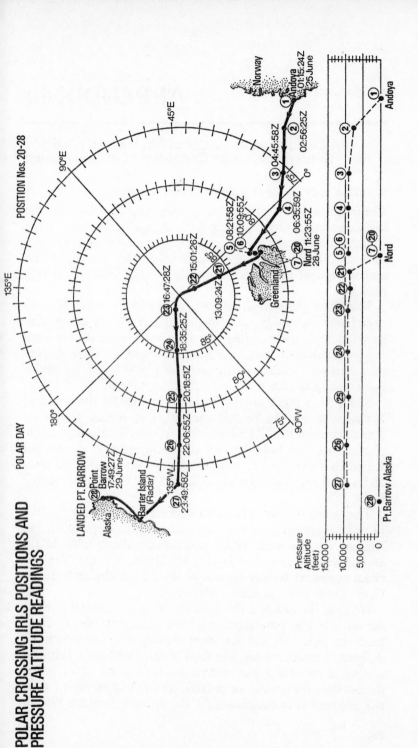

POLAR CROSSING IRLS POSITIONS AND
PRESSURE ALTITUDE READINGS

APPENDIX III

An Explanation of the use of Nimbus and IRLS and
General Instrument Corporation Equipment used

I. SHEILA SCOTT GLOBAL MISSION USE OF NIMBUS IRLS

The frequent periodic collection of scientific data relative to the surface and near surface conditions of the earth is essential to the scientific community. A Polar-orbiting earth-oriented satellite such as NASA's Nimbus is well suited for the collection and storage of data from remotely located fixed or mobile stations.

The IRLS (Interrogation Recording and Location System) experiment was designed to collect location data along with geophysical, meteorological and other experimental data from remote-manned or unmanned stations. Its ranging system permits accurate location of instrumented platforms by triangulation techniques after two successful interrogations.

Miss Scott's flight provided an opportunity for the National Aeronautics and Space Administration to obtain additional data to confirm the IRLS capability with an interesting mobile platform location test. Through the co-operation of the United Kingdom Government, NASA loaned Miss Scott a Nimbus IRLS Balloon Interrogation Package (BIP) for her global flight.

The elements comprising the IRLS experiment were the BIP (a small electronics package weighing about ten pounds), the Nimbus satellite with IRLS experiment, the Nimbus/IRLS ground station located at Fairbanks, Alaska, and the Nimbus/IRLS computer facility located at the NASA Goddard Space Flight Centre, in Greenbelt, Maryland.

When in the range of the specially equipped ground stations the satellite was programmed by the ground station to communicate with selected platforms during the next orbits. At designated times the satellite then interrogated each platform and stored the data. Upon returning to the ground station locale the satellite, on ground command, transmitted its stored data and received new commands for the upcoming orbits. Within one to five hours after interrogation of the Scott BIP system, the data was available at Goddard.

NASA Release

2. BACKGROUND ON GENERAL INSTRUMENT CORPORATION EQUIPMENT FOR NASA ABOARD SHEILA SCOTT'S AIRCRAFT

The BIP or Balloon Interrogation Package is a self-contained receiver, transmitter and digital processing system which was developed for NASA by the General Instrument Corporation. Electronic Systems Division (GI/ESD) located in New York State, USA. Under NASA supervision GI/ESD modified the original BIP equipment and designed additional equipment for Miss Scott's flight.

The sequence of operation that occurred in the BIP equipment located aboard the aircraft is briefly described below. At the time programmed by the computers, the satellite transmitter was turned on and transmitted a unique code which only the BIP equipment located in the aircraft was able to decode. The BIP equipment received this transmission and relayed it back to the satellite. After approximately one second, the satellite transmitted a second unique code which commanded the BIP equipment to encode and transmit all data to the satellite. This ended the interrogation sequence which normally lasted for a long period of less than two seconds. The table below lists the data that was transmitted from the BIP equipment to the satellite.

3. BIP DATA

1. Battery Voltages.
2. Equipment Temperature.
3. Aircraft Altitude.
4. Atmosphere sulphur-dioxide content.
5. Mental response time.
6. Location information (Goddard computers processed this information in order to determine latitude and longitude).

The modifications of the BIP equipment for Miss Scott's flight were:

Redesign of the original antenna for this aircraft application. Also included was the design of a minimum drag radome for the antenna.

NIMBUS 4/IRLS LOCATION PLOTS

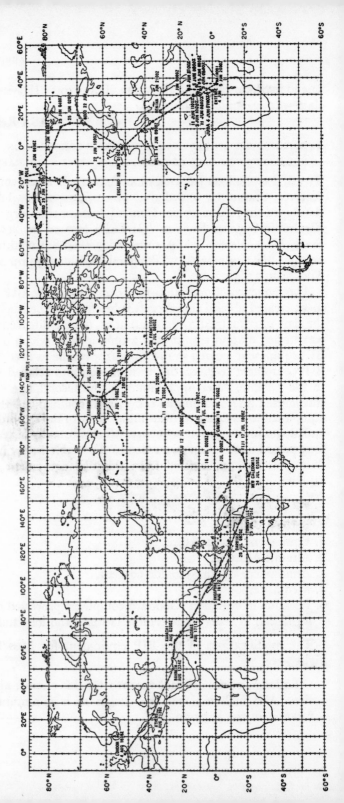

A light in the aircraft cockpit indicated that a successful interrogation had been performed. A special data switch for use by the pilot under special conditions. The incorporation of sensor manufactured by a USA firm, Theta Sensors, Inc, to measure the sulphur-dioxide (SO_2) content of the atmosphere at flight altitudes. Since SO_2 is one of the main byproducts of fossil fuel combustions a profile of SO_2 around the world could be obtained. A pressure transducer was included to give an indication of flight altitude. Battery charging circuiting to maintain the batteries in a charged state throughout the flight. A mental acuity 'busy box' was also included to indicate the pilot's mental state. This equipment encoded the time necessary to perform a specific task. This data was most useful during the long positions of flight.

Sheila Scott flying her Piper Aztec *Mythre* in which she became the first woman in the world to fly solo over the Arctic Ocean and True North Pole 1971. The large extra antennae was part of the IRLS packet which collected the positioning and environmental data transmitted via the satellite Nimbus to Goddard Space Centre, USA.

APPENDIX IV

The Theta Sensor Air Pollution Experiment

THE airborne ambient sulphur-dioxide monitor is an unmanned remote sensing system which provides a voltage proportional to the concentration of sulphur dioxide in the air sample introduced into the system. The three-pound 6″ × 9″ × 5″ box was shock-mounted and served in the only available space left in the cabin—between the pilot's legs!

The output of the black box was telemetered to the Nimbus satellite and then to NASA, Goddard. The unit was chosen because it was small enough and could operate untended for the duration of the flight.

The airborne monitoring unit was developed at Theta Sensors, Inc, Orange, California, by Dr Arnold Miller, Lawrence Winlund and William Conner. It was calibrated using the facilities of the California Air Resources Board Laboratory in Los Angeles. The system is specific for sulphur dioxide.

The operation of the sensor was in the double-blind mode. That is, Sheila did not know the output results of the Theta Sensor—only the ground crew at NASA knew the real-time results. Sheila did record unusual events and times, which we then compared with the pollution data. Hence—burning of stubble in a field, prior to planting, was detected over Nairobi, Kenya. In a sandstorm over Liberia, the burning of sour gas in the wells a hundred miles away was picked up. A forest fire over Fairbanks, Alaska, resulted in high sulphur-dioxide pick-up. Over the Pacific and related places, no sulphur-dioxide pollution was observed.

The most exciting result was the large band of sulphur-dioxide pollution observed over the North Pole. Subsequent to this report, a verification was received from T. J. Henderson of Atmospherics, Incorporated, that a persistent pollutant band had been observed in polar flights using optical means. The pollution measurement is real and is global. Tracking sulphur dioxide was an important quantity on the flight of the *Mythre*. It is one of the chief pollutants from the burning of fossil fuels—coal, oil and wood. Electrical generating plants all produce the pollutant. As the underdeveloped countries expand their power-producing capacity—the sulphur-dioxide pollution levels rise. The question of what happens to these sources of pollution—how it spreads and concentrates over the earth—is important for future control.

From the results of Sheila's flight, Theta Sensors developed several new airborne pollution sensors which were subsequently used by Professor James N. Pitts of the University of California Statewide Air Pollution Research Centre. Bands of very high atmospheric pollution were found over San Francisco, Los Angeles, Long Beach, etc. This verified the stratified layer-like concentrations of pollutants in many areas—at levels much higher than observed on the ground.

Sheila and *Mythre* made a real contribution to the understanding of global pollution.

> Arnold Miller,
> President,
> Theta Sensors, Inc, California

APPENDIX V

The US Naval Air Test Centre's GRAN Experiment

FEW persons in the USA knew Sheila prior to her North Pole Flight in GAYTO. However, in a matter of minutes from her actual Norway take-off the entire US Navy fell in love with Sheila Scott. The Navy orders were simple: "Don't lose Sheila." We tracked her via satellite plotting her course and speed. From her emergency landing on ice, she was off again for the North Pole. Never would this great lady quit and initiate the 'MAYDAY' panic button for help.

Leroy Field,
Communications Specialist,
Naval Air Test Centre,
Patuxent River,
USA.

GLOBAL RESCUE ALARM NET

The Global Rescue Alarm Net (GRAN) was conceived by the Aero Medical Branch, Service Test Division of the Naval Air Test Centre, as a system to save lives by minimising the time interval between the occurrence of a mishap and the initiation of rescue efforts. This system will utilise satellite relay to monitoring ground stations of survivor's distress signals and Omega navigation signals received, and retransmitted by the survivor's transceiver. The GRAN tests were conducted by the Naval Air Test Centre using National Aeronautics and Space Administration (NASA) Omega Position Locating Equipment (OPLE) modified for UHF operation. Satellite relay was accomplished through TACSAT I to a ground station located in Dallas, Texas. The distress sequence consisted of 16 sec of Acquisition and Reference (A/R) carrier followed by 180 sec of Omega signal retransmission. The A/R segment serves as an emergency alarm, and identifies the party or vehicle. The Omega retransmission segment provides localisation information. Reliable satellite relay was accomplished at 0·5 to 1·0 watt ERP during the Omega relay segment when a 4·0 watt, 16 sec A/R alarm was used. Within a 72 nmi Omega lane average localisation errors were 9·5 nmi. Localisation tests utilising the Differential Omega technique showed greatly improved localisation accuracy, i.e. errors of less than 1000 ft were achieved. Satellite relay performance was not degraded until the satellite was lower than three degrees above the horizon. Three satellites will provide continuous coverage of most of the temperature and all tropical zones of the world.

The unique features of GRAN include:

Worldwide, immediate distress incident alert by travellers anywhere in the world utilising satellite relay of alarm signals.

Localisation of personnel in distress with an accuracy of ±1000 ft by analysis of Omega navigation signal relayed to the satellite by the distressed party.

'Rescue Central' knows the exact location of the mishap within three minutes and can vector the nearest rescue vehicle directly to the site in minimum time.

Only one three-minute radio transmission is required.

No voice transmission is required, hence no language barrier is imposed.

The line-of-sight limitations are eliminated.

Civilian as well as military users are foreseen without conflict.

Tests are continuing to develop the concept, establish system parameters and define hardware requirements. Sheila Scott's North Polar Flight was used as one of GRAN's tests. The satellite relay was accomplished through Nimbus to the ground stations in Fairbanks, Alaska, and Goddard, Greenbelt.

APPENDIX VI

Sleep patterns in a lone global pilot
By F. S. Preston, VRD, MB, ChB, DA, AFRAoS and
D. J. Cussen, MA, MD, BCh from the Institute of
Sports Medicine, Ling House, Nottingham Place,
London, W1M 4AX, England

In recent years interest has been focussed on the problems of flying across time zones, particularly in the effect this has on disturbing sleep. In addition, a great deal of attention has been paid to the amount of sleep disruption produced in orbital space missions and more recently in extra-terrestrial and lunar exploration flight. All these studies have concerned themselves with operations involving highly trained crews and planned work/rest periods which enabled the individual crew members to remain at peak efficiency during duty.

One of the authors (FSP) had been involved in the study of sleep disruption in airline pilots and had, in association with Nicholson of the RAF Institute of Aviation Medicine at Farnborough, developed a sleep diary for use by crew members in commercial operations. This method of assessment had already been used by Nicholson in previous studies in BOAC and in the Royal Air Force.

In 1971, Miss Sheila Scott, the British aviatrix, planned a record-breaking solo trip round the world in a Piper Aztec twin-engined aircraft, *Mythre*.

While Miss Scott was planning this epic flight, it was suggested by the Institute of Sports Medicine that a careful record of sleep and duty times should be recorded, and this was readily agreed. She was also asked to make a daily entry—noting the times when in bed and asleep—when sleep ceased—getting up—on duty and off duty, and particularly recording time-zone changes and any associated untoward events. In addition to this a subjective record of fatigue and well-being on going to bed and rising, on a visual analogue scale for subsequent analysis was considered of some importance. This method was first used by Gedye and then by Zeally and Aitken at the University of Edinburgh for the measurement of mood in

JUNE

	G.M.T (Z)
DATE 28th & 29th	
WOKE (LOCAL TIME NORD SAME AS GMT) JUNE 28th	06.50
EST. DURATION OF SLEEP	05.00
GOT UP • PREFLIGHT DUTIES STARTED 0715 TILL	07.00
ON DUTY (FLYING) A.T.D	11.23
OFF DUTY LOCAL TIME BARROW 1749	04.49
IN BED (28 hours later)	11.00
ASLEEP JUNE 29th	12.00

LANDING GEAR PROBLEMS PRIOR LANDING BARROW

TIME ZONE CHANGE = 0 at Nord
13t at Barrow

SECTOR FLOWN: NORD/NORTH POLE / BARROW (ALASKA)

TIRED — FRESH

ON GETTING UP •

ON GOING TO BED †

FRESH — TIRED

A page from Sheila's sleep diary

psychiatry. As such a method of measurement was valid and significant in psychiatry, it was considered suitable for this type of study. A typical page of a sleep diary is reproduced on page 259.

In addition to the study on sleep, Miss Scott was required to carry out during the flight a series of mental acuity tasks designed for her by the General Instruments Corporation using the Polar-orbiting earth-orientated satellite, Nimbus, which had been positioned by the National Aeronautic and Space Administration in the North Polar area. Nimbus was well suited for the collection and storage of data from remotely located fixed or mobile stations. The IRLS (Interrogation Recording and Location System) was designed to collect location data along with geophysical, meteorological and other experimental data from remote-manned or unmanned stations. In addition, by triangulation techniques it provided accurate location information.

Miss Scott's aircraft *Mythre* was fitted with a small electronics package weighing about ten pounds, including a special antenna which transmitted the data through the Nimbus/IRLS ground station located at Fairbanks, Alaska, and the Nimbus/IRLS computer facility located at the NASA Goddard Space Flight Centre at Greenbelt, Maryland.

She was not in voice contact with this system and although the satellite knew her position, she did not while airborne depart from basic dead-reckoning navigation using astro compass and basic direction indicator.

THE FLIGHT

It was planned to start the flight from Nairobi, just south of the Equator flying from there to London, thence to Bodo and Andöy in Northern Norway, across the Arctic Ocean to Nord in Northern Greenland, over the True North Pole to Barrow in Northern Alaska, and on to Fairbanks, Anchorage and San Francisco.

From San Francisco, the flight carried on to Honolulu, Canton Island, Fiji to Townsville in Northern Queensland, thence to Darwin across Indonesia to Singapore. The final phase of the flight took Miss Scott from Singapore across the Indian Ocean to Madras, Karachi, Bahrein, Athens and finally to London. This latter covered the phenomenal distance of 9000 miles and was flown in two and a half days—truly super-human effort as will be seen from the ensuing sleep records she has kept of the journey.

Miss Scott is apparently a natural sleeper and very rarely needs hypnotics to achieve sleep; usually she was so tired that sleep came when the moment presented itself. However, on occasions it was necessary to take a tablet of Mogadon (Nitraze-pam). This is one of the better short-acting hypnotics in that it is fairly rapidly excreted but it is known to produce deficits in response time and inaccuracies in matching visual stimuli. As far as analeptic drugs were concerned, she relied largely on strong coffee and cigarettes and only once resorted to a tablet of Dexedrine on the final stages between Athens and London, an action which she deeply regretted because of the side-effects and inability to achieve immediate sleep on return to London.

SLEEP ACHIEVED DURING TRIP

Table I details the flight as it occurred and includes the hours slept in each twenty-four hours, sleep lost on seven and a half hours (Miss Scott's average sleep at home), cumulative sleep loss, sector flight time and remarks concerning each sector. For simplicity, we have ignored the positioning flight from London out to Nairobi and have only recorded data from Nairobi which was the start of the main record-breaking flight. At this stage, she was already in sleep debt due to the preparation for the flight and positioning the aircraft out to Nairobi from whence she departed on June 11th, being thirty-one hours in sleep debt at that time. We have included this figure in our subsequent calculations (see p. 264).

DISCUSSION

The sheer immensity of the task undertaken by Miss Scott in the flight described above and the resultant total sleep loss in-curred leaves us full of admiration for people of her calibre. Unlike the airline pilot who is carefully cosseted by ground crews wherever he flies and has all the routine of flight planning and meteorology removed from his shoulders, the lone record-breaking pilot has to carry out these duties on his or her own, in addition to supervising refuelling and daily maintenance on the

TABLE I

Date	Day	Hours sleep in 24	Sleep lost (on 7·5 hrs)	Cumulative sleep loss	Flight time	Sector flown and remarks
11/6	1	1·0	6·5	31·0	10·15	Nairobi–Khartoum. Paper formalities delayed T/O due a/c overweight
12/6	2	7·0	0·5	31·5	5·40	Returned Khartoum. Engine trouble. 3 hrs dumping fuel. Khartoum–Benghazi
13/6	3	0	7·5	39·0	3·00	Benghazi–Malta
14/6	4	7·0	0·5	39·5		Crosswinds Malta. Remained Malta weather and other problems
15/6	5	3·5	4·0	43·5	8·00	Malta–Marseilles
16/6	6	7·0	0·5	44·0	5·00	Marseilles–London. Found flat burgled and personal treasures stolen!
17/6	7	6·0	1·5	45·5		⎫ London domestic and aircraft problems occupying long hours of duty
18/6	8	6·0	1·5	47·0		⎬
19/6	9	6·0	1·5	48·5		⎪
20/6	10	6·0	1·5	50·0		⎭
21/6	11	5·5	2·0	52·0		Take-off postponed due thunderstorm activity. Paper work and press interviews
22/6	12	5·5	2·0	54·0	10·30	London–Bodo. Midnight sun and telephone calls disturbed sleep
23/6	13	6·0	1·5	55·5		Bodo—fogged in. Did not fly
24/6	14	7·0	0·5	56·0	1·25	Bodo–Andöy
25/6	15	2·0	5·5	61·5	11·15	Andöy–Nord. Sun all night. Sleep disturbed
26/6	16	10·0	−2·5	59·0		⎫ 24 hrs sunlight. Working on a/c, and trying to make communications. Woken at 0200 (28/6)
27/6	17	6·25	1·25	60·25		⎬
28/6	18	5·0	2·5	62·75	17·00	Nord–North Pole–Barrow
29/6	19	8·0	−0·5	62·25		Barrow. Undercarriage troubles prior landing Barrow
30/6	20	6·0	1·5	63·75	2·30	On ground Barrow, and Barrow–Fairbanks
1/7	21	7·0	0·5	64·25	2·15	Fairbanks–Anchorage
2/7	22	9·0	−1·5	62·75		On ground Anchorage
3/7	23	4·25	3·25	66·0	14·30	Anchorage–San Francisco
4/7	24	7·0	0·5	66·5		⎫
5/7	25	7·0	0·5	67·0		⎪
6/7	26	7·0	0·5	67·5		⎬ Remained at San Francisco. Aircraft repairs, awaiting spare, and dealing with press
7/7	27	7·0	0·5	68·0		⎪
8/7	28	7·0	0·5	68·5		⎪
9/7	29	7·0	0·5	69·0		⎪
10/7	30	7·0	0·5	69·5		⎭

TABLE I (*continued*)

Date	Day	Hours sleep in 24	Sleep lost (on 7·5 hrs)	Cumula- tive sleep loss	Flight time	Sector flown and remarks
11/7	31	7·0	0·5	70·0 }	15·30	} San Francisco–Honolulu
12/7	32	7·0	0·5	70·5 }		
13/7	33	7·0	0·5	71·0		} Honolulu—TV and press
14/7	34	7·0	0·5	71·5		} receptions
15/7	35	0	7·5	79·0	13·20	Honolulu–Canton Isle
16/7	36	6·5	1·0	80·0 }	7·15	} Canton Isle–Fiji. ETA
17/7	37	8·0	−0·5	79·5 }		} Fiji 0700 (17/7). Crossed International Date Line
18·7	38	8·0	−0·5	79·0		
19/7	39	8·0	−0·5	78·5		Remained Fiji awaiting
20/7	40	8·0	−0·5	78·0		} aircraft spares from
21/7	41	8·0	−0·5	77·5		Australia
22/7	42	8·0	−0·5	77·0		
23/7	43	8·0	−0·5	76·5	7·25	Fiji–Noumea (ETA 0252 24/7)
24/7	44	7·0	0·5	77·0 }	8·50	Noumea–Townsville (Australia) (ETA 0730 25/7)
25/7	45	7·0	0·5	77·5 }		
26/7	46	7·0	0·5	78·0		} Remained Townsville
27/7	47	7·0	0·5	78·5		
28/7	48	7·0	0·5	79·0		Remained Townsville
29/7	49	7·0	0·5	79·5	{ 1·00 { 6·05	Took off Townsville, re- turned with electrical fault. ETA Darwin 0815
30/7	50	8·0	−0·5	79·0		} Remained Darwin
31/7	51	7·0	0·5	79·5		
1/8	52	2·0	5·5	85·0	14·13	Darwin–Singapore. Slept on stretcher in Airport offices 0200
2/8	53	1·0	6·5	91·5	13·59	Singapore–Madras
3/8	54	0	7·5	99·0	10·05	Madras–Karachi
					08·20	Karachi–Bahrein
					11·20	Bahrein–Athens
4/8	55	0	7·5	106·5	10·41	Athens–London. Took Dexedrine tablet
5/8	—	7·0		No real recovery from cumulative sleep loss		Sleep disturbed for approx 7 days with cycli- cal swings in mood from 'very high to very low'
6/8	—	7·5				
7/8	—	8·5				
8/8	—	7·5				

aircraft. In addition, there are other pressures such as shortage of money, material support, lack of navigational facilities, poor air to ground communications and the ever-present press and news media who may intervene on essential rest periods.

The lone pilot is subjected therefore to high and continuing levels of work-load not only in the air but also on the ground and in the former situation may spend long hours in a cramped

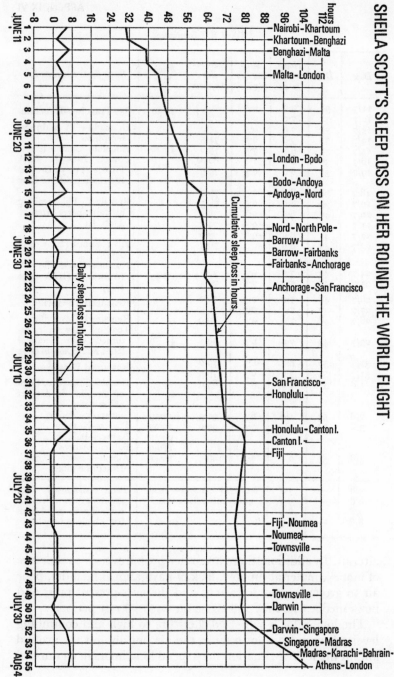

SHEILA SCOTT'S SLEEP LOSS ON HER ROUND THE WORLD FLIGHT

hours
112
104
96
88
80
72
64
56
48
40
32
24
16
8
0
-8

Nairobi-Khartoum
Khartoum-Benghazi
Benghazi-Malta

Malta-London

London-Bodo

Bodo-Andoya
Andoya-Nord

Nord-North Pole-
Barrow
Barrow-Fairbanks
Fairbanks-Anchorage

Anchorage-San Francisco

Cumulative sleep loss in hours

Daily sleep loss in hours

San Francisco-
Honolulu

Honolulu-Canton I.
Canton I.-
Fiji

Fiji-Noumea
Noumea-
Townsville-

Townsville-
Darwin

Darwin-Singapore
Singapore-Madras
Madras-Karachi-Bahrain-
Athens-London

JUNE 11
JUNE 20
JUNE 30
JULY 10
JULY 20
JULY 30
AUG 4

position unable to leave the controls of the aircraft, even for the basic calls of nature. Miss Scott's autopilot did not function over the longer Polar sectors, but was of considerable help to her on the later sectors from Australia to London.

It has been postulated that the sleep patterns of a pilot are related to his duty hours and that the work-load compatible with an acceptable sleep pattern reduces probably in a logarithmic manner. This may be an ideal situation in airline pilots, but was certainly the reverse in Miss Scott's situation where she commenced the most arduous part of the flight at Darwin with a cumulative sleep loss of 85·0 hours in fifty-one days and flew to London on three hours' sleep, her cumulative sleep loss then amounting to 106·5 hours in fifty-five days.

Previous studies by ourselves in BOAC have shown that flight deck crews can incur cumulative sleep losses in the region of twenty-six hours in men in the fifth decade of life, flying on tours extending to fifteen days or so, but we have not been able to carry out any studies on tours longer than this. It is difficult however to assess what effect this sleep loss has on psychomotor functions. The studies by NASA on the Polar sectors of the flight did measure parameters such as heart rate, mental acuity and short memory and reaction time.

In addition, in studies carried out on male and female cabin crews in BOAC we have found that sleep loss seems to be associated more with night flights rather than the effects of time-zone crossing and that sleep loss in some individuals became increasingly severe the longer they were away from the home base. Sleep loss appeared fairly minimal up until the eighth day, thereafter there are very wide variations in individuals.

In Miss Scott's case she was troubled by perpetual daylight in the High Polar summer and this precluded sleep, particularly at Bodo and Nord. Fortunately, or unfortunately, due to aircraft spares problems she was greatly delayed at San Francisco and again at Fiji which allowed her to make up some of her sleep deficit and adjust to local time, although cumulatively speaking she did not reduce her total deficit to any great extent.

Preston, Bateman, Short and Wilkinson have found that reaction time and short memory show a significant decrement in airline stewardesses subjected to time-zone changes which supports the work of Klein who drew attention to the decrement in psychomotor performance found in subjects experiencing six hours' time change. We were unable to measure these parameters in Miss Scott's case, but it is interesting to conjecture how she performed her flying tasks during darkness, particularly when she was in considerable sleep debt.

In summary, record-breaking flights of this kind demand considerable stamina and will-power apart from the necessary flying and navigational skills which go without saying. The degree of sleep loss in such flights is an important factor in achieving success or failure and adequate sleep must be achieved to maintain the record-breaking outlook.

We are deeply indebted to Miss Scott for her help and enthusiasm in keeping a sleep record for us during this epic flight. It was a sad blow to Miss Scott that her record-breaking aircraft *Mythre* should be lost by flood while on the ground in the Washington area during Hurricane Agnes in June 1972.

We are also indebted to Mrs Valerie Sutton-Mattocks, BSc, who has extracted and worked up the data for us, and to Mr Bill Thacker of BOAC for the use of his illustrations in this paper.

APPENDIX VII

Pat O'Hara, General Manager, Engineering
Alexander ('Johnny') Johnson, Company Chief Inspector
Les Baston, Chief Engineer, Aircraft Maintenance
Les Morton, Aircraft Maintenance
Dave Brown, Senior Inspector
Len Oatham, Radio installations
Tony Marchant, Radio installations
Reg Burden, Aircraft charge hand
John Lewis, Installation Fitter
Tommy Thomas, Instructing and test flying with Sheila
Veryell Mitchell, Instructing and test flying with Sheila

BRITISH CALEDONIAN AIRWAYS

Captain David Owen and his operations staff
Alexander Torrance, Chief flight despatcher

SECRETARIAL TEAM THROUGHOUT POLAR FLIGHT

Fiona MacGinley
Christine Stubbersfield
Jackie Williams
Angela Block

DESCRIPTION OF MYTHRE

Mythre is a standard Piper Aztec D (registered in the UK as GAYTO) with two standard Lycoming fuel-injection, 250-hp engines and Hartzell propellers.

Her installations and equipment

The major part of the modification work was performed by
  CSE Aviation Services, Oxford, UK

Her two Cabin Tanks were made by CF Taylor Metal Workers Ltd
Tip Tanks by Metco Air
King Silver 2 × VHF (360 channels)
King Silver 2 × VOR
King Silver ILS
King Silver Marker Beacons
King Silver 2× Digital Radio Compasses
King Silver Transponder
King Silver DME
Pantronics D × 20-RT-HF radio (20 crystals) with static and electric trail aerials
Eveready battery emergency backup electric system
AIM 400 slaved gyro
SG Brown Plantronic Headset
Air Med Headset
Astro Compass
Sperry C11 Compass System (which converted to a simple indicator in the High Arctic where the compass cannot operate accurately. It did not lose a degree and with the astro compass was Sheila's sole navigation reference aid over the Pole)
Heuer Autavia Chronometer
Jaeger Le Coutre Sea Sky
Rollex GMT Master
Wing and elevator de-icers
Prop anti-icers
Heated windscreen panel
3-M anti-static metal strips
Oxygen system
Safety shoulder harness
BAC unbreakable mirror
Beaufort Life Jacket
Beaufort One Woman Dinghy
Burndept Sarbe Survival Beacon Mark V
Champion Iridium Spark Plugs (for long wear)
Park Air Receiver (for team use at London Airport)
Special Moreland Sheepskin seat cover
Electric gloves and socks
Storage box to hold loose equipment and charts

General Instrument Corporation and NASA special installations. BIP
Sign writing by David Cummings

Loose supplies

Duvet and trousers
Lightweight Aquascutum anorak
Moreland sheepskin flying boots
Silk underwear (Smedley's)
Wool underwear and topwear (Pringle)
Sun glasses
Rank Akai video tape recorder (alas stolen)
Konica still camera
Jepson Radio Charts
International Aeradio radio and contact charts
Air Touring Shop Flight Accessories, computers, etc.
Heuer Autavia Chronometer
Jaeger Le Coutre Sea/Sky watch
Tupperware
Thermos flasks
Nestlés coffee, milk, chocolate
Bally Cloud Nine flying shoes
Eveready batteries for all purposes, and climates
Eveready emergency lighting
First Aid kit and survival kit supervised by Institute of Aviation
    Medicine, Farnborough
Optrex
Elizabeth Arden protective and personal make-up
Charles Wyckoff extended range film

ACKNOWLEDGMENTS

There are a great number of people who made the recent flight possible world-wide—in lots of various ways—too many for them all to be listed here—and some wish to remain anonymous.

Kolbjorn Adolfsen
Aeronautical Information Service, UK
Air Registration Board, UK
Air Service Corporation, Hawaii
Air Traffic Control, London Airport
Carl Andressen
Anrite Aviation, Singapore
Ansett General Aviation, Sydney
B.P. Company (British Petroleum)
Jess Bachner
Commander Harry Bain, RN
Lindy Boyes
Bracknell Meteorological Office—Miss Nora Parkinson
British Airports Authority
British Caledonian
British Women Pilots' Association
Butler Aviation
CINCPAC
Tom Carpenter
Max Coote
Theo Cowan
Darwin Aero Club
Peter Denholm
Department of Environment, UK
Geoffrey Edwards
June Eggleston
Eveready Company, The
Far East Fleet
Field Aircraft Services—London Airport
Fijian Hotel, Fiji

Fleet Air Arm
Foreign Commonwealth Office, UK
GPO
GPO Baldock HF telephone
Hamish Goodwin
HMS Jufair—Naval Aircraft Support Unit
Christine Henderson
Katherine Henderson
Holiday Airport Inn, Honolulu
Indian Women Pilots' Association
Institute of Sports Medicine
Auriel Johnson
Capt. Jahn Larsen
Lavco
Robert Lee
Libyan Arab Airlines
London Airport Authority Board
London Airport Meteorological—Mr Farnes and Mr Johnson
Kay MacLean
Mogens Lund
Jimmy Maley, Fairbanks
Pat MacDermott
Mel Air, Alaska
Chuck Miller
Naval Arctic Research Laboratory, Barrow
E.A. Netto
Ninety-Nines around the World
Frances Nolde
Blanche Noyes
Olympic Airways
Elizabeth Overbury
Weldy Phipps
Gilly Potter
Qantas
RAF 90 (Signals)
RAF Northolt
RAF Manby
W. P. Robinson, Navigational Superintendent, BOAC
Royal Aero Club, UK—John Blake
Royal Geographic Society

ACKNOWLEDGMENTS

Ruth Rueckart
SAMTEC
Charles St George
Freydis Sharland
Sikander Ltd.
Tony Smallwood
Jeremy Smith
Bob Snoxall
Station Nord
Sydney Taylor
Col. P. Thorendahl
Townsville Aero Club
Travelodge, Nandi
USA Embassy, London—Major Bishop
US Coast Guard
US Navy
Ugandian Air Services
Harry Yarwood
Fay Gillis Wells
Wilken Aviation Ltd. Nairobi
John Williams
Charles Wyckoff
Zonta International

Index

Sheila Scott long-dist

In `Myth Too´, a single-engined Piper Coma

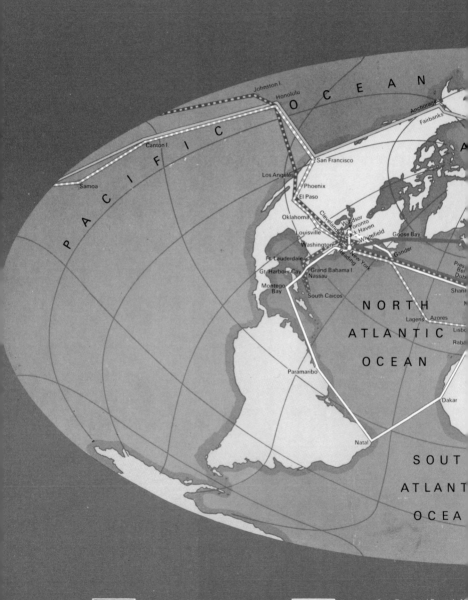

London to Le Hague and return/
Brussels/Paris/Belfast/Dublin 1965.
Fifteen Records within 36 hours.

Round the World Record Flight 1966

London to Cape Town and Records 19

North and South Atlantic Records 196